PRAISE FOR EMMA MILDON AND
THE SOUL SEARCHER'S HANDBOOK

"A totally refreshing look at how to incorporate spirituality
into modern-day life and not feel like you're constantly failing
at it. This book will guide you on the journey of living a more
fulfilling and judgment-free life, introducing you to a myriad of
wonderful practices. Even if you don't consider yourself spiritual
this is a damn good dose of nutrients for the soul. A must read
for the spiritually curious!"

—**PJ Harding**, ZM radio host

"OMG, Emma's new book on modern, life-affirming spirituality
makes me want to fake tattoo my arms in gold feathers and run
off to elope with God. Her offering is a hilarious and sexy primer
for anyone interested in getting started on the spiritual path who
may feel a bit overwhelmed by the breadth and depth of the
options. With humor and rawness, Emma is like a goddessy-
messenger-girlfriend who may just lead you to your inner guru."

—**Katie Silcox**, *New York Times* bestselling author of
Healthy, Happy, Sexy: Ayurveda Wisdom for Modern Women

"A great starter guide for those interested in spirituality
with an integrated approach to body, mind, and spirit.
Written with a healthy dose of humor, combining every day
reality with the search for spirituality."

—**Jennifer Schregel**, marketing manager
BookYogaRetreats.com

"The essential tour guide for any aspiring soul searcher, Emma Mildon is an absolute guru at playfully expanding the consciousness of her readers while offering invaluable been-there-got-the-tee-shirt spiritual guidance. Charming, witty, and undeniably wise, Emma's ode to modern-day soul searching is the perfect way to discover nourishing New Age practices and open your mind to heartfelt spiritual illumination."

—**Cassandra Lane**, editor of
Happiness + Wellbeing Magazine

"If you're looking for answers to the big questions from a modern-day soul searcher, Emma Mildon is the teacher for you. In *The Soul Searcher's Handbook*, Emma will teach you everything there is to know about spirituality and holistic living in a funky, modern, and down-to-earth way. If you wish to be enlightened and have a laugh while you're doing so, you have to read this book!"

—**Michelle Buchanan**, author of
The Numerology Guidebook, Hay House Basics—Numerology, and the *Numerology Guidance Cards*

"Now there's an antidote for those with incurable cases of wanderlust. On your life journey, make sure you pack *The Soul Searcher's Handbook*. It will help you find your way."

—**Jeff Krasno**, founder of the Wanderlust Festival

"*The Soul Searcher's Handbook* by Emma Mildon, is a quick and easy read. She has an upbeat, honest way of writing. Her book is to the point, and not full of prose and preachiness. She explores all forms of soul searching, without bias or judgment. Her open, honest writing encourages you to be free to learn and experience all sorts of healing properties and techniques. We highly recommend this book to everyone in searching for a more empowered lifestyle."

—**The Empowering Team**, My Empowered World

"A warm, wacky, practical guide to everything body-mind-soul. Emma's humorous approach to holistic living is both entertaining, informative, and inspiring."
—**Phillip Mills**, CEO of Les Mills International

"Splitting her pants mid-yoga class so you don't have to, Emma Mildon's outrageously honest advice takes the fear out of stepping onto a spiritual path, soothing any anxieties over the odd 'epic fail,' and arming readers with a wealth of grounded wisdom. Encompassing lashings of inspiration and first-hand experiences, heaps of humor and a whacking great dollop of wit, her light-hearted read reminds us that you don't have to lose your sense of humor on your quest to enlightenment— and had me giggling from start to finish."
—**Rianna Fry**, editor of *Soul & Spirit* magazine

"From aromatherapy to auras, crystals to chakras, Reiki to reflexology, numerology, and yoga, Emma journeys through the world of spirituality, past lives, and the power of dreams. With quotes from famous minds and a wisdom beyond the author's years, this book is a gentle, loving guide that peers into the world of mysticism, wellness, and mindfulness. Woo-Woo scale: variable; I-like-this-book scale: 10/10."
—**Sharad P. Paul MD**, social entrepreneur and author of *Skin, a Biography* and *Dermocracy*

"*The Soul Searcher's Handbook* is a relatable, hilarious guidebook for anyone wanting to dip their toes into the world of spirituality and lead a wholesome, balanced, soulful life."
—**Rebecca Campbell**, author of *Light Is the New Black*

"*The Soul Searcher's Handbook* is an unreserved personal journey full of hiccups and lessons, taking the reader through modern-day Spirituality 101. Emma's uncanny ability to make us laugh allows us to build trust from her experiences and want to sign-up for the next chakra cleanse, angel reading, and past-life regression around the corner. Put on a coat of third-eye mascara, buy a quartz crystal, and get ready to Feng Shui your room in this amusing guide to beginner's enlightenment."
—**Mo McReynolds**, store manager for the lululemon athletica Ponsonby team

"An enlightening and resourceful modern-day guide to optimizing your life."
—**Tiffany Cruikshank**, founder of Yoga Medicine

"*The Soul Searcher's Handbook* is the permission slip you've been waiting for to pull out those Tarot cards, adorn yourself in crystals, and dive headfirst into a soul-fueled adventure of self-discovery. Emma shares her knowledge and personal experiences with integrity, compassion, and humor, making this book everything you need to satisfy your soul-stirring curiosities and explore new age living in a fun, safe, and simple way. Forget Google, this book is your new go to for all things spiritual."
—**Rebecca Van Leeuwen**, founder of Soul Sister Circle

"Emma is a fantastic storyteller. Her cheeky character and honesty make you feel like you're listening to one of your best friends tell you about her amazingly wild adventure of self discovery. This easy-to-read handbook is both entertaining and enlightening, I highly recommend it to anyone who is soul searching and looking for the right path to follow."
—**Michelle Merrifield**, founder of Essence of Living Yoga

THE
SOUL
SEARCHER'S
HANDBOOK

THE
SOUL
SEARCHER'S
HANDBOOK

THE MODERN GIRL'S GUIDE TO THE NEW AGE WORLD

EMMA MILDON

ATRIA PAPERBACK
New York London Toronto Sydney New Delhi

BEYOND WORDS
Hillsboro, Oregon

ATRIA PAPERBACK
An Imprint of Simon & Schuster, Inc.
1230 Avenue of the Americas
New York, NY 10020

BEYOND WORDS
20827 N.W. Cornell Road, Suite 500
Hillsboro, Oregon 97124–9808
503-531-8700 / 503-531-8773 fax
www.beyondword.com

Managing editor: Lindsay S. Easterbrooks Brown
Editor: Anna Noak, Sylvia Spratt
Copyeditor: Gretchen Stelter
Proofreader: Michelle Blair
Cover design: Devon Smith
Composition: William H. Brunson Typography Services

First Atria Books/Beyond Words trade paperback edition November 2015

Library of Congress Cataloging-in-Publication Data

Mildon, Emma.
    The soul searcher's handbook : the modern girl's guide to the new age world / Emma Mildon. — First Atria Books/Beyond Words trade paperback edition.
        pages cm
    1. Occultism.   2. Spiritual life.   3. Women.   I. Title.
    BF1411.M563   2015
    131—dc23

                                                                            2015018843

ISBN 978-1-58270-524-8
ISBN 978-1-4767-8805-0 (ebook)

The corporate mission of Beyond Words Publishing, Inc.: *Inspire to Integrity*

Life is not an experience. It is a journey.
I would like to thank everyone who crossed my path along
the journey to the birth of this book.

This book is dedicated to my soul-sister circle:
Leanne Mulhern, the loving mother, the loving sister.
Rebecca Van Leeuwen, the goddess and soul sister.
Charlotte Desborough, the traveler and Soul Searcher.
Sarah Fletcher-Mare, the well-being junkie.
Toni Thompson, the luminous light seeker.
Amanda Farrant, the earth worker and naturopath.
Erin O'Hara, the golden yogi and homeopath.
Aleisha Coote, the love guru and earth angel.
Sarah Brosnahan, the wellness warrior.

"If there are so many seekers,
why are there so few finders?"
➤Eckhart Tolle

CONTENTS

PREFACE

*"I BELIEVE EVERYONE IS ON A SPIRITUAL PATH—
SOME PEOPLE KNOW IT, SOME DON'T. THE ONES THAT KNOW IT
CALL THEMSELVES RELIGIOUS, SPIRITUAL, OR SOUL SEARCHERS."*

So, you're here. You're fired up. High five for being ready to connect all the dots of your personal spiritual constellation!

If you've been asking those big questions—like *Why am I here? Is there a god? or What's the deal with reincarnation?*—or slightly smaller questions—like *Is yoga really that great for you, or is it just a fad? Coconut oil: yes or no? Is crystal healing real? or Holy patchouli, Batman: why do people wear it?*—welcome to my world. You, like me, probably wish life came with a handbook on this stuff—a book to guide you and shine some light on how to harness your spiritual, intellectual, and physical potential; to fuel your life purpose; and to show you how to become more awakened to and connected with the world. A how-to guide to navigating the labyrinth of modern-day life, a handbook reminding you how to ground, center, and reconnect to your inner and higher self.

Alas, life did not come with said guide. And at some point several years ago, I realized this oversight. So I wrote one—a guide that mostly covers the slightly smaller questions, so you can answer the bigger questions for yourself.

I'd like to invite you to think of me as a personal assistant for your soul. My epic fails, lessons, and growing pains on the path of my spiritual evolution have all been to benefit you: the boss, the seeker, the learner, the soul's pupil, the reason why I chose to write this book. So, dear soul, I present myself as reporting for duty, like your own spiritual crash test dummy.

Have you ever given yourself a sneezing fit by dousing yourself with too much patchouli oil? Have you ever pulled a muscle in your butt trying to perfect your King Pigeon Pose? How about getting stared at by your confused neighbor while performing a crystal-cleansing ceremony in your backyard? I did all this and more when I ditched my spiritual training bra and dove headfirst into the world of modern holistic living—successfully managing to simultaneously face-plant midheadstand, choke on chia seeds, and stab myself with a few clear-quartz pendulums along the way.

I'm *that* girl, the one that things happen to—and to a no-longer-surprising degree. I had wanted my entrance into modern spiritual living to be graceful, breezily effortless, and instantly gratifying. What I got was the spiritual version of a self-titled, never-ending, off-Broadway show full of epic fails and sheepish shrugs on my quest for enlightenment—a quest full of stumbles and falls, but also one full of learning. The truths I learned along the way were messy, funny, difficult, embarrassing, joyous, and most of all, real. That realness—in all its crystal-wielding, farting-in-yoga-class, kale-in-your-teeth glory—is what spurred me to write this book.

As your soul searching PA, I feel that I should share my CV with you, so you can check that I am qualified. Think spiritual *Survivor.* I have drunk *ayahuasca* in the depths of the Amazonian rainforest seeking an enlightening vision and experienced what looked like a rainbow vomiting from my mouth—some would say not fun. I say it's a spiritual experience all the same.

I have met with past-life-regression experts and found out I am not the reincarnated soul of Elvis or Cleopatra, but rather of a grumpy, fuddy-duddy in Serbia. I will admit to some disappointment around that. I totally wanted to have been Elvis. On the plus side, in another lifetime, I was a disciplined Thai monk, meditating under the sun for hours on end, blissfully content, and surrounded by a sea of orange robes and sunlight.

I have had my tea leaves read in Ireland, my palms read in Spain, my stars read in New Zealand, my numbers counted in Miami, my future read in Australia, my auras read in Peru, and my chakras cleansed in the Caribbean. I have pored over, underlined, scribbled on, crossed out, Post-it-noted, and dog-eared nearly every how-to guide to spiritual and holistic living out there. Along the way, there has been one constant: I have never stopped being astonished by how many ways there are to be spiritual.

The more I tried to work out what spiritual category I slotted into, what label I could bestow upon myself, the more it dawned on me how impossible it is to define spirituality. Seriously, try to think of a definition—no cheating with a dictionary. When I tried this little exercise, I tried for something universal, something that would resonate with you, me, and everyone—something all encompassing, kind, holistic ... And there it was! To me, *spiritual* has come to mean simply a life lived holistically—a wholesome, balanced, soulful life. A life lived well.

In my efforts to begin living a wholesome life, I had to consider all facets of life—body, mind, and spirit—as one. Energy, be it positive or negative, influences our health, love, adversity, joy—embodied through our everyday thoughts, actions, and choices.

What the mind, body, and soul are looking for in life, intentionally or otherwise, ripples outward, through everyone and everything we touch.

I mean, let's face it: with every act, you're either lifting the world around you with the good shit, or polluting it with pure ick, pure and simple. Once I'd come to terms with what the word *spirituality* meant for me, I realized that the next big question I should be asking myself was: *Am I a purifier or a polluter?* I had to look at my every action, word, breath, and smile as a single whole and consider how it impacts me, others, the earth, and life in general. That's what *holistic* means: the big picture. So it dawned on me that once I adopted a holistic attitude, I would feel a whole lot better about life in general.

For me, the first step was to incorporate spiritual elements into my daily life. Once I started to figure this out, I felt more grounded, my heart felt more inspired and satisfied, my body felt at peace, my brain learned how to shut it and take a break, and my spirit positively oozed good vibes. I felt like an angelic hippie chick with some earth mother–slash–spiritual savant thrown in.

"Um, Emma?" you might say. "Declaring yourself a divine being of pure love and enlightenment's all well and good, but what does it actually mean to live it?" Soul sister, boy do I hear you. Because just saying that you're wholesome doesn't automatically make it so, which is a bummer. Getting real, spirituality isn't an inborn superpower. It's about having the power to live a spiritually connected and authentic life day to day, in small, practical increments. This stuff takes work.

I'll readily admit that I had some problems with this myself—and still do. I mean, do we all truly have to rock a real, honest-to-goodness wholesome lifestyle *every day*? Sometimes I switch out my herbal tea for caffeine and my mudras turn into middle fingers. I am a human, and I am spiritual—like with most things in life, there's balance to be had between the earthly and the divine.

So, what does *holistic* and *spirituality* mean in practical terms? What does it mean in the context of our hyper-fast-paced, super-plugged-in, ultra-evolved, modern-day lives? Even just asking these questions sounded like crazy amounts of work that I wasn't sure I wanted to do. Considering that I—probably just like you—value time as currency, I already considered myself time poor. I was stretched out and overworked, a busy, working-class bohemian looking for a quick, easy spiritual fix that could solve all my soul's aches. So I did what any self-respecting modern girl would do. I googled "how to be spiritual."

Anti-surprise! This didn't exactly yield the results I was looking for. I was bummed to find that, no matter what Google might want us to believe, we can't plug our spiritual hunger into a search engine. Instead, apparently there's this whole "search within" trend that has been happening (according to Google) since the dawn of humans being humans. This created an immediate bit of stress. I mean, I *googled* it. All of my questions should have been found. Even the all-knowing great and powerful Wikipedia failed me. *Middle finger!*

What I finally did discover via other, more real-world-based experiences, was that incorporating practical spirituality into your daily life doesn't necessarily mean you need to go have a full body, mind, spirit time-out and meditate for days on end like Elizabeth Gilbert in *Eat, Pray, Love* (props to her though). Phew, right? I wasn't quite ready to go there at that juncture on my spiritual path either.

Over time, what I have found is that anyone, including me, can live a spiritually nourished lifestyle if they know how to locate and use the universe's spiritual tools. And I also found that even when it felt like I didn't have any of those tools, I totally did—and they're out there for everyone. And this is another reason why I wanted to write this book. I thought that perhaps it would be nice to have a stack of those tools neatly organized in a little spiritual toolbox that my fellow soul explorers could access anytime. Sisters, I've got your backs.

"But why soul search at all these days?" you might ask. "Who's got the time, the energy, even the desire—even if we do have access to the tools?"

You do have the time. If you have even five minutes, you have the time. You're reading this book! If you have the time to do that to encourage your spiritual growth, you have time to spend five more minutes of your day (or five minutes of your reading time) on your soul-searching journey. Remember, in five minutes you could learn one thing that changes your perception on everything.

Now, I'm not here to dictate to you how to live your spiritual truth. This search of ours is less to do with "do this" and "do that," and everything to do with "explore this" and "try that"—finding your kit and putting it to use is all about trial and error (emphasis on *error* in my case, I don't know about you), and the journey really is a beautiful one. I want you to feel free to note, check off, cross out, read, circle, tear up, download, and highlight the bits of pieces explored in the pages to come that speak to your soul's curiosity—in my experience, that is the only way to find your path. Be as flexible as you dream of being in yoga class, as free flowing as the smudge stick you use to cleanse your apartment—so carefree that you completely ditch deodorant altogether and board the one-way train to Au-Naturels-ville. (Well, maybe not *that* carefree—don't forget to pit sniff, Soul Searchers.)

In truth, there is no right or wrong, no knowers of all, no framework, no experts—I ascribe to the idea that we all know what we are meant to know and, more importantly, all come into the information that we need at the right time and in the right place. So while I have indeed done the research and written the book, your own soul is going to be your guide. Again, spirituality should encompass what's deeply personal to you—whether that's boho chic, hipster, religious, woo-woo, nomad, wanderer, or simply seeker.

Me? I came out of the spiritual closet a few years ago. I believe in kindness and karma—which could make me a Buddhist. I believe in mystic healing and crystals' powers—which could make me a witch. I believe in truth, honor, and forgiveness—which could make me a Christian. I even believe in the existence of past lives and that each and every one of us is watched over by guides from the other side—which, to some, would make me totally *woo-woo* squared.

Up until fairly recently, I have always let others define my spirituality. I have been called a hippie, a boho hipster, a witch, a crystal licker, and just plain weird. I have proudly embraced them all. From a young age, I was drawn to Tarot cards, candles, angel sculptures, and aromatherapy. I was artistic, emotional, and very much a black sheep adopted into a down-to-earth New Zealand family. I am the product of an atheist mother (who was spiritually open to my *woo-woo*-ness, however always considered me a little eccentric); a Catholic father who lives in a very black-and-white, nine-to-five world; and a quiet, humble sister who has always been content reading and observing, taking life as it comes.

But not me. No way. If I wasn't telling tales about mermaids or faraway lands, I was imagining past lives, talking about my dreams that were brimming with mystical magic and cosmic revelations, or sketching and scribbling about my experiences. Little did I know back then, but I was already developing into the spiritual being that had always lived inside of me. There was not a time I can remember when I just woke up and decided to explore spirituality—I was born with it.

I have taken what resonates with me from different religions, different cultures, and different traditions, and created a sense of holistic living that works for me, which I have dubbed "spiritual living." I sleep with my head facing east (an Ayurvedic practice to invite in positive energy), I meditate when I get pissed off, I use aromatherapy to de-stress, I focus on manifesting beautiful things into my life, and I am constantly downloading new spiritual insights from my surroundings that allow me to forever better my life. The point is everyone is spiritual, no matter her definition of *spirituality* and no matter how she practices it.

I have to share with you that one of the things that shocked me to my core while researching and writing this book was how judgmental some "spiritual" people can be. It really opened my eyes when I discovered that some of the most well-known New Thought thinkers who you would expect to have big, fat, juicy egos in fact didn't, and that the people I expected to be down-to-earth, work-your-way-to-the-top spiritual folks were the judgey-wudgey ones who thought it was their way or the highway. That's what I get for judging before I have all the facts.

Upon embarking on your journey, I implore you: please try to remain open-minded, understanding, and in a universal frame of mind, and remember that not all elements of spirituality speak to everyone. Take what you need and leave the rest, simple as that. You're also going to run into people who will judge you for the choices you make on your spiritual path. When this happens, acknowledge it, investigate it if you feel it's necessary, and then release it and move on—please do not let it back you up. Everyone's got spiritual constipators in their lives. Don't give them any more time than you have to.

There are a few things I found while researching this book that seem to resonate very strongly no matter the belief and the practice. I traveled across the globe, meeting yogis, gurus, and religious leaders of all sorts—healers, celebrities, shamans, and many more like-minded individuals—all in the quest to put together a single source of practical, universal wisdom for the modern-day Soul Searcher. I connected with masters, specialists, experts, and leaders to hear about their knowledge on a range of spiritual topics, allowing me to pass on their teachings, their experiences, and their wisdom to you.

Across all the beliefs, all the religions, all the scriptures, stories, and people I met along the journey, one element connected them all: a belief, a curiosity, a hunch that there is something more to life—a universal spark to seek, to know, and to be enlightened.

We usually get to enlightened states via learning combined with one of the most powerful forces out there. Some call that force *veda* (Sanskrit), conscientia (Latin), *Zhīshì* (Chinese), or simply *wisdom*.

Wisdom has both a universal and personal quality to it; some things that others find wise, I might find a little superficial, and in the same way, some things that have blown my mind have totally underwhelmed my best friend. Everyone has their wisdom list somewhere in their heads. Here's a sampling of some of the wisdom that I learned while traveling ye olde globe:

▷ Goodness is, well, good. Get you some. Stick with it.

▷ Epiphanies happen. Just roll with them; it saves time.

▷ Laughing and crying are both beautiful. Sharing both is also beautiful.

▷ Wisdom and assholes: everyone has them, but it's only sure that one gets used daily. Try to go for both.

▷ There is no one way; there's only a soul's singular, unmapped path.

▷ We're all pretty weird and that weird is all kinds of spectacular.

▷ Wonder is the emotional equivalent of eating the best ice cream ever.

▷ Yay!

▷ After your soul is switched on, there's no going back.

▷ Since all of life is a journey taken one step at a time, shoes do, indeed, matter.

Listening to all of the people I met along my journey, I found that epic takeaways are the best things. Ever.

With that in mind, consider the book you are holding in your hands right now your invitation from the universe to get it on with epic takeaways. This is a warm welcome to the Soul Searchers' tribe, where others like you will read, learn, and grow together, a tribe where all quirks, weirdo rituals, and definitions of spirituality are unified and accepted—where lessons, tips, and stories that will leave your soul singing out "Me too!" will come to life.

Consider what's next as a sweet kiss warmly planted on your forehead, a blast of fresh morning light sending prisms throughout your soul, a cosmic wind that whispers you awake while somewhere across the globe the monks are gently humming, and right outside your window, the birds are brightly chirping nature's anthem in honor of your awakening—all welcoming you to your new day, your new life that is jam-packed with spiritual goodness.

Consider today the day you are crowned whole. Why? Because this book in your hands means, you, my friend, are about to become a Soul Searcher.

INTRODUCTION: YOUR JOURNEY

*"TO BELIEVE IN COINCIDENCES, TO BELIEVE IN FATE—
IT TIES INTO THE SPIRITUAL REALM, TO THE IDEA THAT THERE IS SOMETHING
UNIVERSAL OUT THERE, SOMETHING LOOKING OUT FOR YOU,
WATCHING OVER YOU, GUIDING YOU."*

Welcome. You are about to make the shift toward a holistic approach to life, healing, and well-being. First off, I request a Buddha belly bounce (this is the New Age version of the chest-bump athletes give each other after a good play)—go you! Next, and before we go any further, let's take a peek at that word *holistic*. *Holistic* has many definitions—some call it *"woo-woo,"* others "spiritual," others "educated."

I like to think of a holistic life as a good life, pure and simple. What we think, do, say, eat, practice, believe in, and act on are all reflections of how we choose to live our lives. A holistic approach to your body, mind, and soul cannot only transform your health and well-being, but it can also benefit your relationships; make you more patient, understanding, and loving; and generally help you to become more awake as a person in your day-to-day life, which will result in more love, energy, and abundance all around.

Wherever you are on your spiritual journey right now, it's where you need to be—even if it doesn't feel that way just yet. And one more thing before you go any further: do yourself a huge favor and leave your ego and any lingering cynicism at the door. (I like to think that judgments happen when our souls are constipated. Ew, I know. But it is a way of our soul telling us we need to open up, let it go, and let it out! So consider this an enema for any negative, cynical, narrow-minded, judgey-wudgeyness within you. Let that shit go.) I'd bet everything I own that when we first start exploring this stuff, most of us think we've gone off the deep end a bit—how many times have we rolled our eyes at spiritual practices, from horoscopes to past-life regression, thinking it's just a *liiittle* too woo-woo for us to get into? Don't stress. You're certainly not alone—but that judgmental gunk in your gears is possibly due for a cleaning. The good news is that this is a great place for that too. The more you allow yourself to be open to all ideas and all angles and approaches to life, the more wisdom and *dharma* (existing in symbiosis with the divine laws of the universe) your soul can consume. So shush that voice in your head telling you to stay static, and allow yourself to crack open and let the light of the universe, in all its many forms, into your mind, body, heart, and soul.

In this world, there are doers, believers, dreamers, and thinkers. You, dear friend, are what I like to call a seeker—a curious, open, aware, and intuitive human. You were drawn to this book and listened to the urge to pick it up, open it, and read this introduction because you know there is more to your life, there is more for you to discover. These words you are reading are the first footsteps on your spiritual journey, and like many before you, you are beginning with the desire to seek.

> "SPIRITUALITY IS ABOUT ONENESS—ONE LOVE, ONE SEEKER, ONE SOUL,
> AND ONE SPIRITUALITY THAT SPEAKS TO ALL PEOPLE.
> NO MATTER A PERSON'S FAME, FORTUNE, OR FAITH, THEY ARE ONE WITH YOU."

When you think of a spiritual person, whom do you picture? Is it a sandalwood-fragranced, unruly-haired old hippie who desperately needs a pedicure? Is it someone who drives a rusted, old VW Bug that runs on discarded fryer oil and is plastered with bumper stickers that say things like "I break for wood elves"? Or is it a yogi, bone-thin and bearded, silent and wise? Newsflash, friends—you have just as much spiritual essence as all of these peeps. We all do. Spirituality, wisdom, and love are our birthright—they can be hard to keep in mind and access when our day-to-day lives feel like they move faster than the speed of light, but that doesn't make it any less true.

With the advent of the New Age movement and the increasing desire to live a spiritual existence separate from traditional organized religions, the last barriers to getting your eager little mitts on spiritual wisdom have rapidly broken down.

Today, spiritual people look no different than anyone else. Their homes and cars, the books they read, even the clothes they wear are no different from their neighbors. And unless they suddenly open up and start sharing their spirituality and beliefs with you, you might never know. In fact, chances are the majority of the people you interact with every day—from your mother to your boss to the barista who makes your morning coffee—believe in something spiritual, whether that be angels, magic, a higher power like God or Allah, astrology, fate, miracles, or even ghosts. You may be even more surprised at the sheer number of people who are already on or are about to embark on a spiritual journey just like yourself. I bet you will look differently at Marjorie, the accounts lady, when you notice her crystal necklace, or your boss, when you notice the subtle yin-yang tattoo you never spotted before.

Today, more people than at any other time in history believe in something bigger: a universal presence, a connection, a guiding power, an energy greater than the concrete world we see and feel around us—and that's what I call a great opportunity if there ever was one.

> "Though we may know Him by a thousand names,
> He is one and the same to all of us . . . "
> **>Mahatma Gandhi**

Some kiss the earth with their forehead; some sit in wooden pews watched over by stained-glass windows; others put their fingertips on their third eyes or mark their foreheads with red bindis; some have quiet conversations and whisper in their minds with angels and guides; while others sit cross-legged, listening to nothing, thinking of nothing, becoming one with nothing. Spirituality has long been defined by religion, but the key to all religions and what is at the core of all beliefs, the thing that makes religion spiritual is their *lifestyle*—the day-to-day rituals, behavior, and beliefs that transform a simple way of life into a way of being.

What lies ahead in these pages aims to cover the basics of everything you've ever wanted to know about living a holistic, spiritual, fulfilled life without having to become a full-time yogi or get your doctorate in spiritual studies (phew, right?).

In the pages of this book I've combined my real-life experiences (I've offered my spiritual virginity to many a new age practice), with practical how-tos (I've road tested this stuff for you), to help you explore the big-picture questions and answers that best resonate with you (chose your own adventure, yay!). We're going to discuss soul education (yup, health ed was a waste of time) and we're going to talk about what it might mean if it did indeed have the ability to heal and communicate with us through our energy levels, illnesses, and other physical, mental, and emotional cues. We will explore universal wisdom and its ability to be creative and visionary, and what the soul means to each of us and its untapped abilities to be intuitive—not to mention checking out our stars, numbers, names, smells, environments, thoughts, passions, dreams, guides, and destinies.

How to Use This Book

How should you approach this book? However you dang well please! Really. Think of what's to come as a choose-your-own spiritual adventure where you can pick and choose which practices you explore based on which ones resonate deepest and most immediately for you. Think crystal healing's super awesome but aren't so hot on yoga just yet? More spiritual power to you, friend. You'd rather work on contacting your spiritual guides than on Feng-Shui-ing your apartment? No worries. This book is about doing what's right for you at this moment. Plus, you can come back to these pages again and again, depending on where you're at on your spiritual path.

To help you along the sometimes-bumpy path to everyday enlightenment, I've broken the book down into three parts: Body, Mind, and Spirit. From there, each part is further broken down into sections that cover a variety of beliefs, practices, and good ol' fashioned general factoids that are handy to have in your back pocket for trivia night.

I've also developed what I like to call the Woo-Woo Scale. It's exactly what it sounds like: a scale to give you a heads-up on how wacky, weird, or wonderful a certain practice might feel the first time you try it out, because let's face it—some of this stuff feels pretty bizarre the first (or second . . . or fifth) time around! But nothing good ever came from dismissing the weirder parts of life just because we were feeling scared or embarrassed or judgey, and often the most wonderful breakthroughs we can experience are hidden behind a patina of the peculiar.

Each major practice or belief will begin with where the subject falls on the Woo-Woo Scale based on my experiences with it, as well as where I think it falls on the Explore-It Scale: with 1 being "you should probably check this out before you die" and 10 being "OMG. GET ON YOUR SPIRITUAL BIKE RIGHT NOW, PEOPLE." You get the picture.

By the time you close the back cover, you'll have experienced twists of fate, visions of truth, and revelatory discoveries both personal and universal. You will have become a healer, yogi, dreamer, stargazer, crystal holder, teacher, physic, Tarot reader, and, most importantly, Soul Searcher. To me, a Soul Searcher is someone who is spiritually active. Yep, you are about to get curious and experimental, and find out how to push all your spiritual buttons. Soul Searchers are people with their lights switched on—we are awake, alert, and active. With an activated spiritual GPS that leads our souls toward new experiences, wisdom, dreams, people, and resources, we start to develop a wholesome understanding of the world—a truly holistic and universal way of living. Soul Searchers pick up on the "warmer...hotter...hot" whispers from the universe as they get closer to uncovering everything that living a spiritually active life holds.

New Age Beliefs for a New Age

"SPIRITUALITY IS A UNIVERSAL CURRENCY. IT IS PART OF EVERY RELIGION, EVERY FAITH, AND EVERY PERSON. EVERYBODY HAS A BELIEF SYSTEM."

So here we are. Meditation and chakras and past-life regression, oh my! Mix all that in with a healthy (or not-so-healthy) dose of cynicism, sleep deprivation, stress, and the countless other elements of the daily grind most of us are constantly dealing with, and you've got the perfect recipe, not for spiritual success, but rather disenchantment. Sure, some of us squeeze in a half hour of yoga before bed and read our horoscopes over our morning coffee, but these days, when it comes to seeking out what makes our souls truly complete, most of us raise our shoulders and sigh, "Huh?"

Believing in a way of life but not actually living that life is an all-too-common affliction these days. Like many things in modern society, our lives have become possession rich but time poor, and the demand for instant knowledge, communication, and results is higher than ever before, including when it comes to spirituality. We seek instant answers, expertise, and results, but what many of us do not realize is that spirituality is more accessible than it's ever been—we've just been wandering around with sunglasses on in the dark while looking for it.

Modern-day spirituality is increasingly branching off from organized religion and has become more and more accessible on a personal level. Despite the many barriers to spiritual enlightenment the world throws at us every day, our technology-obsessed culture actually enables our spiritual growth far more than we give it credit for. While some still search for a higher self or creator in a chapel, synagogue, mosque, or temple, many find what they seek by looking inward—through quiet reflection in meditation or yoga, by educating themselves about spiritual practices across history and cultures. Some find it in online communities or through books, films, or even apps on their smartphones. There are now more ways to watch, read, download, and share spiritual wisdom across multiple platforms than ever before. The age of tailored, individual spiritual enlightenment has truly arrived.

Still, there's the burden of choice to contend with: the more choices one has (cars, gadgets, where to go to dinner—we all know how this goes), the harder it can be to move forward. But if we can harness the many paths stretching out before us without becoming overwhelmed—considering it a spiritual sampler, as it were—we can ride the wave of higher consciousness one Soul Searcher at a time.

Through technological advancements that so often seem to keep us farther apart, our ability to connect with wisdom, to get and gift guidance, to collectively hurt and heal, teach and learn—both instantly and collectively, across states, countries, and oceans—will only be amplified. What used to only be taught from guru to acolyte, teacher to student, is now universally accessible. Perhaps most importantly, we are at a unique place in history where we have the opportunity to take this wealth of knowledge and incorporate it into our daily lives in ways that work for us.

In this book, you will learn about tuning in to daily spiritual messages like they are a radio station; you will explore speaking with your spirit guides, or the universe as a whole, as quickly and easily as texting a friend; and you will get to know your body, mind, and soul like never before.

You will find out about reading your destiny in the stars and communicating with your past selves across the barriers of time and space. You'll be able to see how to diagnose an imbalance in your energy centers quicker than you can google an illness. In fact, think of this book as the Google of spirituality.

You can browse different pages, reading about everything from crystals to chakras, meditation to aromatherapy, and yoga to spirit guides, to identify and incorporate the practices that work best for you.

You can add more of what enlivens and develops your spiritual journey and leave what doesn't add to your growth and happiness by the side of the road, and you can connect with other like-minded Soul Searchers across the globe, giving "spiritual connection" a whole new meaning.

> "You have to grow from the inside out.
> None can teach you, none can make you spiritual.
> There is no other teacher but your own soul."
> ❯Swami Vivekananda

Challenge Yourself

When I was a kid, my reply nine times out of ten was "But why?" My dad's response was always, "Because Y's a crooked letter and Z's no better." Um, rock on, Dad. Solid way to impart (some kind of confusing) wisdom!

We are taught from childhood to question, justify, and make sense of things that shouldn't, by their very nature, make sense. As our brain processes sensory experiences, it looks for patterns and then seeks out meaning in those patterns. This phenomenon, known as *cognitive dissonance*, shows that once we believe in something, we will try to explain away anything that conflicts with it. I personally just like to call this narrow-mindedness; it makes it hard for some people to be open to learning about other possible beliefs, ways of life, cultures, traditions, and experiences—typically these people have learned this through their upbringing or an inherited belief system.

Few people choose to "reset" their beliefs, but my experience is that those who do are destined for some big stuff—they are the inventors, pioneers, adventurers, teachers, and leaders of our time. Humans can't help but ask big questions. The best teachers are our own souls, and the best way to let our souls teach us what they want us to know is to feed them the good stuff! You get out what you put in, and that's what we're going to do here.

If there were some sort of super-badass underground Soul Searchers organization (move over, Fight Club) the first rule would be to challenge yourself. The second rule would be to do it again. The third rule would be—especially if it's your first time soul searching—that you have to ask the big question: What is it that you seek?

Then, when you know what that is, you have to grab your chakras by the horns and hold onto your cosmic handlebars!

Meaning? Belonging? Understanding? Love? Fulfillment? Peace? What's your destination? I have been exactly where you are now, trying to figure it all out. The only difference between you and me is you were smart and savvy enough to pick up this book. I fiscally skewered myself by empting my bank accounts to buy a one-way to ticket to the other side of the world to find myself, which ended up working for me but doesn't work for everyone.

You bet your ass I laughed/cried mine right off when I found out the answers I sought were inside me the whole time. But the truth remains: I challenged my fear of the unknown and took that leap of faith that is needed if you want to be rewarded with unclouded answers.

Everyone has a different path to tread on their journey toward spiritual enlightenment. Throughout this book, you will find anecdotes from myself and from my friends, family, and others I've met along the way who've tried out these practices and, in turn, have unique perspectives to share about the good, the bad, and the lessons to be learned about everything from meditation to crystal healing to star signs. You will also find "Explore This!" moments that offer suggestions on ways to dip your toe in the new age pool so you can float back and soak up all that spiritual goodness.

Every Journey Starts with a Story

Throughout time, life's eternal truths have been hidden, buried, burned, covered by rocks and dirt, and even sunk to the bottom of lakes. According to legend, Padmasambhava, also called "Lotus Born" or known to many as the second Buddha, believed humanity was not ready for his spiritual teachings in the eighth century. Almost six hundred years later, his hidden scriptures were found, stumbled upon by a Soul Searcher—a spiritual student just like you.[1]

Today, this scripture is one of the most popular spiritual books of all time: *The Tibetan Book of the Dead*. It has been translated into many languages, and its concepts continue to prove themselves universal. Why are they universal? Because everyone wants to know more about the soul, about our life's purpose, and about what happens when we die.

All good soul searches start with a story—the story we hear about a friend whose life has changed drastically for the better after they've taken up yoga, the tale your parents read to you as a child about an adventurer who explored far-off lands, even that offhand anecdote from your coworker who just learned about past-life regression that sparked your curiosity. In the spirit of storytelling, what tale of spiritual enlightenment is more inspiring and surprising than that of the great Buddha? It was one of the first stories I read when I became spiritually curious, and it is one all Soul Searchers should know:

An expectant mother had a vivid dream one night just before her child's birth. In her dream, she was visited by a white elephant which told her that her son would be offered two paths in life. On the first path, he could become a king and ruler. The other path was that of a healer and spiritual teacher. When she shared news of this dream with her husband, the king, he vowed to make the baby his successor and committed himself to making sure nothing would get in the way of his son's future rule.

The prince grew up in the confines of a palace, drowning in lust, riches, and power—a fake utopia free of any aging, illness, or hurt built by the king to make sure his son never felt a need to ask questions or seek out the meaning of life.

Fooled and distracted by the king's false world, the prince married and fathered a healthy baby boy. Being a father can be quite a sobering experience; however, for the young prince it was the spark that set his latent need to soul search alight, making him curious about life, its meaning, and his purpose.

With the permission of the king, he was allowed to venture outside the kingdom and deep into the city on the other side. However, prior to his venture into the unknown world outside the walls of the palace, the king had swept the streets of anything that would cause the prince to ask more questions; the sick, the poor, the elderly were all hidden from the prince's view—all except one. One frail old man sat on a street corner, and he immediately caught the prince's attention. The prince was captivated by the old man—his tales, his experiences, his age, and most of all, his suffering. The meeting had a profound impact on the prince, showing him a world he had never known existed.

> "You can search throughout the entire universe for someone
> who is more deserving of your love than you are yourself,
> and that person is not to be found. You yourself, as much as anybody
> in the entire universe, deserve your love and affection."
> **>Sharon Salzberg**

The more the prince learned about suffering and despair, the more his soul urged for more from his life, until one day he wandered into the forest, stripped off all his finery, cut off all of his hair, and left everything he was attached to behind. During this part of his journey, he surrounded himself with wise men, spiritual leaders, teachers, and gurus, but he was always left wanting more. One day, he stopped searching and settled, sitting under a tree, and began to meditate. Hours and then days passed as the young prince spent time not just with himself but within himself. After days of meditation, the prince reached enlightenment—and from that point onward, the young prince was known as Buddha. His teacher of enlightenment had been his soul.[2]

Most stories have a beginning, middle, and an end; however, a spiritual journey really only has a beginning, because self-discovery and learning is never ending. It all starts with a question, a desire to know more, understand more, see more, to explore and journey into the unknown. For you, the first step on your spiritual journey may very well have been picking up this book. Like the Buddha did, you seek knowledge, information, and wisdom.

You don't have to be a prince or a princess or strip away all your worldly possessions and go meditate endlessly in the forest—you certainly *could*, but nobody's asking you to become the next Buddha. The point is this: spiritual exploration and experimentation allow us to develop a deeper understanding of life and its inner workings, which in turn leads to peace, patience, and kindness.

When we say, "enlightened," we are referring to a lighted soul, one that is calm, connected, and concerned with both the suffering and the growth of others. Yes, this sort of growth can be painful at times. In fact, you may have been drawn to this book because of hurt, confusion, or a sense of incompleteness.

In truth, a soul search usually starts when someone feels lost, off track, or stuck. Rumi, an ancient spiritual mystic and poet said, "The wound is the place where the Light enters you," meaning that our human experiences—the suffering, the pain, and the growth—all contribute to our enlightenment.[3]

You, dear friend, are about to walk out of the confinement of your walls—the walls built by society, your parents' teachings, and everything you have grown to think and believe about the world. Your soul search will present you with far more roads to travel down than you even knew existed. Some will be silly; some will be profound. Some will make you laugh, and some will make you cry. Some you'll decide you don't feel like walking down after all, and others you'll continue down for the rest of your life. The important part is that you take the first step.

We are about to journey deep into your childhood and beyond, into past lives, where your soul lived in other countries, spoke other languages, and learned lessons your soul might still be seeking to learn again today. You will learn a variety of ways to connect and listen to your soul, feed your body and your mind, and connect to the hidden truths of the universe. You will dust off memories long forgotten in your subconscious and that hold the key to your life's purpose, and most importantly, you will learn tips on how to incorporate modern-day spirituality into your everyday life using the whole package: your body, mind, and soul.

So grab your bag of crystals, your yoga mat, and maybe a goji-chia snack or two, and come with me as you turn the pages and journey deeper into your spirituality.

What are you waiting for? Let's go!

"SPIRITUALITY IS NOT A RELIGION OR A TREND—IT IS A LIFESTYLE.
IT IS A LIFESTYLE OF AWARENESS THAT COMBINES THE UNDERSTANDING OF
FAITH, BODY, MIND, AND SOUL, ALLOWING US TO LIVE MODERN-DAY ENLIGHTENED
LIVES IN SMALL AND BIG WAYS."

WHAT KIND OF
SOUL SEARCHER ARE YOU?

This simple quiz will help you discover what type of Soul Searcher you are, guide your soul's purpose on its journey, and help you discover the meaning behind your search. Are you a

GODDESS?   SPIRITED HIPPIE?

YOGI?   LIGHT WORKER?   GURU?

WANDERER?   EARTH ANGEL?

Goddess, an Earth Angel, a Yogi, a Light Worker, a Spirited Hippie, a Guru, or a Wanderer? For the best results, go with your first instinctive answer, and listen to your whole body, not just your head. The less you think about it, the more accurate your results will be.

The first spiritual thing I experienced in my life was:

A festival (7)

A book or TV show (3)

Seeing or meeting a spiritual teacher (2)

An inner spiritual knowing (1)

A friend or family member shared religious or spiritual
   wisdom with me (4)

Reading a horoscope (6)

A yoga or meditation class (5)

In my downtime, I make time to:

Be alone in my sanctuary (1)

Practice yoga, hike, surf, or other physical activity (3)

Read (2)

Meditate and relax (4)

Socialize (7)

Decorate or make something (6)

Be in nature (5)

I became spiritual when:

I experienced a life crisis (3)

I was born spiritual or brought up with spirituality (1)

I traveled (6)

I learned that there was more to life in some way (2)

A relationship ended or I lost a loved one (4)

I began practicing yoga or meditation (5)

I embraced a more bohemian lifestyle (7)

When it comes to work:

It is just a way to pay the bills (7)

I am self-employed (1)

I am a full-time mother (6)

I am trying to work out a way to follow my purpose in life
   through my profession (4)

I have taken the leap and am following my purpose through
   my profession (2)

I love my job because it helps to support me financially (3)

I think about quitting every week (5)

I feel connected when:

I eat well and exercise (2)

I meditate, pray, worship, and/or talk to my guides (1)

I travel (5)

I am surrounded by like-minded people (7)

I can dip my feet in water or feel grass between my toes (3)

I am spreading love and wisdom wherever I go (4)

I am surrounded by beauty in any form (6)

I can pick out another spiritual person by:

Their openness to talk about all religions and spiritualties (1)

What they wear (7)

Their lifestyle (4)

How happy someone is (2)

The music someone is into (6)

What they do for a job (5)

Things that they say (2)

**The spiritual leader I would most like to meet
would be:**

Russell Brand (7)   Your yogi (2)

Oprah (5)   Buddha (3)

Gandhi (1)   Your personal angel or

The Dalai Lama (4)   guide (6)

**When I was a child, I would have most liked to
meet:**

A mermaid (4)   A bear (2)

A unicorn (7)   A princess (6)

An orca whale (1)   A turtle (3)

A fairy (5)

Guru: 7–11 You are an old soul. An observer, a listener, and a guide for others, your journey involves learning patience, forgiveness, and imparting wisdom to those whom you can identify as your pupils. You can create a ripple effect: start with one, then heal and transform many. The Guru's journey is all about staying centered, stable, and grounded no matter what storms you may have to endeavor. The Guru's life can come hand in hand with sacrifice, and you are often challenged and tested, tempted by the lure of turning your back on your purpose because sometimes the easy road is the one more traveled. Remember, you are destined for the one less traveled.

Earth Angel: 19–25 You are a sensitive and intuitive soul. You have had more life experiences than most people you know and you have a natural gift for rapport, communicating and inspiring others. Your journey is to become a messenger, a leader, and a teacher to others, which could see you in the public eye as a writer, speaker, teacher, instructor, actor, singer, or artist. Like other Earth Angels, such as Mother Teresa, Princess Diana, Jane Goodall, and Gabrielle Bernstein, your life lessons are love, nurturing, and leaving a trail of kindness throughout your journey.

Goddess: 31–38 You are a nurturing, angelic, vibrant soul. You have an organic aura of beauty that surrounds you that lots of people comment on. People are drawn to your company, and because of that, you are very social and popular. You have an inner calling to sisterhood, and feel most empowered when you are surrounded by like-minded souls, especially women. Your soul lessons will be connected to friendships, relationships, and family, and mastering the art of human love, teaching, and guiding other soul sisters and goddesses alike.

Wanderer: 45–49 You are a free-spirited and brave soul. Others admire and comment on your liberation and your ability to follow your heart and dreams. You love to laugh and seize life, and your journey involves seeking fulfillment in each and every day. You have an affinity for travel, and you often feel most at home on the road, when you have nothing holding you back. Your soul grows with every brave leap you take. Your journey involves forging new paths, venturing into the unknown, and challenging yourself to step out of your comfort zone.

Yogi: 12–18 You are a playful, pure, and energetic soul. You are open to new ideas and believe in always expanding your mind, stretching to new limits, and pushing yourself to continue to grow, develop, and reach new spiritual heights. Your journey will involve experiences that challenge you to transform and evolve. Just like the art of mastering a headstand, your life involves bravery, growth, new experiences, and movement. You are not afraid of the unknown—in fact, you invite it into your life and understand it is the key to your soul teachings and spiritual growth.

Light Worker: 26–30 You are a healer and are gifted with the ability to transform lives. You have a connection to Mother Nature and often find yourself looking for ways to help people. Light Workers make excellent counselors, healers, doctors, or life coaches, often working in communities where they can reach and touch people's lives. Like the proverbial moth to a flame, people are drawn to your brightness—you light up a space, shine light on people's dark spots, and often have a natural gift for leaving others feeling freer. You live bright, and the world needs your light.

Bohemian: 39–44 You are a gifted and beautiful soul. Beauty attracts beauty, so it is not uncommon for bohemian spirits to be attracted to crystal jewelry, perfumes, aromatherapy, and fashion. You leave a trail of fairy dust after every step you take on your journey. Your path is about seeing the beauty in all things, all experiences, and all people—you always see the bright side, come out smelling roses, and have a natural glow that attracts others to you, you little beauty, you!

Spirited Hippy: 50+ You are a wild flower child whose soul is here to feel joy and love, while spreading joy and love to those in your company. At times, others find you overwhelming because you are so honest, connected, and straightforward in your approach to life. You get the big picture and believe in enjoying every aspect of it—the good, the bad, and the offbeat! The ones who stick around love being in your company because you help people let their hair down and can teach people to disconnect from their egos. Your journey is all about helping people have fun with their life, helping those around you open up, loosen up, and move to the beat of life.

PART I

HEALTHY BODY

One thing I've learned on my spiritual journey is that my soul's number-one tool is my body. The school of thought I personally lean toward is that our souls use our bodies to communicate with us. The soul talks to us through sensations—our energy levels, illnesses, and aches and pains are all ways our souls give us signals that something is out of whack.

For both my personal purposes and the purposes of this book, I define *soul* as your essence; the voice in your head that says things you haven't thought of; the driving force behind your desires, impulses, and dreams; that almost magical element of your being that both transcends mental and physical boundaries and plays a vital role in their well-being. The soul is the calling within you to seek, search, and discover everything you can channel, create, and master in this lifetime.

If our souls could take control of our bodies, mine would probably kung-fu chop that aspi-

rin bottle I reached for this morning, and yours would probably derail that Netflix-and-junk-food binge you went on to soothe the aches and pains of a long workweek; instead, they'd make us focus on the eloquent language of our bodies that so many of us have forgotten how to speak. There are underlying reasons why we get those headaches, eye twitches, backaches, and cold sores. So I challenge you to stop masking those reasons and stop acting surprised when they keep coming back to bite you in the butt! I invite you to get to the core issues of what your body and soul are telling you.

If we pursue the idea that our bodies are also reflections of our minds and our souls, then our thoughts, feelings, emotions, experiences, and energy are all reflected in how we nurture and love (or not) our bodies. It follows that how we feed, nurture, and even present ourselves to the outside world all reveal our spiritual state. If we act from the core understanding that our souls choose our bodies, actively inhabit them, and, most importantly, need those bodies to thrive, then we can identify when our souls are warning us, telling us when our souls are tired, when we're off track, and when we're out of tune.

So pay attention when hairs stand on end, goose bumps blanket your skin, and shivers tickle down your spine—all of these may well be signs of intuitive communication from our souls, telling us that something is happening that we should pay attention to. The more connected we become to our souls, the more in tune we will become with our bodies, and vice versa.

The question of whether we do, in fact, have a soul or not has been asked through the centuries by philosophers and everyday folks—like us!—alike. Pythagoras believed the soul left clues in numbers and studied numerology—numbers that dictate a soul's journey in life—even giving a "soul number" to every individual. Plato believed the soul was a person's spiritual essence. Aristotle believed the soul was the essence of a being's personality and nature. Immanuel Kant believed in the ever-evolving soul through immortal reincarnation. Carl Jung spoke often about the power of the soul, and the miracles and unexplained cosmic force it held in each of us.

The world of medicine and the healing arts—doctors, researchers, scientists, light workers, and holistic healers, to name a few professions in that field—is another area where the relationship between the body and the soul is a hot topic. Some believe that when we die, the soul leaves the body, that the body is simply a host for our journey on earth. Others believe that what we call the soul is snuffed out like a candle the moment our corporeal selves stop functioning. Many in the science and spiritual communities study the balance and effects of imbalances in the body, mind, and soul, and how these imbalances can be directly linked to illness and disease. From out-of-body experiences to phantom limb pain, the body's intrinsic connection to this thing we call the soul is—however mysterious—undeniable.

What a lot of us have lost touch with is how much of an impact our bodies have on our moods, thoughts, and overall energy and essence, which in turn has an enormous impact on how we feel and heal. Broken down into its etymological parts, *disease*, after all, is *dis* (lack of) and *ease* (physical comfort, undisturbed state of the body; tranquility, peace of mind). When we're sick or otherwise in a state of physical discomfort, we're much more likely to focus on negative emotions and actions as well—not exactly a happy diet for your soul to subsist on! When we have been hoarding emotions, we can expect our souls to feel bloated, irritated, grouchy—again all symptoms of a constipated soul—which also makes for a great spiritual insult, e.g., "It's okay that she's behaving like a royal b*io*tch. Her soul's just constipated."

> "The main purpose of life is to live rightly, think rightly, act rightly. The soul must languish when we give all our thought to the body."
> **>Mahatma Gandhi**

Someone once told me that, just like our day-to-day experiences and challenges hold keys to our wider journey, so too do our bodies and any bodily problems or illnesses we may be facing. Just like when our minds and hearts decide it's time to move on from hurt, resentment, or hostility, the same goes for our bodies.

The point is, if we don't let go of all that crap, where do we keep it? Inside ourselves, is where (and where actual crap's concerned, quite literally!). When we choose to suppress and hang on to negative emotions, they can manifest internally as illnesses and disease, or become catalysts for unhealthy lifestyles. That's when you've just gotta shake it off—like Taylor Swift would.

> "The way you think, the way you behave, the way you eat, can influence your life by thirty to fifty years."
> **>attributed to Deepak Chopra**

As I did my own spiritual exploring, it became clear to me that there are three key aspects in our control when it comes to nurturing our bodies: what goes into our bodies, how our bodies interact with the world, and our attitudes toward our physical selves and how those attitudes influence the overall spiritual health of our souls. In this section, you will learn how to communicate with your body through its own language, to seek out the best possible combination of spiritual self-care.

Whether it's through finally perfecting your downward dog, understanding the potential of homeopathic healing, or experimenting with aromatherapy to combat stress, the point here is to experiment with what works for you. Play around, explore, mess up! I sure did . . . and so will you. Embrace it! In fact, it will make you feel better: If you learn from making mistakes, why wouldn't you want to make some? Hell, I must be a genius considering some of the world-class crashing and burning I managed while learning some spiritual doozies. Genius, I tell you!

Life's a journey, and each Soul Searcher's path is different with rest stops and info booths along the way. The info both we're headed to in the next few chapters is simply this: spiritual well-being through physical bliss.

1

YOUR BODY BALANCE

Ever fallen asleep while reading something on your iPad in bed only to have it fall from your fingers and smack you in the face?

I think we've all been there, or some version of there, whether we admit to it or not. What if it's not just sleep clumsiness? Maybe little technology elves are trying to send us a blunt-force message of the go-the-f★★k-to-sleep variety.

Magical mischief makers or not, we could all use a wake-up call once in a while to remind us to give our body the good lovin' it deserves— whether that love manifests in the form of getting more rest, engaging in more physical exercise, eating right, or feeding the connection between our bodies, minds, and spirits. Consider this chapter your wake-up call from your ol' bag of bones.

I (and most everyone else at this point) have noticed over and over that, in today's world, we are taught to "just do it," to "never give up," and we are living busier, fast-food-saturated, sleep-deprived,

instantly downloadable lives surrounded by lights, energies, frequencies, and stressors that we've never before encountered as a species. While there are major benefits to all the innovations of modern life—amazing advances in medicine and green energy, the ability to form partnerships and friendships across the globe, opportunities to do more and be more than ever before—the "should've done it yesterday" mentality is also taking a heavy toll on our mental, emotional, and physical well-being.

Unlike our phones and tablets, we cannot simply plug ourselves in to recharge our batteries and, no matter what anyone tells you about energy drinks and wake-up pills, a magic, quick-fix recharge just doesn't exist.

The things you are about to explore spell the imminent demise of your romance with your energy Band-Aid of choice. With the encouragement of your body, you are about to break up with your quick fix, so start working out how you are going to dump your pseudo-energy crutch now. It's not you; it's the crutch. And, hopefully, you're just not that into it anymore . . .

Our habit of being constantly connected and finding ways to artificially rev ourselves up doesn't just impact our rest. Privacy has gone the way of the dodo bird. Our lives have never been more public, making solitude a rarity and self-care nearly nonexistent. Today, we often find ourselves consumed by society's penchant for over-delivering on work results and undervaluing quality of life. As a result, many of us feel like our lives, minds, and bodies are spinning out of control.

Happily, concepts like "mental health days" and the integration of practices like office fitness programs, along with a general acceptance of holistic health practices, are becoming more widespread. People are finally beginning to see the benefits of feeding their souls with things that fuel their happiness, relax their minds, and most importantly, leave their bodies feeling more balanced.

Some practice yoga or meditation; some seek out alternatives to traditional Western medicine. I've noticed there is one unifying factor across those practices: they bring our bodies back into equilibrium with our minds and souls.

What works for you isn't necessarily going to work for me or your mom or your best friend; it's all trial and error (emphasis on the *error* at times, right, you little genius?), but without experimentation, no one would ever leave the damn house in the morning! So roll up your sleeves and get your hands dirty here. Your body will thank you for it.

Finding Balance: Holistic Practices

I had a handful of epic fail moments when I began to dip my toes into holistic practices (as I have already stated, and you're welcome, by the way). I am happily stripping my soul bare for you, so feel free to learn from my spiritual stretch marks and holistic cellulite. From my own experiences, here is my up-front list of stuff to just avoid, right off the bat—start as you mean to continue, I say.

Yoga is not a marathon. Go slow and steady. I almost put my back out trying my first Bridge Pose; it made me briefly consider trying some warm-up stretching before the yoga stretching to limber up.

Always, but always, when you are detoxing, make sure you are close to a restroom—you do not want to have the nearly-didn't-make-it-to-the-toilet situation that I had on my hands when I was midway through a cleanse. (FYI: the movie cliché is true; you do actually hold your ass as you run to the toilet.)

Crystals, oils, smoke, and other scented things are never a substitute for soap. My loving friends staged a much-needed intervention to talk to me about my "aroma-therapy vs. soap" issue, and I was finally able to admit that I did, indeed, smell.

All of these were huge moments for me, laughable, embarrassing learning curves on my journey to holistic living, and all vital to my continued spiritual growth. My point here is that if you ever find yourself in a similar muscle-spasm-y, butt-clench-y, body-odor-y situation, don't sweat it too much and keep two things at the ready—an open mind and a sense of humor. You'll work out pretty quickly what will work for your lifestyle and what won't, and remember: laughter is one of the best natural medicines out there.

Over the years, I've dabbled in all the fields below—some of which have stuck with me as constant companions to my physical well-being, and some that I've tried once or twice and then bid farewell to because they didn't serve me the way I needed. Again, this journey is all about curiosity, experimentation, and fun; you will not find a one-size-fits-all spiritual checklist on this path. It's also important to remember the place of Western medicine in this dance, and that if you have serious symptoms that you're concerned about, please consult a licensed medical professional as soon as possible.

Below is a range of holistic healing techniques that I've experienced in my soul search, and I hope that there's something for every Soul Searcher here. Let's get started!

Chiropractor

WOO-WOO SCALE: ▲▲▲▲▲▲▲▲▲▲
EXPLORE-IT SCALE: ▲▲▲▲▲▲▲▲▲△△

A chiropractor specializes in a form of alternative medicine that involves realigning and balancing the body by readjusting the spine, usually resulting in pain relief, better body movement, and helping the immune and nervous systems. Chiropractors address everything from headaches to foot aches, which are usually signs that your body is out of balance in some way, whether from stress, an injury, or an illness.

EXPLORE THIS!

Oh, snap! Yes, getting popped and cracked can be kind of scary the first time, but trust me, once you feel the benefits of being properly aligned, you'll wonder why it took you so long to try it. I know I sure did. Put aside any fears or skepticism you may be harboring and give a chiro a call!

Naturopath

WOO-WOO SCALE: ▲▲▲▲▲▲▲▲▲▲
EXPLORE-IT SCALE: ▲▲▲▲▲▲▲▲▲▲

A naturopath practices alternative medicine based on your body's vital energies, and focuses on holistic and preventative healing using a combination of general lifestyle advice, diet advice, relaxation techniques, and herbal tonics, supplements, or oils to help balance out the body. You may benefit from visiting a naturopath if you have allergies, suffer from low energy, have a compromised immune system, or struggle with arthritis, to name a few.

Homeopath

WOO-WOO SCALE: ▲▲▲▲▲▲▲▲▲▲
EXPLORE-IT SCALE: ▲▲▲▲▲▲▲▲▲▲

A homeopath, similar to a naturopath in some ways, practices alternative medicine using diluted tonics or tablets made from plants and minerals to help trigger the body's natural healing systems. Many people who struggle with issues such as fatigue, infertility, anxiety, depression, and bowel problems have said that they find visiting a homeopath beneficial. I've found that this practice also tends to be a lot gentler on the body, and cheaper than supplements from health food stores or concentrated tonics from naturopaths, which is always a plus!

EXPLORE THIS!

Google "basic reflexology chart" and take yourself through a mini-crash course on reflexology right there at your computer. Want more? See if a holistic healing center, massage center, or other health-care facility offers reflexology services in your area.

Reflexology

WOO-WOO SCALE: ▲▲▲▲▲▲▲▲▲▲
EXPLORE-IT SCALE: ▲▲▲▲▲▲▲▲▲▲

Reflexology is a zone of alternative medicine that focuses on the feet, hands, ears, and other parts of the body. When massaged, pinched, or pressed, certain trigger areas of the body can help shift energy and blockages in corresponding areas. For example, gentle pressure applied to the mound of the palm can aid with digestion, and pressure to the pad of the thumb can help with headaches.

Acupuncture

WOO-WOO SCALE: ▲▲▲▲▲▲▲▲▲▲
EXPLORE-IT SCALE: ▲▲▲▲▲▲▲▲▲▲

Game for being a real life voodoo doll? Acupuncture is an alternative medicine that involves retuning or balancing the body by using fine needles inserted into the skin at energy points to help heal, align, and prevent imbalances in the body. This ancient healing technique is known to benefit circulatory disorders; nose, ear, eye, and throat disorders; immune, addiction, and emotional disorders; and to relax muscle tension as well as joint and arthritis pain. Getting stuck full of pointy things doesn't sound super-appealing, but man, does it work! At least it has for me in the past. Plus, the needles are so thin (seriously, look up a picture of them—you can barely see 'em!) that you hardly notice the prick of one entering your skin.

Massage

WOO-WOO SCALE: ▲▲▲▲▲▲▲▲▲▲
EXPLORE-IT SCALE: ▲▲▲▲▲▲▲▲▲▲

Alternative healing massage combines the benefits of touch, muscle relaxation techniques, and often aromatherapy. Massage helps the body recover, reset, and relax, and it can relieve back pain and general muscle pain, boost immunity, and release endorphins, all helping to restore natural balance in the body. Who doesn't love a good massage? Chances are if you don't, you've either not tried one yet or haven't found the right practitioner. Make sure to tell your therapist what you're looking for (hard/soft pressure, problem areas, and comfort level with being touched) and don't be afraid to shop around until you find the right fit.

"Begin to see yourself as a soul with a body rather than a body with a soul."
>attributed to Wayne Dyer

Detoxing Stress

WOO–WOO SCALE: ▲▲▲▲▲▲▲▲▲▲
EXPLORE–IT SCALE: ▲▲▲▲▲▲▲▲▲▲

Stress is a killer. Literally. But instead of getting all doom and gloom about it, let's look at it from the perspective of healing rather than hand-wringing, shall we? A major key to honoring and loving up your body is fighting stress, and while it's nearly impossible to completely eliminate stress from a modern-day lifestyle (I can hear y'all laughing your asses off right now at the mere thought), we can use some of the techniques below to help us relieve the effects of stress by relaxing the body, mind, and spirit. Think of them like a de-stress soul aid kit. You know, for when you just want to tell the world to go smudge itself.

Below are some simple stress-relief techniques I have tried and come to trust to help center, ground, and relax me in times of stress, anxiety, and depression. (They're like the three-headed dog that guards the gates of the underworld for me—one hardly ever shows up without the other two!) Also, why not use more than one de-stress super-power at a time to fight your stress monsters. I use a lot of these techniques when my wheels have come right off altogether, or sometimes when I've just hit a bump in a road.

Based on my own experiences and the experiences of those close to me, it seems that people tend to quickly connect with one or two stress-coping tools that suit their level and flavor of stress (if only stress came in mint chocolate chip or praline pecan), and the key is to remember everything has to be balanced—you can't always be flying high, and that's okay. You're gonna have low days, weeks, sometimes even months, but happiness and well-being will come when you learn how to manage your stressors in sustainable ways; your lows won't be so low and so long.

The number-one hurdle where coping with stress is concerned is time. First question I ask stress addicts: "Do you believe you have no time to de-stress?" It can become a vicious cycle if you're not careful. We think, *I need more time to focus on reducing my stress*, which in turn, stresses us out more. So here's my challenge to you for this section: take ten minutes. Just ten. That's it. Every day, preferably at the same time every day, devote those ten minutes to a stress-reduction technique of your choosing. Try out all of the ones below or just one or two, but promise me this: stick with at least one of them for a week, and then a month . . . and then two—onward until those precious ten minutes are your go-to time to focus on you and give some love and kindness back to your incredible body.

Breathe

WOO-WOO SCALE: ▲▲▲▲▲▲▲▲▲▲
EXPLORE-IT SCALE: ▲▲▲▲▲▲▲▲▲▲

(For the record, if you think breathing is *woo-woo*, then maybe we should go over the four things we all must do to survive: sleep, eat, drink, and breathe. All mandatory for living, so it ranks a zero on the *Woo-Woo Scale*.) Crazy simple, right? Yes, I'm really telling you to inhale oxygen into your lungs and exhale carbon dioxide. Think about it: When was the last time you took a moment to really just breathe?

Mantras

WOO-WOO SCALE: ▲▲▲▲▲▲▲▲▲▲
EXPLORE-IT SCALE: ▲▲▲▲▲▲▲▲▲▲

Negative self-talk can be the quickest catalyst to spark a stress-out. When our minds start going a hundred miles an hour with the thinking, processing, and worrying, our bodies' adrenaline response can also kick into overdrive. Quiet the negative self-talk by having a mantra or affirmation that helps you collect yourself. I often tell myself simple mantras such as, "Keep life simple," "It always works out," and "Zoom out for a minute." We'll learn more about mantras later in the chapter.

Zen

WOO-WOO SCALE: ▲▲▲▲▲▲▲▲▲▲
EXPLORE-IT SCALE: ▲▲▲▲▲▲▲▲▲▲

Zen exists and you can go there! Think of it as your inner garden of peace, your sanctum where negative weeds of thought cannot grow and where you nourish and cultivate loving, peaceful, fulfilling thoughts and actions. Change your thoughts and focus your energy on yourself, recharging and fueling

EXPLORE THIS!

The quickest, cheapest, and most beneficial way to help alert your body that it no longer needs to be in a state of panic is just to simply to breathe. Take one deep breath through your nose, allowing your chest (but not your shoulders) to rise. Hold your breath for few seconds and then powerfully exhale through your mouth, trying to make the exhalation longer than the inhalation (in for four, hold for five, out for seven is ratio that works well for me). Do this five to ten times and feel your body begin to calm itself. You can do it anywhere too: your car, in a coffee shop, at your computer, wherever you happen to be. Hurrah for breathing!

your positivity. Take five minutes of Zen time a day among the chaos to check in with yourself—incorporate them into your ten minutes of stress self-care or take another five specifically for your Zen time; it's up to you. Are you tense? Are you hungry? Are you tired? Ask your body these questions with a still and caring mind, and your body will be honest with you. Serve your body's needs, listen to what your body has to say, and remember that it operates best when it is relaxed, fueled, and centered.

EXPLORE THIS!

One of my coworkers at an old job made a little sanctuary in his cubicle under his desk at the office. It was a high-stress job by nature, and we all needed coping mechanisms in place for days when it got really rough. His was definitely my favorite. He brought in a yoga mat, pillow, face mask, blanket, battery-operated Christmas lights, and some aromatherapy oils in tiny vials (learn more about the powers of aromatherapy in chapter 3) and made himself a little Zen nest right there under his computer, phone, and baseball player bobblehead doll collection. Most days, and especially after a particularly grueling phone call or meeting, he'd crawl under there, put in his earbuds, dab some oil under his nose, put on his face mask, and simply be still for five or ten minutes. Sure, some of us thought he was a total fruitcake, but I'd bet anything that he was the most relaxed person in that high-stress job, so you could argue he was the one winning at life.

Meditation

WOO-WOO SCALE: ▲▲▲△△△△△△△
EXPLORE-IT SCALE: ▲▲▲▲▲▲▲▲▲▲

Stop! It is that easy. For real. Remember those ten minutes? That's all you need, trust me. If you want to go further and have the time, do it. But start with ten minutes every day. Sit, stop, relax, breathe, and allow your mind to completely go with the flow. Just allow your thoughts, emotions, and breath to be. If you find your mind wandering off, bring your attention back to the in-and-out rhythm of your breath entering your nose and then leaving your mouth. Breathe into your belly and lungs, not your shoulders and neck. Take a few minutes to be in a state of natural nothingness. Allowing your body time to regroup like this is a chance to reset your body's major systems—nervous, cardiovascular, and digestive—and to start fresh when your day may be cluttered with stressors and burdens. Instead of checking your messages or email, or picking up a magazine in a waiting room, sit with yourself in silence, peace, and rest—every minute helps. Learn more about meditation later in this chapter.

Yoga

WOO-WOO SCALE: ▲▲▲▲▲▲▲▲▲▲▲
EXPLORE-IT SCALE: ▲▲▲▲▲▲▲▲▲▲▲

Some say that when we take care of our bodies, we also take care of our souls and would I agree with that mostly because of my experience with yoga.

Yoga has been used for thousands of years as a practice to strengthen and unite the mind, body, and soul, with the purpose of keeping everything in balance. On this journey toward everyday emotional, physical, and spiritual healing and enlightenment, yoga offers ways to ground the body while helping to strengthen and tone it as well. These poses can be used as in-the-moment coping strategies to relieve anxiety and bring awareness back into ourselves in a world where we're constantly feeling like we're spinning off into outer space.

Before we dive in, I feel compelled to include a small disclaimer here. Your first yoga class might stress you out a bit given that it'll be a new environment with new people and involve new physical demands placed on your body. You'll get more out of it if you can enter a chillsville state of mind before you start. Trust me. Don't worry about how you look in yoga pants, how sweaty you get, or how ridiculous you feel in your first Downward Facing Dog. Everyone feels a little goofy in their first handful of Downward Dogs. It's called Downward Dog, for the love of Pete, and your ass is in the air. How can you feel anything else? Just be proud of yourself for giving it a go. Also, feel free to giggle.

One other note: people fart during yoga. There, I said it. It's embarrassing, it's hilarious, and it totally happens. All that twisting and bending is bound to give your intestines a workout. If it happens to you or someone in your class, laugh it off (at least inside your head), shake it off, and keep going. Stay aware of your body and your breath while you learn the yogic ropes, and cut yourself and others some slack—even when someone has cut the cheese.

Below are some simple yoga poses that can be incorporated easily into your daily routine. Try to hold each pose for at least five breaths (breathe in for four or five seconds and out for the same). The type and method of breathing varies throughout different styles of yoga, the basic breath (*Ujjayi*), is done with the mouth closed and a slight constriction in the throat. A more advance form is *Kundalini*, where for each breath, slowly and deeply inhale through your nose and exhale out your mouth. Do not keep holding a pose if it is hurting you in any way. The more you relax into a pose, the better the stretch will be. Also, a quick, me-being-stern moment: don't beat yourself up if you're not a master yogi instantly! This stuff takes time. Start with the easy poses (there's literally a pose called "Easy Pose," dudes) and then work your way into deeper, longer, more complex poses and routines.

Easy Pose/Sukhasana

They weren't kidding when they called this the "Easy" Pose, because wow, is it ever. Calm and focus is required to maintain the posture and breathing, which makes it ideal for both prevention and in-the-moment coping for those who experience anxiety.

Those who are feeling displaced or confused can mindfully envision the body as being rooted to the ground like a tree. I find this imagery very calming and beautiful, and it helps me feel connected not just to myself but also to the earth below me.

Downward Facing Dog/Adho Mukha Svanasana

Famous for its easily recognizable ass-in-the-air position, Downward Facing Dog is what I like to call a turbo-button pose. A powerful stretch that helps fight fatigue and stimulates the body, Downward Facing Dog promotes healthy circulation and relieves lower back pain. By bending the knees, you can get into a deeper and often more comfortable pose.

This pose helps you take time to check how you are feeling.

Plow Pose/Halasana

Yes, another ass-in-the-air pose, but this time you are sheltered from the stares of those behind you! This pose helps to calm the nervous system and strengthen the immune system. The stretch uses the weight of your legs to gently loosen the lower back and spine.

Plow Pose is also helpful in relieving symptoms of menopause and can help with stomachaches too.

Tree Pose/Vrksasana

The tree: strong, solid, stable. Are you? By perfecting this pose, you can be as rooted as an old oak. I'm more like a droopy, underwatered, bathroom potted plant most of the time, which is why this pose is a goody because it challenges you to use your body strength to balance, helping to strengthen your legs and core as you ground yourself.

The emphasis on balancing helps you to stay in the present moment and focus your body and mind while holding the pose steady.

Bow Pose/Dhanurasana

I hear Missy Elliott's "Get Ur Freak On" every time I do this pose—it's just so bendy. But fear not! This pose isn't as hard as it looks. Bow Pose is a perfect full-body strengthener, helping to lift the chest and strengthen the body from the chest and shoulders down to the groin and ankles.

Holding the pose helps to stimulate the organs in your core and awaken the body. It also helps to improve posture and confidence.

Triangle Pose/Trikonasana

All right, you. If you haven't been brave enough to pick a pose yet, this one is it. The training wheel of all poses, triangle pose opens the chest and shoulders, and your hand can reach as far down as the floor, depending on your flexibility level. This stretch stimulates the lower abdominal organs, aiding digestion, and also helps give you a feeling of greater space by widening your legs and lengthening your arms.

Camel Pose/Ustrasana

Take this bad boy nice and slow because chances are your back and neck are going to be holding a lot of your daily tension. This pose stretches the entire front of the body by arching the back and pushing forward with the hips, stretching along the thighs, groin, chest, and throat. The stretch helps lengthen the spine and helps with posture by strengthening the back.

Cobra Pose/Bhujangasana

For the more low-key of the yogis, the cobra is a gentle stretch that is perfect to do in between your other poses. This pose is a great one for opening the lungs and heart and has been known to benefit breathing and combat fatigue, and kick asthma's ass.

Schools of Yoga

WOO-WOO SCALE: ▲▲▲▲▲△△△△△△
EXPLORE-IT SCALE: ▲▲▲▲▲▲▲▲▲▲

Hatha Yoga
Perfect for beginners and advanced yogis

Hatha is a slow-paced, flowing style of yoga that focuses on meditation; breathing; and strength-building, stretching, and balancing poses.

Benefits include: exercise, flexibility, strength, balance, stress relief, and improving circulation.

Ananda Yoga
Good for beginners and advanced yogis

Ananda focuses on combining silent affirmations while holding various Hatha Yoga poses. The poses and movements are designed to prepare the mind, body, and soul for meditation.

Benefits include: stimulation of blood flow and energy to the brain.

Vinyasa Yoga
Good for beginners and advanced yogis seeking more strength

Vinyasa focuses on sun salutations (Google "basic sun salutation" and incorporate this short sequence into your morning!) and a series of other poses that connect you with your breathing. The poses are held for a series of breaths, calling for greater focus on strength and challenging mind over matter.

Benefits include: flexibility, strength, stress reduction, and reducing high blood pressure and cardiovascular issues.

Anusara Yoga
Good for intermediate yogis seeking alignment and
both physical and spiritual growth

Anusara focuses on the body, mind, and spirit as one, and is essentially a more modern day, integrated approach to Hatha yoga. This style of yoga can be very therapeutic and brings our awareness to the body's attitude, alignment, and action.

Benefits include: pose refinement, general health and well-being, a deeper integration of Hatha yoga benefits.

Ashtanga Yoga
Good for fit, healthy yogis looking to get in touch with their spiritual side

"Power yoga" is adapted from Ashtanga, and it is known as "vinyasa" as well. Ashtanga yoga consists of six athletic pose sequences known as "series or eight-limbed yoga." Ashtanga yoga combines a series of poses, lunges, and push-ups. The length of one full breath dictates the length of time spent transitioning between asanas, or poses.

Benefits include: better coordination, strength, core conditioning, fewer back problems, and weight loss.

Bikram Yoga
Good for beginners and advanced yogis
(also good for people with certain injuries)

Bikram is sometimes referred to as "hot yoga" because it is practiced in a room heated to 95–100 degrees, though other types of yoga can be referred to as "hot" as well if practiced in a heated room; if you're looking for a specific type, be sure to check the description of the practice to know for sure. Bikram consists of practicing the same twenty-six poses in the same order every time, and the heat allows the muscles to relax, allowing for a deeper stretch, and the humidity makes you focus more deliberately on your breathing. It's kind of uncomfortable at first, but can soon grow addictive!

Benefits include: flexibility, detoxing and cleansing the body; can speed up the recovery process for certain injuries and strains.

AcroYoga
For intermediate and advanced yogis

AcroYoga combines yoga and acrobatics, and is performed in partnership with another yogi.

Benefits include: strength, concentration, balance, massage, and focus.

Rhythm Yoga
Perfect for beginners and the advanced yogi alike

Rhythm yoga is a mix of Vinyasa yoga, meditation, breathing, and dance. This type of yoga tends to be free flowing and organic, and focuses on the dance and movement aspects of the practice.

Benefits include: relaxation, flexibility, stress reduction, strength, circulation, and balance—not to mention fun!

Kundalini Yoga
Perfect for beginners and advanced yogis who are interested in the more spiritual or relaxation side of yoga

Also known as "Laya yoga," Kundalini focuses on compassion and mindfulness through yoga. Through breath and movement, energy is released from the base of the spine, heating up the body and challenging you physically, mentally, and emotionally to connect with your spirit. No two Kundalini classes are the same, and this form of yoga is best experienced with an open mind and no expectations.

Benefits include: physical and emotional grounding in the body, increased awareness and compassion for the self and others, increased overall spiritual health.

Tibetan Yoga
Good for both beginners and advanced yogis looking for all-around Zen

Tibetan yoga is a combination of gentle exercise, breathing practices, and self-massage. Classes are not very common in the Western world, but some poking around online should lead you to more information on this practice.

Benefits include: bringing together the body, mind, and spirit and unifying them in health.

The possibilities, combinations, and opportunities yoga provides are nearly endless, and I invite you to explore. I also strongly recommend joining a class to help you with technique. You will be introduced to new postures as well as different types of yoga, not to mention like-minded yogis as well.

Yoga may seem like a fad at times, but its benefits are undeniable, and most people find that once they push past that initial frustration and resistance that comes when learning any new skill, yoga is an immensely rewarding practice that supports all sorts of spiritual growth.

Another practice that may seem like a fad, but is really just fabulous, is meditation. Drawing a blank can seriously rock, especially when done for at least ten minutes a day while in a relaxed position.

Schools of Meditation

WOO–WOO SCALE: ▲▲▲▲▲▲▲▲▲▲
EXPLORE–IT SCALE: ▲▲▲▲▲▲▲▲▲▲

Meditation sounded super-intimidating to me before I tried it. Spending minutes or even hours just sitting there, thinking about *nothing*? Are you kidding me? You know the old adage "Don't knock it until you try it"? Turns out that it's an über true adage, especially regarding my experience with meditation.

Put it this way—spiritual peeps have been practicing meditation for over five thousand years. I'm talking the oldest, the wisest, and the most enlightened, awake, and spiritual Soul Seekers throughout time, from the Vedas in ancient India and the Tao in China, to the Buddhists of Japan, and all the way up through to the Beatles, who learned transcendental meditation while traveling in India in the sixties.[1]

You are about to tune in to a meditative vibe just as spiritual and cultural juggernauts Deepak Chopra and Oprah have, as well as funny folks with a soulful side, such as Russell Brand, Jim Carrey, and Ellen DeGeneres, who all fit a bit of quiet time into their hectic schedules with meditation.

Ancient and modern Soul Searchers alike understand that meditation can be daily hygiene for the soul, clearing out stress, anxiety, and emotional blockages from our mind and body. I have often heard meditation referred to as a "mental shower," cleaning and cleansing the mind.

As you explore this awesome tool, think of meditation as flipping the bird at your daily stressors, because when you incorporate meditation into your routine—remember it can totally be short bits of time; sometimes all it takes is ten minutes a day—you may not end up with less to stress about, but you'll sure end up better equipped to combat those stressors when they rear their ugly heads. Sayonara, chill pills. Hello, natural Zen.

Mindfulness Meditation

An adaptation of Buddhist Vipassana meditation,[2] this is a popular form of meditation because it can be performed pretty much anywhere. Mindfulness meditation is when you cultivate an awareness of everything surrounding you and yet also acknowledge nothing, simply letting sounds, smells, and thoughts flow freely through you.

Spiritual Meditation

This practice is often linked to religion and is the act of prayer or worship to a god or belief. It offers you time to reflect and seek what you truly desire or need, and then to ask for assistance—or simply to give thanks.

Mantra Meditation

Mantra meditation incorporates a repeating chant, affirmation, or om, known as a mantra, that helps keep you focused and present during meditation. Read more about mantras later in this chapter.

EXPLORE THIS!

Sit on a mat, chair, or flat cushion with your back straight and your eyes closed. Focus on your breathing—how it moves in and out of your lungs, how your chest and belly expand with each breath, and how each part of your body feels as oxygen flows through it. If your mind wanders away from your breath, acknowledge it, don't judge it, and slowly bring your awareness back from the distraction and to your breathing again. Try this every day for ten minutes or so and observe the results. Do you feel more calm, centered, and aware? Do you feel less stressed as you face your rigors of the day? Are you sleeping better?

Guided Meditation

A guided meditation incorporates music, sounds, or a voice to help talk you through a meditation, from relaxing the body and quieting your mind to helping you let go of passing thoughts, often including connecting with guides or spirit animals. We'll learn more about spirit guides in chapter 10!

Transcendental Meditation

This Vedic tradition (the Vedas are a body of texts originating from ancient India and are the oldest Hindu scriptures in existence) is an easy-to-learn and natural way to relax the

EXPLORE THIS!

My bad for playing favorites, but trust me: your soul is practically begging you to give this a whirl. While writing this book, I was encouraged by the CEO of the business I work for (Yes, she too is a total Soul Searcher, one of us. We're everywhere—mwahahaha!) to learn Transcendental Meditation (TM), an easy, mantra-based meditation that, when practiced regularly, will help return you to a comfortable and natural state of being. By practicing TM for twenty minutes, twice a day, I became more tolerant, more agile, and more efficient; I slept better while also sleeping less, and I had tons more energy. Though we live in a time-poor society, I was suddenly meditating twice daily for 20 minutes and found myself time rich and I had become more efficient and proactive.

One of the things I find most rewarding about TM is that the practice teaches only good comes from meditation. There's literally no bad side to this practice. As we rest and transcend into a deeper state of relaxation, we flush negativity out, cleaning the body of stress, doubt, anxiety, worry, and disease. Once these toxic elements are released, usually they're gone for good. There hasn't been one person I've talked to who has tried TM who has not felt a profound impact on their lives.

Here's another challenge for you: open up your internet browser, and search "transcendental meditation classes" to see if there's a free introduction session available near you. You won't regret it.

mind. Allowing the brain to rest for twenty minutes, twice a day, through meditation helps the mind recharge and rest in a meditative state deeper than a deep sleep.

Mudras

WOO–WOO SCALE: ▲▲▲▲▲▲▲▲△△△
EXPLORE–IT SCALE: ▲▲▲▲▲▲▲▲△△△

Sometimes meditation in general can be challenging, especially for people with busy minds and exhausting lifestyles. Mudra-based meditation can help lend focus to your meditation by centering on a specific need.

A mudra is a symbolic gesture seen most commonly in Hindu and Buddhist cultures. A *hasta mudra* is a spiritual hand gesture that is known as a "seal" or *mud* (Sanskrit for joy) and *dra* (to bring toward or draw in). There are over a hundred mudras that are used in meditation to show your intention. The best thing about a mudra is that you can use it anytime, anywhere—at your office desk when you need to focus, when you're stuck in traffic, or even in bed before you catch some shut-eye. I usually pick a mudra that reflects my soul's needs at the time, to help me focus my energy during meditation or to just gather my thoughts for a few moments.

Below are some mudras for you to try out in your next meditation.[3] I find I really connect with these mudras when I can feel a pulse beating through my fingertips. If you are having trouble focusing your attention on your breathing, feel for your pulse and repeat a mantra.

Think of these mudras like yoga, hand-gesture style! Often used throughout yoga practice, these hand poses are also powerful on their own. Flipping someone the bird can be considered a mudra, but let's aim to spread the love instead, yeah?

Lotus Mudra/Vessel Gesture
*Opening your heart—great for new beginnings
and attracting love and opportunities into your life.*

Bring your hands in to meet in front of your heart; palms open with thumbs and pinkie fingers remaining touching, your wrists becoming the base of the flower and your hands forming a lotus. This mudra also helps to open the crown chakra. Check out more on chakras in chapter 4.

Anjali Mudra/Namaste Gesture
Gesture of peace, gratitude, and humility—the divine in me salutes the divine in you.

Bring your palms together as in prayer and rest your thumbs against the middle of your chest, so that your arms from elbow to elbow run straight along your chest. This is an excellent mudra to thank those watching out for you and to show how grateful you are to a teacher or for a lesson.

Gyana Mudra/Guru Gesture
Gesture of wisdom, understanding, and knowledge— symbolizes focus and transformation

With both hands, make a circle by bringing your thumb and index fingertips to touch, leaving your other three fingers extended. Rest your hands on your knees, palms facing up. This is the mudra for reflection, calmness, and knowledge, perfect for meditation. This mudra is also good for grounding and supporting the root chakra.

Mahakranta Mudra/Power Gesture
Gesture for self-love, recharging, and balancing your energy centers

Bring your hands up toward your face; align your hands, palms inward, with your cheeks but keep them away from your face, so they do not touch. Your elbows will point down to the floor. This is an excellent mudra for when you are feeling flat, worn-out, or unbalanced.

Hakini Mudra/All-Seeing Eye Gesture
Gesture for protection, communication, and connection to your guides

Fingertips on both hands align and touch to create a triangle, which can be held up to your chest or down by your abdomen. This is a good mudra for when you need to ask for assistance or share a concern with your spiritual role models or guardian angels.

Shivalinga Mudra/Om Gesture
Gesture for balance and harmony

Place the left hand palm facing up in front of your bellybutton. Do a thumbs-up with your right hand, pointing your thumb up, and place it on top of the left hand. This mudra helps realign the body and clear out any blockages in our energy centers. It can bring newfound confidence and contentment.

Anahata Mudra/Love Gesture
Gesture for the heart, love, and healing

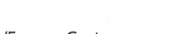

Softly clench your right hand into a loose okay sign so the thumb and forefinger meet and rest over your heart/chest. Rest your left hand on your knee or thigh. This is a simple but powerful mudra good for helping ease heartache, conflict, or any negativity. This mudra also helps clear the heart chakra.

Kundalini Mudra/Energy Gesture
Gesture for recharging, awakening, and revitalizing the body

Clench both fists and stack your left fist on top of the right one; bring them up by your heart, so your elbows point outward and your arms run in a straight line from elbow to elbow. Kundalini mudras are most often used with Breath of Fire. This quick breathing technique starts by relaxing your abdomen as you inhale then pulling your navel in tightly as you powerfully exhale through your nose. As you utilize your abdominal muscles your breathing will sound loud and fast but don't worry, this is normal! An important instruction for Breath of Fire is that the inhale and exhale are balanced in strength and length. It is like panting through the nose, with the mouth closed. It is also important that women know not to practice Breath of Fire during their moon cycle (that's yogi speak for menstrual cycle) or after the 120th day of pregnancy. This is an excellent mudra to do when you want to awaken your soul and body.[4]

Buddha Mudra/Contemplation Gesture

*Gesture to quiet the mind, relax, and reflect; a unique mudra different
for both women and men.*

Men place the left hand palm up in the lap and the right hand in the left palm up.
Women reverse the hand positions.

Place the left hand on top of the right hand, gently cupping hands
and bringing your thumb tips into touch. Rest your hands in this
mudra gently onto your lap. A popular mudra for meditation and contemplation. This Mudra also connects with the sacral chakra.[5]

Combating Physical Illness with Spiritual Care

WOO–WOO SCALE: ▲▲▲▲▲▲△△△△
EXPLORE–IT SCALE: ▲▲▲▲▲▲▲△△△

Your brain is an organ, just like your heart and your skin. When bad thoughts get in
there—considered by some to be toxins for the mind—they can negatively impact your
good vibes in a number of unpleasant ways, just like bad food are toxins for the body.

On the next page is a chart that lists key diseases and illnesses that may affect one's
body throughout a soul-search journey[6]; as you explore, you might start seeing links
to the overall condition of your body, mind, and spirit. Accompanying this information are affirmations that can be used to help cleanse and balance the negative energy
that may be contributing to these conditions.

Over time, if you decide to make spiritual care a part of your self-care regimen, you
will become increasingly aware of your body's ways of telling you something is wrong
and be able to spot a variety of symptoms. And, with the tools you've gained in this
chapter, you will then be able to combat and overcome a number of issues you weren't
previously comfortable confronting or even identifying. Whether it be through meditation, yoga, exercise, a form of holistic healing, or all of the above, be your own spiritual
love doctor! You always come first. Permission to be a positive-energy hog granted.

I just want to take a moment to acknowledge that some of these affirmations can
feel, well, cheesy, if not full-blown lame. I say: own the crap out of that cheese. Live
it up, consider it a cheese spread: you have your soft cheese, your hard cheese, sweet
and savory cheeses, and even stinky cheese. Throw in some fruit, bread, and wine, and
you have a cheese party. The point of these affirmations is to identify the underlying

emotions that these physical ailments can bring up and, in doing so, acknowledge and release them. This helps to prime your body to heal itself.

Let's celebrate the cheese and get our affirmation on, ya big cheese ball.

One of the quickest, easiest, and most straightforward ways of staying in tune with your soul is to drink lots of water—around six to eight glasses every day is the widely accepted amount—to help cleanse and flush the system of toxins. Throughout nearly every spiritual script, water is referenced as the pure essence of cleanliness, purifying and reawakening, not just through consumption or rituals such as baptism, but also as a way to journey through adversity and onto calmer shores through the imagery of oceans and storms.

> "When you view food as nourishment, your whole world changes and you are naturally drawn to making better food choices."
> **>Dr. Libby Weaver**

While we are flushing and cleansing our system with water, we should also be fueling the body with natural nutrients by eating as healthfully as possible. When you can, choose organic. When it's available, eat whole foods instead of processed. It's not always possible to do so in today's world—and hey, sometimes what your soul needs is a bowl of mac and cheese, let's be real—but the more healthy choices you're able to make, the better your body will feel, and the happier your soul will be.

The three questions to consider when making a new well-being mantra are: Does it help me live well? Does it nourish me? How does it impact me and the world around me?

Mantras should help you look at yourself as a whole—body, mind, and soul in unison—and help you become more aware of your day-to-day choices and how they impact your well-being. If they aren't doing that for you, switch them up or look at one of the other practices in the "Body" section of this book.

A thing to also keep in mind if you hit an unwholesome wall is to listen to what your body is trying to tell you—aches, pains, illness, stress, and cravings all have meanings. Embrace wellness by tuning in to your body and becoming better acquainted with what sets you off and what fuels you. You body is your best teacher, friends, so be a good pupil and listen up. Just say no to firing spitballs at it and it will stop sending you to energy detention. It's time for all of us to be good to ourselves—our bodies will thank us for it.

Illness/Problem Area	Spiritual Meaning	Healing Affirmation
Acne	Dislike for one's self image, not seeing your individual beauty.	*I love and accept me for me.*
Ankle Problems	Rigidity, inflexibility, guilt, in a rut.	*I deserve to enjoy life and its pleasures.*
Anxiety	Distrust and control of the natural order of life.	*I trust the process. I am safe.*
Back (lower)	Guilt, feeling overloaded, stressed, financial stress.	*I am doing everything I can and all I need will be taken care of. I can relax.*
Bowel Problems	Fear of letting go.	*I easily let go of the old and welcome in the new.*
Breathing Problems	No acceptance, fear of growth and giving.	*It is my birthright to live fully and freely.*
Cancer	Deep hurt, secrets, and grief.	*I forgive and release the past. I choose to fill my life with joy and love. Life flows through me.*
Cold Sores	Festering, angry words, and fear of fully expressing your true feelings.	*I am safe to say and release anything that does not serve me.*
Depression	Anger, sense of helplessness.	*I let go of my fears and don't believe in limitations. I create my own life.*
Ear Problems	Failure to listen, not wanting to hear, too much anger.	*I hear with love. I accept what I hear.*
Flu	Responding to mass negativity, putting too much faith in statistics and influence.	*I am beyond group beliefs. I am free of congestion and influence.*

Illness/Problem Area	Spiritual Meaning	Healing Affirmation
Headaches	Self-criticism, failure to accept current situations.	*I am loving and approving of myself and look at things with love.*
Neck Problems	Refusing to see another side, stubbornness.	*I am peaceful with life. I accept all views of life.*
Weight Issues	Lack of emotional protection, struggling with insecurity, running away from true feelings.	*I create my own security. I love and approve of myself.*
Sore Throat	Holding in angry words, feeling unable to express yourself.	*I release all restrictions, and I am free to be me.*
Stomach Problems	Dread, fear of the new, or not feeling nourished.	*I digest life with ease.*
Teeth Problems	Indecisive, not being able to think clearly and decisively.	*I live my truth and follow my soul's decisions. I trust my decisions.*
Tumors	Nursing old emotional anguish and trauma.	*I lovingly release my past and focus my energies on my future.*
Ulcers	Fear and negative self-talk.	*I love and approve of my life, my successes, and myself.*
Urinary Problems	Feeling pissed off, usually at a partner or romantic/sexual interest.	*I release the pattern that creates this energy in my relationships. I love and approve of myself.*

YOUR CRYSTALS AND GEMSTONES

Crystals and gemstones have long intrigued humankind with their gorgeous glimmering colors in a variety of shapes and sizes. If the first time you saw a crystal you had the impulse to yell out "SHINY!" and run toward it with "gimme" hands, I totally get you because me too! We're a bunch of curious, spiritual little magpies.

Throughout time, crystals and stones have been used as symbols of power by kings and queens, worn as jewelry, shown off in home ornamentation, praised in sacred ceremonies, held during prayer and meditation, and used for their healing properties in Reiki (a Japanese stress-reduction, healing, and relaxation practice), massage, and cleansing. Today it's more common than ever to see boho fashion accessories of crystals and gemstones on rings and long necklaces. Come on—seriously, who doesn't love sparkles?

But those pretty pebbles have more to give than simple sparkle. The first few gemstones I bought were clear quartz, rose quartz, and angelite. To be honest, I didn't even know what they were for. I just thought they were pretty.

Again, when we go with what feels natural, what resonates with us when we listen to our souls, we will be drawn to the things we need most and the things that will help us most on our journey. It turned out that I needed the exact energies that those gemstones offer at that exact moment in my life—at the time, I was going through a string of turbulent relationships and was experiencing a lot of negativity in my life in general. I was also looking to get answers by learning about connecting with my guides. (We'll be talking more about them in chapter 10.)

You can imagine my surprise when I began to research the three stones I'd spontaneously picked up and discovered their powers to aid with the healing of hearts, clearing negativity, and communicating with your angels. From that moment on,

I never looked back where acting on instinct is concerned, and whenever I stumble across something that jumps out at me and practically yells "Hey, girl, pick me!" I listen. Because of the above experiences and the benefits I have received by working with crystals, I strongly recommend and firmly believe that every Soul Searcher should try working with them, or even just keep a handful of gemstones or crystals somewhere in their living spaces.

Often the first thing about a crystal or gemstone a Soul Searcher is drawn to is the color. If you looked in your wardrobe right now, what color would you see most of? What color do you always gravitate toward? Can you see certain styles and colors you wore more when you were going through hard or happy times? I'm not judging your goth phase, or your everything-is-awesome fluorescent phase, by the way. If I could send you a Snapchat of my wardrobe to make you feel better about yours, I would! Put it this way: you can see my spiritual evolution as my style shifted from brown, cold, and corporate to hipster, to hippie, full of noise and color.

> **EXPLORE THIS!**
>
> Think of a color you are drawn to—visualize it in your head; imagine yourself wearing it; even imagine holding it as a glowing ball of colored light in your hands. How do you feel? Let's see what that color represents and why your subconscious mind directed your brain to plant that color in your thoughts.

Think about what your favorite color was as a child. When we are children, we tend to be more in tune with, connected to, and undistracted from our higher selves. Even that one color of crayon we constantly picked out (and maybe drew all over the walls with) can reflect who we were as a person and point to what our purpose in this lifetime is. Each color has a deeper meaning that can tell us something about ourselves. I've collected some of the colors with their meanings for you on the next couple of pages.[1]

Now that you know your color and its meaning, let's check out what that meaning reflects in a variety of contexts, for example in a career sense. Red, gold, and orange lovers are likely to be entrepreneurs and leaders who forge ahead with new ideas and developments in whatever roles they fill. Yellow, purple, and white folks are usually more nurturing sorts—healers and creative types likely to be working in health care, the arts, or counseling. The browns, grays, and pinks tend to learn the most from life through their challenges, which influence the directions of their lives and make them strive for stability and a rooted lifestyle at work and at home.

While colors have a strong influence over our moods and energy (which we'll be exploring in depth when we talk about Feng Shui in chapter 5), they also play an important roll in focusing energies, particularly in meditation. When we gravitate

PURPLE

Magic, mystery, royalty, spirituality

Enthusiasm, endurance, thoughtfulness

ORANGE

GREEN

Fertility, nature, well-being

Action, vitality, confidence, drive

RED

Truth, youth, spirituality, inspiration

PINK

Nurture, love, self-care

YELLOW

BLUE

Joy, creativity, happiness, healing

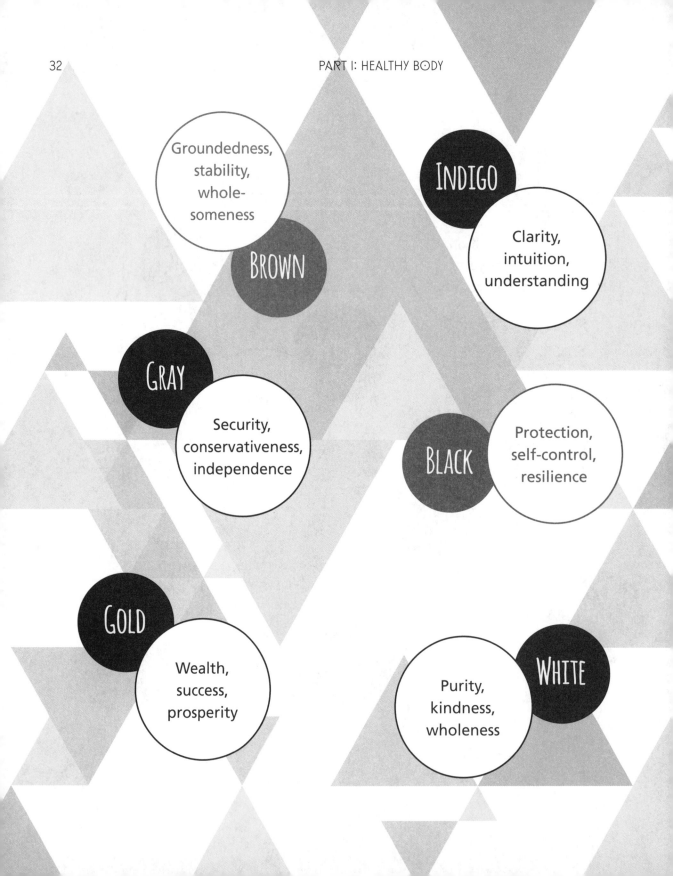

Groundedness, stability, whole-someness

BROWN

INDIGO

Clarity, intuition, understanding

GRAY

Security, conservativeness, independence

BLACK

Protection, self-control, resilience

GOLD

Wealth, success, prosperity

WHITE

Purity, kindness, wholeness

toward a gem or crystal, it is both the color of the stone and the energy the stone emits that our higher self is calling for. So what is it that your soul's yammering on about? It could be anything from healing or clarity, to communication or wealth—the key is to pay attention to what your soul's saying and to know how to give the soul what it's asking for.

Crystals and gemstones can illuminate your thoughts, wishes, emotions, and dreams—they're basically Mother Earth's spiritual magnifying glass. On the following pages are crystals and gemstones to help with some common challenges and desires that I encountered during my soul search, and that many others no doubt run up against in life from day to day.[2]

The simple presence of crystals can bring calm and serenity. We wear crystal jewelry, hold crystals in our hands, keep them in our pockets, bras, socks—wherever we can stuff 'em. (No, not *there* . . . Well, you *can* put crystals there, actually. Have a glass of organic wine and Google "jade eggs.") We display them in our homes, hang them in our cars, or place them by our computers or under our pillows. After a while, crystals can become as natural and comforting a presence in your life as that pair of old beat-up sneakers you just can't give up or your favorite coffee mug.

EXPLORE THIS!

My first experience with crystal healing was during a Reiki session while in the Caribbean. I was nervous, clueless, and had to hold back holy-crap-that's-cold giggles when the crystals first came into contact with my body. You could say I handled the whole experience like an amateur, but then something happened—something big. Halfway through the session, I exploded into tears. Consoling me a bit later, the practitioner told me that he had been working over my hips when Niagara Falls suddenly decided to spring forth from my face. He explained that the hips are where many women store emotional baggage and that the sort of reaction I'd had was not uncommon. I had so much excess baggage stored up in there that my emotional health probably resembled a fat groundhog stuck in its hole—there was simply no more space for anything or anyone to fit into my life because I was bursting at the seams with negative emotional weight. With that release of tears and a follow-up cleansing session, I had all the space and flexibility back in my hips and was back up and running emotionally and physically. I recommend trying out a Reiki session and seeing what comes up for you . . . even if it's tears!

Crystals and Stones for Healing

WOO-WOO SCALE: ▲▲▲▲▲▲▲▲△△
EXPLORE-IT SCALE: ▲▲▲△△△△△△△

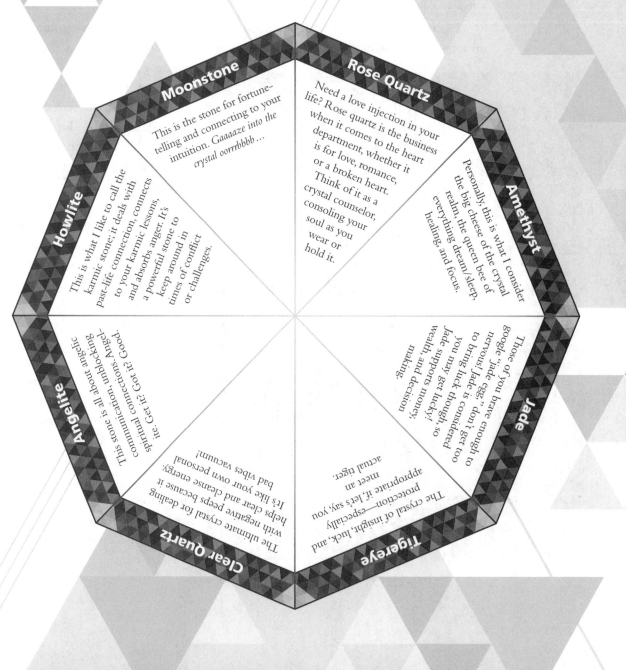

Moonstone

This is the stone for fortune-telling and connecting to your intuition. *Gaaaaze into the crystal oorrrbbbb …*

Rose Quartz

Need a love injection in your life? Rose quartz is the business when it comes to the heart department, whether it is for love, romance, or a broken heart. Think of it as a crystal counselor, consoling your soul as you wear or hold it.

Howlite

This is what I like to call the karmic stone; it deals with past-life connection, connects to your karmic lessons, and absorbs anger. It's a powerful stone to keep around in times of conflict or challenges.

Amethyst

Personally, this is what I consider the big cheese of the crystal realm, the queen bee of everything dream/sleep, healing, and focus.

Angelite

This stone is all about angelic communication. Angel-ite. Get it? Got it? Good. It's all about unblocking spiritual connections.

Jade

Those of you brave enough to google "jade egg," don't get too nervous! Jade is considered to bring luck though, so you may get lucky! Jade supports money, wealth, and decision making.

Clear Quartz

The ultimate crystal for dealing with negative peeps because it helps clear and cleanse it. It's like your own personal bad vibes vacuum!

Tigereye

The crystal of insight, luck, and protection—especially appropriate if, let's say, you meet an actual tiger.

The most interesting and rewarding thing that I've found out about crystals is that they look pretty. Just kidding. It's their potential to heal. If you ever feel out of balance, lost, worn down, ill, or just plain bitchy and in need of a break, I recommend trying out crystals and gemstones in healing meditation and Reiki, and see if you notice a benefit.

Labradorite

The perfect stone for any mystic, crystal ball, tarot lover. Labradorite brings with it magic and physic energy. This is an intuitive stone.

Aquamarine

This stone always reminds me of the Atlantis era. Think meditation, spiritual connection, and discovery, like discovering new spiritual shores!

Jasper

Feeling like you are about to lose it? We've all been there. This stone is all about stability and aiding in eliminating emotional stress.

Smokey Quartz

All smoke and mirrors? This stone will bring you back down to earth. It's a cleansing and grounding stone that removes negative energy while adding to your survival instincts. Helps you to keep a clear mind.

Obsidian

Think black sponge! This shiny black stone sucks off negativity and shields you against it, working as a bad vibe vacuum. Obsidian is the ultimate cleansing stone.

Citrine

Had your confidence knocked? Citrine will help with self-esteem and protecting with negativity. To supercharge it, use it in conjunction with positive affirmations.

Ruby

Think about the royal awesome that you are. Ruby is totes your crystal! Vitality, strength, passion ... rawrr.

Fluorite

Absorbs and neutralizes negativity. (And cavities! No, wait ... that's fluoride.) Just like bad breath needs neutralizing, fluorite will help bring your vibe back into balance.

EXPLORE THIS!

Make a concentration crystal cocktail for finals week, presentation day, or when you are faced with looming deadlines. Place fluorite, clear quartz, amber, and a crystal that speaks to you particularly strongly, in a cloth bag. Keep them with you while you study, work, and sleep, and then take them with you on the day you need them most. You'll feel like you have a tiny crystal guru in your pocket, protecting you and cheering you on. Plus, it's not like you're going to get kicked out of an exam for cheating because you had some rocks in your pockets!

What follows is an overview of some common physical conditions and ailments and their corresponding crystal, gemstone, and placement to get you started.

If the idea of lying around with a bunch of rocks strewn all over you makes you giggle or groan, never fear: trying new things is supposed to be uncomfortable—even silly. And seriously, what have you got to lose? Mix and match; try out one and skip another, whatever works for you!

Disclaimer: I can't believe I am going to say this to you, and I know this is a little bit Captain Obvious of me ... but ... I had an awkward situation with someone swallowing crystals and stones to help heal them. It kind of doesn't work like that. In fact, that brings new meaning to the idea of a constipated soul! Please do not eat them. Seriously, no nom noms.

Addiction

There are many different forms of addiction: smoking, alcohol, drugs, sex, or overeating, to name a few. Hands up, all you emotional eaters, or chocolate-bar wrapper hiders out there—it'll stink if you leave me high and dry with my hand in the air alone! Good news though: using smoky quartz or sugilite can help to ease symptoms of addiction such as cravings, especially if they are worn as a bracelet or necklace or carried in an easily accessible pocket. This way, in moments of stress, boredom, social pressure, or any other triggering situation, you can hold the stone between your fingers as a gentle reminder to stay strong.

Allergies

I am a specialist in allergies. I rock the eyes puffy, noise sniffy, Sean Connery vocals in springtime, so listen up from a seasoned (Get it? Get it?) sneezer. Think hay fever, dust allergies, pet allergies, and food allergies. Ugh. By using a carnelian stone, you can help reduce or even eliminate the itching, scratching, rashes, and sneezing associated with most allergies. If the allergy affects the skin, try to either wear the stone on that location, against the skin, in the form of jewelry or hold the stone to the affected area. For example, if you're experiencing an itchy nose or irritated eyes, wear earrings or a necklace featuring carnelian.

Boils

Boils—yeah, they're about as pleasant as they sound—are often the body's signal that you have a blocked energy center. In most cases of boils, it means violently blocked! By holding a sapphire and imagining your body's blockages breaking down and dissolving, your boils will likely begin to pack their bags and go. This is the perfect exercise to do just before you go to sleep.

Childbirth

Related to pregnancy, birth, and post-pregnancy healing, stones such as agate, bloodstone, pearl, moonstone, and jade all work with the body's sacral chakra. Using these stones is said to help support fertility and pregnancy, ease labor pains, and to soothe, heal, and support the body post labor. These stones are great carried around in the pockets of pants . . . or even down your underpants!

Concentration

I do not think I know anyone who does not struggle with concentration these days. Oh, sorry, what? What were we talking about . . . oh, yeah . . . When our attention's being tugged in every direction—like those dog walkers I've seen in Central Park attached to a zillion yammering pooches— is it any wonder that we can't ever seem to focus? To support concentration, get your

EXPLORE THIS!

Jade eggs are said to have been used by the Chinese for centuries in aiding sexual health, childbirth, and the overall strengthening and tightening of the vaginal and pelvic floor muscles. The ancient Chinese even believed that the feminine chi (creation energy) was strengthened and increased by incorporating jade egg exercises into a woman's routine.[3] If you're down to get a little freaky with your crystals, think of it as a goddess workout.

hands on a simple quartz, which provides mental clarity and focus, or carnelian, which clears and reins in the wandering mind.

Amber is thought to stimulate memory, and lapis lazuli is a powerful amplifier of thoughts to help boost creativity. Like amethyst, lapis lazuli (sometimes just called lapis) can settle the mind when you're struggling with a headache and also promote mental clarity, helping you visualize and focus on realistic goals. This is a great stone for meditation, too, believed to soothe the nervous system and aid in neural transmission.

Fluorite is an excellent aid for focusing on and recalling facts when studying, as it is believed to balance the functioning of the brain hemispheres. Deep blue stones such as sodalite can aid in communication and pave the way for understanding difficult concepts and ideas.

Digestion

Includes bowel irritation, stomachaches, cramps, bloating, and food allergies. By placing stones such as obsidian, pearl, and labradorite on your stomach or solar plexus and focusing on smooth, flowing, and balanced energy, you can begin to channel new power to heal any imbalances in the digestive system.

Ear Trouble

Ears are my kryptonite. In general, they love to act up, so these are good tips for people who have hearing or ear setbacks. Ears can affect not only our hearing, but also our balance and focus. Stones such as amber and onyx work particularly well at helping heal ears when worn as earrings. Personally, I think someone should invent crystal and gemstone headphones. Just saying—two birds, one stone!

Eyesight

Eye issues can indicate not wanting to face your future, or not accepting the reality of an unsatisfactory situation. To help heal your eyes and your internal vision in one, check out stones such as aquamarine and cat's-eye. Tigereye, opal, and emerald can help with failing or aging eyesight problems, and cat's-eye is also great for people who struggle with night driving.

Headache

Need a head check? Headaches are triggered by lots of different things, and which crystal or gem you use is dependent on the trigger. Most headaches are caused by issues with diet, stress, or lack of sleep.

A tension headache—You know that band of pressure-pain around your skull that makes you kinda want to crawl under a blanket and rock back and forth forever? Yeah, that's a tension headache—can be cleansed and balanced by using amethyst, amber, or turquoise as earrings, on a necklace, or placed near the head on your pillow while you rest. Lapis lazuli has also been used for centuries to help treat migraines.

Another common cause of headaches is an imbalance between head energy and the solar plexus chakra, usually from built-up stress or the negative effects of an all-around frantic lifestyle, including poor diet and lack of sleep. (Or sometimes just from being around too many dickheads.) If you suspect stress to be the cause of your headache, and especially if you have a headache accompanied by an upset stomach, use a stone that helps to balance the solar plexus chakra such as citrine, moonstone, or amethyst—all three together are a great crystal cocktail for a headache and stomach-ache. So much better than a dirty martini. Maybe.

Inflammation

This category can include sports injuries, sprains, back pain, and even flu aches. Stones for inflammation are best used when slipped into a bandage or compression wrap to help stay connected to the area that needs healing. Stones such as bloodstone, emerald, garnet, and pyrite are great at combatting inflammation.

Liver Trouble

If you suffer from liver ailments or simply went a bit too hard at the wine over the weekend, these crystals can be placed in your water to help cleanse the liver: jasper, topaz, aquamarine, and beryl. Word to the wise: don't *actually drink* the stones.

Sleeplessness

Again, the crystal depends on the cause. What's keeping you up at night? Like headaches, trouble sleeping can often be linked back to stressors in your waking life. If you believe this may be at the root cause for your lack of sleep, place a crystal such as chrysoprase, rose quartz, citrine, or amethyst by your bed or under your pillow to calm and sooth. You may need to experiment, as a stone that works well for one person may not work for someone else.

Some people swear by a snack before bedtime while others swear off food after sunset. Whether you're a nighttime snacker or an evening faster, if you believe your restlessness could be the result of overeating or of an overall unhealthy turn in your recent diet, iron pyrite or moonstone can be used to calm the stomach. As with the stress-fighting crystals above, place them by or in the bed before you drift off to dreamland.

If nightmares are causing your grief, protective stones such as tourmaline or smoky quartz can promote nighttime protection and peaceful sleep. These stones should be placed at the foot of the bed. Labradorite is also an excellent stone for kicking nightmares in the backside, as it is thought to chase away any unwelcome feelings and thoughts.

Toothache

These stones can be kept in a glass of water or under your pillow while you sleep. Malachite and aquamarine are known to ease toothaches and help heal gums, teeth, and jaw aches. If only I'd known to get my hands on some malachite when I had my wisdom teeth out!

The fun doesn't have to stop here, my friends. Oh no, crystals have got so much more to give if you're ready to receive. Just remember you may get deemed as that "crystal-lady" if you start prescribing your friends crystal cures, so watch out for that one!

Crystals in the Home

WOO-WOO SCALE: ▲▲▲▲△△△△△△
EXPLORE-IT SCALE: ▲▲▲▲▲▲▲▲▲△

My home is riddled with crystals. You can find them under pillows, on my coffee table, in my undie drawer—I even have a clear quartz hanging in the east window of my living room that radiates rainbow prisms and positivity throughout my sanctuary every sunrise. I have given hanging crystals to friends for everything from baby shower gifts to bachelorette party baubles; I even sneak them into tiny terrarium gardens so the plants have crystals for company. After all, plants and crystals are both products of Mother Earth so it seems natural to have a crystal hanging from the bedroom curtain rod, as it is to have a potted plant on a table in your living room. Orienting from the primary entrance to your home and its rooms, you can choose locations for your crystals that will help awaken and positively influence the following areas of your life:

▷ Wealth and abundance—the far left corner
▷ Relationships—the far right corner
▷ Wisdom—the near left corner
▷ Friends and travel—the near right corner
▷ Fame—the far center wall
▷ Family and Health—the left center wall
▷ Children—the right center wall
▷ Career—the near center wall

There's nothing quite like the subtle sparkle of crystals catching the morning light as it filters into your living space—surrounding you, protecting you, and energizing you for the day ahead.

Wearing Crystals and Gems

WOO-WOO SCALE: ▲▲△△△△△△△△
EXPLORE-IT SCALE: ▲▲▲▲▲▲▲▲▲▲

There are tons of ways to wear crystals that enhance their healing and protective qualities while making you look like a total boho babe in the process. Wearing rings, bracelets, and necklaces featuring crystals or gemstones is becoming more and more trendy—not only are they beautiful, but wearing crystals and gems is also the most simple and effective way of utilizing their powerful healing energies, as we explored a bit a few sections ago.

I also like wearing chakra jewelry to help stimulate the body's energy centers and help align and fuel my energy levels. It's important to remember that when you are wearing a crystal pendant or necklace, the length of the chain will determine which chakra it is connected to and which chakra will be most stimulated and balanced. For example, wearing crystal earrings can help to balance the energies of the throat, neck, and head, while wearing an anklet can help with grounding. We'll be learning lots more about chakras in chapter 4.

Healing with Crystal Pendulums

WOO–WOO SCALE: ▲▲▲▲▲▲▲▲▲△△
EXPLORE–IT SCALE: ▲△△△△△△△△△△

This is an ancient technique that can be used to remove energy imbalances and blockages from the body's chakras and auras. A clear quartz or amethyst pendulum will work as an all-purpose healer, as they both have a wide range of healing properties. Other crystal pendulums will focus their balancing actions on the key chakra, energy, mood, or illness it is known for healing.

Here's how it works: The patient (that's you, my dear) lies down, and the healer stands or sits to the side of the patient. The pendulum is held lightly and firmly between the thumb and forefinger. The healer then allows the wrist to relax. The pendulum is hovered a few centimeters above the body, just below the feet and in line with the central axis of the body. The pendulum starts swinging in a line back and forth. This is known as the neutral swing. Have the healer move the swinging pendulum slowly up your body, along the centerline, toward the head, paying close attention to the chakra centers.

When the pendulum changes its back-and-forth movement, the healer simply stops at that point until the neutral swing returns. When the healer reaches a point above the head, they move back to the feet and repeat along the front and the back of the body.

Laying on Stones

WOO–WOO SCALE: ▲▲▲▲▲▲△△△△△
EXPLORE–IT SCALE: ▲▲▲▲▲△△△△△△

This sort of cleansing or healing is most commonly practiced through Reiki or a crystal chakra balancing process by placing crystals and gemstones along the chakras of the body. The healer goes chakra by chakra, moving from the feet to crown and placing the appropriate-colored gemstone on the corresponding energy center.

Healers usually choose one of two options. They can go to the head and begin a hands-on healing—Reiki or energy healing. With this, the healer will cover the stones with their hands carefully in order to not scatter them. While each chakra stone is covered, the healer visualizes the bright color of the gemstone entering the chakra, envisioning it as balanced, centered, and healthy. Usually these colors will flood into your thoughts too as you are healed. The healer will do this visualization until they feel confident moving on to the next chakra. Often healers will flick fingers, wash hands, or rub or wipe hands to release any negative energy before moving to the next energy center.

In option two, the healer sits beside the patient and simply waits, allowing the gemstones and surrounding energies (like your spirit guides—more on them in chapter 10) to do the healing at the patient's pace. As the patient's chakras (your chakras!) and aura absorb and are balanced by the crystals' and gems' energies, the stones begin to roll off one by one. When all the stones are off, or when you feel finished with those that remain, the healing is complete.

Every healer works differently and intuitively, so be open and try to leave behind any judgment to ensure you get all the benefits of a cleansing.

This form of healing can be quite intense for patients—like, way intense. Trust me on this—and is a unique experience for each person. There is often a major shift in a person's energies during a crystal-chakra cleanse. Frequent emotional releases, both current and past-life trauma openings, and other transformative events can be triggered, released, and healed through the cleansing process. After a healing session, there may also be a physical detoxification process that can continue for up to a week. The key tip to benefiting from a cleanse is to flush the system and drink plenty of water post cleansing. Be aware of what is happening and acknowledge, accept, and and release anything that comes up for you. Change can be a challenge, but in the case of a crystal cleanse, it's change for the better.

Using Crystals to Connect to Energy

WOO-WOO SCALE: ▲▲▲▲▲▲▲▲△△△
EXPLORE-IT SCALE: ▲▲▲▲▲▲▲▲▲▲△

Crystals and gemstones have their own unique sound, vibration, and energy—and when these connect with your bodily energy by being placed on your chakras, held during meditation, or even placed in your aura, their energy can change and balance yours. I find that when I hold crystals or gemstones while relaxing, breathing deeply, and thinking of what I would like healed by love and light, I can feel my pulse in the hand that holds the stone.

We have seven major energy centers, or chakras, which can help you connect to the energy of your stones. Your chakras may be open or closed based on your mental, emotional, and spiritual state, and often when any one of these chakras is blocked, we are thrown out of alignment and stop operating at full capacity. Often, we Soul Searchers will feel fragile, sensitive, overly emotional, or strangely empty when we're out of alignment. The important thing to remember when you start to feel this way is that we all get knocked on our butts sometimes in life—sometimes every couple of years, sometimes even daily when stuff gets especially challenging. However, when we know how to realign and reconnect our energies, life can get back on track surprisingly easily.

Chakra is the Sanskrit word for wheel, symbolizing how our chakras should be rolling—free flowing and smooth. To get your chakras rebalanced, you can visit a trained Reiki practitioner who will realign your body, mind, and soul, and unblock anything that needs unblocking (again, more on chakras in chapter 4). In fact, realignment should be seen as required for your soul's fitness, and done periodically when possible.

EXPLORE THIS!

A great chakra-balancing cheat is to get your paws on a blue kyanite crystal. This crystal is renowned for realigning chakras automatically and immediately, with no conscious direction.

On your own, you can maintain and recharge your chakra centers by using your crystals or gemstones to help focus your energy on the chakra and issue at hand.

Use the chart on the next page to play around with and get to know the many healing and realigning properties of your crystals.[4]

CROWN CHAKRA

Our ability to be fully connected spiritually.

CRYSTALS: Clear quartz, Amethyst

LOCATION: The very top of the head.

EMOTIONAL ISSUES: Inner and outer beauty, our connection to spirituality, pure bliss. I like to carry around a clear quartz with me at all times to keep my connection to my spiritual nature close at hand—literally.

THIRD EYE CHAKRA

Our ability to focus on and see the big picture.

CRYSTALS: Amethyst, Sapphire, Turquoise

LOCATION: Forehead between the eyes. (aka Brow Chakra)

EMOTIONAL ISSUES: Intuition, imagination, wisdom, ability to think and make choices. Big life decisions giving you a headache? Sleep with an amethyst under your pillow and wake with the conviction and clarity you need to kick any doubts to the curb.

THROAT CHAKRA

Our ability to communicate.

CRYSTALS: Aquamarine, Turquoise, Angel stone

LOCATION: Throat

EMOTIONAL ISSUES: Communication, self-expression of feelings, the truth. Consider keeping this chakra open and clear with a turquoise pendant or aquamarine necklace.

HEART CHAKRA

Our ability to love.

CRYSTALS: Rose Quartz, Fluorite

LOCATION: Center of chest just above heart.

EMOTIONAL ISSUES: Love, joy, inner peace. If this chakra were an animal, it'd probably be a purring kitten. Make sure to care for it accordingly!

SOLAR PLEXUS CHAKRA

Our ability to be confident and in control of our lives.

CRYSTALS: Citrine, Amber, Topaz

LOCATION: Upper abdomen in the stomach area.

EMOTIONAL ISSUES: Self-worth, self-confidence, self-esteem. Shower the solar plexus chakra with healing attention when your stores of self-love are running on empty.

SACRAL CHAKRA

Our connection and ability to accept others and new experiences.

CRYSTALS: Hematite, Carnelian, Moonstone

LOCATION: Lower abdomen, about two inches below the navel and two inches in.

EMOTIONAL ISSUES: Sense of abundance, well-being, pleasure, sexuality. Rev your engines, people—the sacral chakra's the pleasure-seeking joy-magnet at the table.

ROOT CHAKRA

Represents our foundation and feeling of being grounded.

CRYSTALS: Jasper, Garnet, Onyx, Ruby

LOCATION: Base of spine in tailbone area.

EMOTIONAL ISSUES: Survival issues such as financial independence, money, and food. You know how your hips hurt like hell after a hard day of working? Yeah, it's time for some sacral chakra attention.

Birthstones

WOO–WOO SCALE: ▲▲▲△△△△△△△
EXPLORE–IT SCALE: ▲▲▲▲▲▲▲▲▲▲

Our astrology, numerology, name, and even our Feng Shui choices in our homes and workplaces can all be tied to our birthstones. The stones and colors you love may well be the stones and colors you were programed to love from birth.

Think back to the beginning of this chapter, when I asked you to visualize a color. Now think of the gemstone you are drawn to the most. Next, check out any connections to your birthstones on the birthstones chart on the page to the right.[5]

Once I acknowledged the intense, almost instinctual pull I feel toward my birth-stone, I realized that I'd been subconsciously surrounding myself with that color my whole life. Whether it's through the intense reds of rubies or the deep, calming depths of aquamarine, your stones will find their way to you.

Caring for Your Crystals

WOO–WOO SCALE: ▲▲▲▲▲▲▲▲△△
EXPLORE–IT SCALE: ▲▲▲▲▲▲▲▲▲▲

There are some important things to know about how to care for your crystals and gemstones that are essential to any Soul Searcher's survival kit. Trust me, this seemed full-scale *woo-woo* factor the first time I learned these crystal pointers. But if you find crystals to be your thing, then you'll want to take care of those puppies.

Firstly, stones and crystals can store and transfer energy—both good and bad—so it is important to cleanse them and recharge them when needed. How do you know when your crystals need some TLC? Use your intuition or gut—they'll let you know.

Even simpler than that: if someone else touches your crystals or stones, consider them tainted. Sounds harsh, right? Well, maybe "tainted" is a little rough (unless your friends are the type to skip washing their hands after they use the bathroom or something), but the point still stands. What your crystals being "dirty" in this context means is that another person's energy has touched and changed them, and they need a spiritual bubble bath to get them back to ground zero.

When I first learned that crystals could be tainted and needed regular cleansing after another person's energy came into contact with them, I would get pretty pissy when friends, random acquaintances, and even strangers on the street would grab at my jewelry and compliment me on my crystals. For me, it became the equivalent to reaching out and honking one of my breasts—jeez, people, look but don't touch! But one thing that helped me on this particular journey was remembering that they were just trying to compliment with positivity and didn't know any better. When something

January
Garnet
Lighthearted, loyal, affectionate

February
Amethyst
Power, royalty, a leader

March
Aquamarine + Bloodstone
Peaceful, serene, a protector

April
Diamond
Loving, enduring, patient

December
Turquoise + Zircon
Sensitive, intuitive, spiritual

May
Emerald
Hopeful, wise, reasoning

November
Topaz
Confident, strong, charismatic

June
Pearl + Moonstone
Pure, intuitive, connected

MONTH BIRTHSTONE MEANING

October
Opal + Tourmaline
Lucky, fortunate, connected

September
Sapphire
Joyful, devoted, dedicated

August
Peridot + Sardonyx
Lighthearted, easy, stable

July
Ruby
Popular, loving, passionate

like this happens, take it as a gesture of positive energy but always cleanse your crystals thoroughly after Mr. or Mrs. Grabby Hands has their way with them.

Cleansing can be as simple as holding the gemstone or crystal under running water for a few minutes—or, to save time, take 'em into the shower with you. You can then choose to recharge your stones or crystals in the sun or full moonlight, but be careful when using the sun as it can fracture and crack a crystal if it becomes too hot. Alternately, you can hold them in your right hand and imagine a bright white light beaming through your head, down your body, into your arm, and then consuming your hand. From there, program your crystal to get the most out of it by simply saying out loud while holding it, "This crystal connects with me and empowers me to (whatever you wish your crystal to aid you with)." Okay, there's a whole lot of *woo-woo* there but, hey— nothing ventured, nothing gained, yes?

Here are some other options for cleansing your crystals and gemstones.

EXPLORE THIS!

Try hanging your gemstone necklaces in a tree where the moonlight can cleanse them. When the weather is good, this does double-duty as yard art. I personally do not recommend ever placing your crystals and gemstones in the sunlight; many stones tend to fade their colors in the sun. Also, internal fractures may cause your stone to crack or break if placed in the sun.

Smudging (a little different from mastering the perfect smoky-eye look)

A quick way to cleanse your healing stones is to smudge them with burning cedar or sage. Smudging is an excellent way to make sure your stones are purified. Simply hold the burning sage or cedar stick while passing your stone through the smoke. I usually do this a couple times to ensure cleansing. I also like to cleanse my stones by smudging after every healing.

Moonlight (moonlight makes everything 100 percent more awesome— a tried-and-true fact known by romantics and werewolves alike)

Moonlight is another way of cleaning your gemstones. Simply place them outside in a safe place, from the full to the new moon. Waning moons are good times to clear crystals and dispel old energies, but any time works. The amount of time varies with the sensitivity of the healer and the amount of material the stone needs cleansing from.

Burying (usually when we bury stuff—emotions, bodies, and similar—it's not for the most positive of reasons, but this kind of burying's exactly the opposite!)

Burying your crystal in a cupful of dried herbs will also clear it. Suggested herbs for this are rose petals, sage, frankincense, myrrh, and sandalwood. You can usually find these at low cost at many co-ops or herb stores. This is a gentle, pleasant, and usually great-smelling way to clear crystals.

Crystals can also be buried in the earth. This is my personal favorite way to cleanse my sparklies, and it is especially helpful when you feel deep cleansing is needed. Outdoors, simply dig a hole the size of your crystal in the earth, place your crystal point down, and cover with soil. The amount of time needed is your choice.

Breath Cleanse (like gentle kisses for your crystals)

Some like to use this method of "blowing away" any negativity from the stone by simply holding the stone in your hand and blowing on it. While blowing, ask your higher self to cleanse the crystal. Visualize it all blowing away with your breath.

EXPLORE THIS!

Be sure to place a Popsicle stick or some other marker in the ground to ensure you find your stone again! I'm sure a crystal garden will one day sprout up in my back lawn with the amount of buried and lost crystals I've got out there. I'm like a squirrel hiding and then forgetting about nuts for winter. One day, somebody's dog will have a major treasure-hunt dig-a-thon, I'm sure. For apartment-dwelling Soul Searchers, use a flowerpot to bury your stone in.

Angel Stones

WOO–WOO SCALE: ▲▲▲▲▲▲▲▲▲△△
EXPLORE–IT SCALE: ▲▲▲▲▲▲▲▲△△△

Different crystals and gemstones can help us facilitate our communication with the angelic realm (cue choirs of angels singing). It sounds a bit loopy, but certain stones such as seraphinite, selenite, celestite, charoite, angelite (go figure, right?), and danburite are considered to possess vibrations that closely match angels (many also call angels "spiritual guides") and can be used as a gateway or bridge between our existence and

EXPLORE THIS!

Hold an angel stone in your hand or place it on your third eye (your brow) while meditating. Use any form or style of meditation you feel comfortable with and try to relax and open your mind. Welcome your angels or guides and make sure you are in a grateful state of mind. Greet them, thank them, and then feel the joy. Stay quiet, calm, and patient as your guides communicate to you through words, pictures in your mind, sensations, and emotions. Let the angel stones be your anchor throughout the meditation.

theirs. Angel stones can help us open our inner vision, so we can perceive our own personal angels (more on these helpful guys in chapter 10).

Your crystals and gemstones can even be used to attract angels into your life, not because the angels need us to holler at them (angels and guides are always believed to be present with us, whether we know it or not), but rather because we may not yet be receptive and present to them. Most of our angels are just waiting for an invite. Having these stones around you or on your body bridges the gap between our world and the angelic world and acts as a sort of on-air light flashing over your head, letting your angels and guides know that you are all ears.

Crystals and gemstones are believed to resonate in large part because they are a product of Mother Nature herself—growing in the Earth's crust for thousands, even millions, of years, accumulating abundant energy (You know that New Age-y thing "vibration"? That's what we're talkin' about!), wisdom, strength, and their own unique personalities.

For a Soul Searcher, crystals and gemstones can be a fantastic way to start communicating with your highest self and to gain clues as to what you really need in life. As you grow your knowledge and understanding of gemstones and crystals, you will be able to make up different crystal cocktails, utilizing a selection of stones that all work in harmony to recharge, reconnect, and realign whatever's out of sync for you.

The way you look at people's rings, necklaces, and even choice of colors in their wardrobe will never be the same. Once you've gained this wisdom, you can never go back—and why would you want to? You will be the resident quartz doctor, offering various gemstones or crystals for friend's issues, sneaking gemstones under pillowcases, or gifting gemstones at birthday parties and holiday get-togethers. Embrace your newfound wisdom, channel your energies to a higher power, and share this abundance with others.

I was über excited to share my crystal and gemstone knowledge with those who crossed my path and suffered from illness, stress, or negativity, but while I was always offering tips for the right reasons, not everyone agreed with the potential healing properties of crystals and gems. Often the expressions on my loved ones' faces were gobsmacked confusion of the holy-shit-she's-gone-completely-crazy variety, which definitely stung a little.

My only advice on this front is to keep an open mind and heart, and remember that skepticism is natural and to be expected. After all, there is no medical proof that gems and crystals have healing properties, and medical professionals, scientists, and skeptics regularly dismiss crystal healing and gemstone therapy as a "pseudoscience." The healing effects of crystals and gems are often said to be placebo effects, wishful thinking, or cognitive bias.

My answer to that is this: So what? Seriously. So what if the link between crystals and healing hasn't been scientifically proven? The link between what we think, how we feel, and how these things manifest in our physical being is undeniable, and if something makes our bodies and minds happy, then our souls are gonna be happy too—and in the end, my friends, that's all that matters. We're all on this interconnected roller coaster of energy exchange together, so let's not disparage each other for holding different beliefs or practicing different methods of satisfying our spiritual appetites. Where's the fun in that?

A rock is just a rock . . . or is it? Now that you've got a foundation of knowledge about how crystals and gemstones can be used to further your soul-searching journey—whether that journey is focused on healing, growth, adventure, protection, cleansing, love, or any other pursuit—you know that there is a crystal to serve your soul's every desire. The next time you happen to stumble across a pretty piece of rose quartz or a glimmering orb of moonstone, listen to your intuition, pick out that one that sings to you, learn about it, and grow with it. One day, you'll look at your crystals and realize you've cultivated a collection without even realizing it. So go find the first stone!

YOUR AROMATHERAPY

Aromatherapy is one of my favorite elements of spirituality. Something to know about me, and another notch on my oh-this-chick-is-a-teensy-bit-of-a-weirdo-but-I-am-digging-her-openness-and-honesty belt is that when I meet people, I give them a good sniff. (And, just for the record, I am not like a butt-sniffing dog. I am classy about it. Well, as classy as you can be, I guess. Oh, side note: if you decide to start sniffing people when you first meet them, it's best to just power through the awkward moment that follows). You can tell a lot about someone by his or her scent. I especially do it when seeking a partner; if I am attracted to their scent, it will last longer than if their scent repulses me. Try it. Trust me. It works …

I love the fact that scents can elicit so many different responses in people for so many different reasons—one person smells fresh-baked muffins and is reminded of weekend brunch at their grandma's house when they were little, and another conjures up the bakery down the street from their first apartment—and that each person has a unique relationship to the smells they love, and the ones they hate! I personally can't handle patchouli (it smells like bad BO to me, yuck!) even though it's one of the most widely used scents in incense around the world (a mystery never to be understood). When we connect with the scents we enjoy, however, they can instantly pick us up, calm us down, or transport us—kind of like Mother Earth's version of drugs without the nasty side effects. I also think aromatherapy is one of the quickest, easiest ways to incorporate a level of spirituality into your life—like a spiritual life hack.

Think of a weed. Now, a weed is called a weed because it grows where it is not wanted. But one person's weed is another person's wild flower. Take the common dandelion—a pest to many gardeners, and yet to others, a key healer and natural medicine used in teas, salads, and an essential oil that helps to relieve muscle pain and tension. When I first was learning about dandelions, it made me start to think about a lot of weed-like things (metaphorically as well as literally) and as I deepened my exploration of all of these kinds of things, it shifted how I looked at the world around me. When I stopped seeing weeds as weeds, it was a spiritual shift for me.

When people outside the spiritual realm hear about aromatherapy, many don't realize that they already practice some of the key elements of aromatherapy in their day-to-day lives. Candles, incense, diffusers, and even perfume are all modern-day aromatherapies. A modern-day Soul Searcher does not need to smell frankincense and myrrh or have the thick smoke of incense billowing out of their home to qualify as a card-carrying aromatherapy enthusiast. In fact, just as you set aside skepticism to experiment with and embrace crystals and their many beneficial properties (kudos to you, by the way), I now invite you to follow your nose further into personal spiritual growth through aromatherapy.

People have used natural herbs, flowers, incense, oils, and perfumes throughout time to connect body, mind, and spirit in a sweet-smelling cloud of spiritual wellness. Today, aromatherapy can be as simple as a spray from your favorite perfume bottle or the heated intensity of an essential oil burner.

As you begin to explore, you will start to notice that we live in a world full of deodorants and sprays that are pumped out by the hundreds. Because of this, it's important to identify scents that speak to you on a personal level and, through these personal connections, find ways to incorporate aromatherapy into your daily rituals.

Diving into the world of aromas, let's start with perfumes. The word perfume is actually Latin for "through smoke," originating from the fragrance of incense that is commonly used in spiritual rituals. The Egyptians have long been considered to be the preeminent perfumers, mastering how to extract essential oils from everything from flowers, grass, leaves, fruit, trees, cedarwood, and cinnamon long ago. They connected perfumes with the gods, spirituality in general, and physical and mental health—like so many elements of spirituality, the body, the mind, and the spirit united.

The ancient Chinese, Hindus, Israelites, Carthaginians, Arabs, Greeks, and Romans all practiced forms of aromatherapy, as well. While the earliest use of perfume bottles in Egypt date to around 1000 BCE, it is believed that the art of aromatherapy itself actually originated from both the Greeks and the Chinese. Greek mythology maintains that the knowledge of fragrance and perfume was something only the gods were gifted, and that knowledge of aromatherapy and its ability to influence health and moods was a sign of status.[1]

To this day, scent is connected with celebrity, which I believe comes down to the simple fact that when we wear a fragrance, it lifts our mood and sometimes makes us feel almost royal. Perfume, beauty, and confidence all go together, and many of us Soul Searchers are drawn to beauty in all its forms, including scent. It is every Soul Searcher's right to know the power and benefits of different scents and oils. Aromatherapy will uplift your spirits and calm your mind and body, making you more open to exploring, enjoying, and growing from other spiritual lessons along your path.

> "Happiness radiates like the fragrance from a flower
> and draws all good things toward you."
> **>Maharishi Mahesh Yogi**

If aromatherapy becomes your go-to spiritual practice or even if it is something you decide to only occasionally dabble in, knowing which smells are connected to what mood triggers and which scents transform the feeling of your surroundings can allow you to alter and channel different energy levels with just a few drops of powerful potion.

Aromatherapy: A Primer

WOO-WOO SCALE: ▲▲▲▲▲▲▲▲△△
EXPLORE-IT SCALE: ▲▲▲▲▲▲▲▲▲▲

I once picked up a bottle of essential oil while traveling through Egypt. I had become fascinated with the stories of ancient medical masterminds and altars still masked with the scent of perfumes from hundreds and even thousands of years ago. My soul was drawn to a perfume and essential oil shop. Walking in, my eyes lit up as I scanned the large room plastered in tiny glass bottles holding a wide array of yellow and clear oils. All the bottles were unlabeled, allowing me to follow the direction of my nose rather than be bombarded with glitzy marketing blurbs (sure, Gwyneth Paltrow looks great skipping through a field of flowers in a ball gown while being chased by a pack of golden retriever puppies, but is that really how I want to smell?), pretty bottles, or packaging. I selected the scent that resonated with me the most and rubbed the oil into the pulse point of my wrist in a circular motion, heating it up against my skin. When I took the blank bottle up to purchase it, a labeled bottle was presented to me with what essential oil it was. I smiled when I read the handwritten label: "Lotus Flower Essence." Under the label it read: "Open and expand spirituality and meditative insight." It really does pay to follow your nose!

Below are a few natural oil blends that stimulate and transform different moods to get you started.[2] These oils can be burned into the air of your surroundings, placed onto your temple or shrine if you have one. They can also be rubbed into your pulse points, put on a cotton ball and slipped into your pillowcase, or added to water and sprayed as a mist on your hair and clothes. The trick to working with aromatherapy is to go with your gut (and your nose, of course), and use scents that you enjoy. This step on your search is almost all about pleasure, so relish it! Sniff it all in.

Mood	Blends & Benefits
Fatigued, unmotivated, unfocused, confused, and lost	orange, jasmine, grapefruit, rosemary, sandalwood, peppermint, lemon, ginger, basil, frankincense
Stressed, overworked, and run down	vanilla, ylang-ylang, lemon, orange, chamomile, bergamot
In need of a boost to your self-esteem, nurturing, love, and self-care	jasmine, orange, rosemary, cypress, bergamot
Dealing with sadness, grief, loss, and change	frankincense, rose, orange, lavender, jasmine, clary sage, sandalwood, ylang-ylang, bergamot
Angry, agitated, mean, having trouble finding forgiveness	chamomile, lavender, mandarin, sandalwood

If you decide to embrace aromatherapy in your day-to-day life, it can help empower and inspire you to be more connected, sympathetic, and loving.

Just as scent blends can be used to shape our moods, similarly, families of scents can tell us a lot about the scents themselves and why they do what they do. Read on to discover which fragrance family your scents fall into and what that may mean.

Which Soul-Search Fragrance Family Resonates with You?

WOO–WOO SCALE: ▲▲▲▲▲▲▲▲▲△△

EXPLORE–IT SCALE: ▲▲▲▲▲▲▲▲▲▲

"A woman's perfume tells more about her than her handwriting."
>**Christian Dior**

Dang, Dior is not wrong! Just as much can be said about the keynote scents in your perfume as what essential oils you are drawn to.

The fragrance wheel splits classes of fragrances into sister groups to help cluster similar scents and blends. What family of scents you connect with can hold keys to your soul's personality types, past lives, careers, and how to best recharge yourself. For example, someone who likes fresh-smelling perfumes such as Miyake's L'Eau d'Issey or Davidoff's Cool Water may have had a past life heavily connected to the water (check out chapter 11 for more on past lives) and will often feel they can collect themselves or reconnect by having a bath, shower, swim, or surf.

Floral

The largest and most popular category is created mainly from flowers, such as roses, orange blossoms, gardenias, jasmine, and carnations. These are often blended to produce a distinctive floral bouquet.

Oriental

A heady mix of spices, amber, balsams, and resins marks this type. Suggestive of warmth and exotic sensuality, people either love or hate the oriental smells.

Fresh

Derived from citrus fruits such as lime, lemon, tangerine, and mandarin, this fragrance type projects a sharp, tangy aroma. Naturally refreshing and uplifting, citrus blends work well for people who like light scents.

Woody

Sharp, grassy, earthy notes blend with pine, juniper, leaves, and herbs to create memorable perfumes. Sporty and brisk, woody scents are deep and spicy.

Key Notes	Perfumes	Benefits
Floral—lily, rose, jasmine, vanilla	Chanel Chance, DKNY Be Delicious, Givenchy Amariage Marige	For the earth angel: romantic, uplifting, calming, comforting, and balancing.
Fruity—ylang-ylang, lemon, orange, chamomile	Chanel Coco Mademoiselle, Guerlain Mitsouko, and Dior Miss Dior Cherie	Fruits of the goddess: awakening, refreshing, alerting, motivating, uplifting, and restoring.
Aquatic—jasmine, orange, rosemary, cypress, bergamot	Aramis New West for Her, Davidoff Cool Water Woman, Issey Miyake L'Eau d'Issey for Women, Davidoff Cool Water Game Woman	Atlantis aromas: cleansing, purifying, uplifting, euphoric, and refreshing.
Spicy—frankincense, orange, lavender, clary sage, sandalwood	Chanel Coco, Sonia Rykiel Belle en Rykiel, Estée Lauder Youth Dew, and Yves Saint Laurent Opium	Spirit siren: sensual, energizing, passionate, strengthening, and centering.
Musky—chamomile, vanilla, mandarin, sandalwood	Aramis Always for Her, Calvin Klein CK Be, Jette Joop Jette, Lanvin Rumeur, Bulgari Blv, Donna Karan Gold, Kenzo Amour, Sarah Jessica Parker Lovely, and Stella McCartney Stella in Two Peony	Mystic motivator: invigorating, anchoring, strengthening, and purifying.

Each group of scents has different keynotes and different benefits associated with its use as outlined in the chart on page 58.[3] See if you can trace the keynotes in your favorite fragrance.

You will be surprised what connections can be drawn between what scent you are attracted to and your past lives, your personality or mood, your astrological sign, your numerological personality—these will all share the same underlying theme. For example (going totally *woo-woo* on you), my past-life connections to Atlantis, and my love for surfing, diving, and generally being in the water is reflected in my choice of perfume—they all have aquatic keynotes.

As I explored the world of smells and spirituality, it was really brought home that smells—from a personal blend of perfume to that particular brand of post-run stink feet give off—tell a story about who a person is. Some smells are gross, some are divine, but all of 'em are yours. And so are the scents we choose to complement our natural odors.

I say that a Soul Searcher is not fully dressed if they are not wearing perfume or essential oils. Consider your personal scent blend like a little black dress for your soul—essential. The belief that a scent is as specific to a person as a signature is an old one. Add a dash of spirituality to that heady idea and you can see how the use of scents can also be used to create a tangible soul signature.

> "The fragrance of flowers spreads only in the direction of the wind. But the goodness of a person spreads in all directions."
> **➤Chanakya**

Consider letting the first thing people experience about you be your signature scent. Let it be one of the many ways you leave beauty everywhere you go, and one of your tools for recharging, reconnecting, and expressing yourself. Spiritual expression through fragrance is the reason that aromatic herbs and oils have played a part in religions across a variety of cultures throughout history. Multiple aromatic

EXPLORE THIS!

Pop into a perfume, naturopathic, or aromatherapy shop near you and test out some oils and perfumes. Here's the challenge: don't look at any of the labels! Or even better, go with a fellow Soul Searcher and spray them for each other, so that the smeller has no connection to the bottle, just the scent. Poke around until something strikes you as just right; then buy it and walk out of the store. Only then should you look at the label and see what scent your soul has latched on to.

EXPLORE THIS!

Use the appropriate oils in baths or with compresses to loosen muscles, relax the mind, and de-stress after a long day. Add some Epsom salts in there and you'll feel like a new person when you emerge from the waters.

botanicals are referenced in the Old and New Testaments for an assortment of uses including anointing oils, perfume, incense, and medicinal, hair, and beauty oils.[4] Many of the oils and fragrances mentioned are still used in traditions today.

On the nonsecular side, aromatherapy is a quick and fun way to enlighten your senses and get flirtatious clues about your soul's character, desires, and purpose. Look at the following chart for a few common scents and their spiritual meanings and uses.[5] I'm a total frankincense freak and ylang-ylang junkie myself, and have an organic perfume balm that has both of these fragrances in it that I place on my wrists, behind my ears, and across my heart every morning.

Spiritual Scents	Uses
Aloeswood	Meditation, calming, entrancing
Juniper	Cleansing, purifying, eliminating
Jasmine, ylang-ylang, bergamot, citrus	Giving thanks, gratitude
Cypress, frankincense, sandalwood, rosemary	Enlightenment
Bay laurel, cinnamon, lavender	Aid spirituality, faith

Aromatherapy and Healing

WOO-WOO SCALE: ▲▲△△△△△△△△△
EXPLORE-IT SCALE: ▲▲▲▲▲▲▲▲▲▲▲

Another confession: while writing this book, I used lavender oil on my third eye to help me channel and connect with what the content of this book should be. Forgetting I had anointed myself with lavender goodness, I ventured out to visit my darling grandmother who proceeded to lick her thumbs and rub it off, saying, and I quote, "Oh dear, your hormones must be going haywire. What an odd place to be oily." Thanks, Nan!

Just as crystals can aid in healing, so can essential oils. For example, just as blue kyanite can immediately and automatically realign chakras, so too can the essential oil lavender. Below is a compilation of common illnesses and emotional challenges and the oils or blends that can help with the healing and care process.

Anxiety, Depression, Stress, Fear

Rescue remedy anyone? Chamomile oils are used to help soothe anxious, overactive minds that may lead to trouble sleeping or exacerbate depression. Other relaxing oils include valerian, sandalwood, and lavender. There are also a handful of oils that cannot only rebalance a negative state of mind but can also help you get into a more uplifted and happy mood including bergamot, orange, and jasmine oils.

Relaxation and Sleeping

There are lots of elements that need to come together in order for someone to feel relaxed and have a good night's sleep. Similarly, oil blends work best to solve the multifaceted problem of insomnia—blends that include rosewood oil, which is grounding and relaxing, and has antiviral properties. I recommend blending rosewood with frankincense, which is a mood balancer and de-stressor, and ylang-ylang, which is an excellent oil for restoring the balance of your energies and recharging your energy centers.

Muscles and Inflammation

If you're sorer than a triathlete after a big race or puffed up like a pissed-off blowfish, I'd recommend searching for oils that increase circulation and reduce inflammation. These oils can be added to coconut oil and be rubbed into problem areas. Basil is one of the key essential oils for healing muscle inflammation—yeah, the same herb you put on your pasta! Basil oil can be placed directly on problem areas or diffused. Eucalyptus oil is the perfect "anti" oil, working as an antiviral, antibacterial, antifungal, antiaging, and anti-inflammatory agent. If you dilute it in equal parts water and then diffuse it, the oil will even help to kill airborne bacteria. Like many other oils, a few drops can also be rubbed directly into the problem area. Just the tiniest drop of eucalyptus always makes me feel like I've strayed into the most luxurious of spas and am being waited on hand and foot. *Ahhhh.*

General Bone Pain and Aches, Fractures, and Breaks

There are a handful of essential oils that are fantastic for bone pain. These oils can be blended, or you can use the one scent you enjoy the most. Peppermint, wintergreen, spruce, palo santo, and eucalyptus are all oils that can be used to soothe bone pain of most kinds.

Burns and Sunburn

For any burn (note: we're talking sunburns and burns from your hair straightener, not third degree here!) you'll probably want to use oils that have natural anti-inflammatory and analgesic (pain relieving) properties. Oils that contain a combination of these healing elements include lavender, rose, Roman chamomile, eucalyptus, rosewood, lemon, helichrysum, and Idaho balsam fir oils.

A great blend for burns that I rely on is one with lavender, rosewood, and ylang-ylang oils. Together, they provide anti-inflammatory help, pain relief, and act as a relaxant or sedative to help calm the nervous system and heal the skin. Next time you overdo it at the beach, I'd recommend having this blend on hand.

Disinfectants

The uses of natural oils don't stop at the body—they're great for the home too. Going green in your home includes using natural disinfectants. Here are some oils that have disinfectant properties: tea tree, grapefruit, lemon, Melrose, eucalyptus, lemongrass, and citronella. Make your own cleaning products by mixing water and oils in a spray bottle. Ensure you mix up your routine and vary your disinfectant to ensure you confuse any bacteria in the home. Bonus: ants hate citrus. Spritz some lemon oil on the little critters and watch them instantly run for cover (hopefully cover far, far away from your kitchen).

Vomiting and Stomach/Intestinal Issues

A variety of oils can help ease the stomach and soothe vomiting. Peppermint oil and lavender oil are great essences to breathe in or diffuse to help nausea. Oils like nutmeg and fennel are also commonly used to help stomach problems, as they are natural stomach protectants and laxatives, which can help flush the system of any crap—literally—that's mucking up your internal machine.

Abuse or Abandonment

These oils are great if you're dealing with the emotional impact of events like a divorce, a family member's passing, or extricating yourself from an abusive relationship. These blends will release negative emotions and help clear your energies. I'd recommend combining frankincense, lavender, spruce, and sandalwood for emotional trauma. Combine ylang-ylang, blue tansy, and sandalwood oils to release negative experiences and energies from the body. Combine lemongrass, citronella, and rosemary oils to clear spaces of negativity.

Anger or Hate

These oils are perfect when diffused to help clear any hostility, tension, or conflict from a workspace or home. Blend bergamot, ylang-ylang, jasmine, mandarin, and coriander oils and diffuse throughout whichever space needs a bad-feelings kick in the butt. These oils are also a great addition to a bath or added to vegetable oil for a relaxing and de-stressing massage.

Concentration, Focus

To focus, we must balance and center the mind, so a delicate balance of oils is what we're going for here. Each oil adds a unique benefit to this blend, including frankincense oil, which elevates the mood and helps us to rewind from stress; helichrysum oil, which helps with circulation as well as with the unblocking of thoughts and ideas; sandalwood oil, which is an antidepressant and mood balancer; cedarwood oil, a purifier; lavender oil, which helps to release tension from the whole body; and finally blue cypress oil, which helps stimulate the body and awaken the mind. Citrus oils of all sorts are also great to help give the mind the spring-cleaning it sometimes needs to get your focus back online.[6]

Aromatherapy and Chakra Healing

As you will learn in the next chapter, aromatherapy is deeply connected to chakra healing, and using the two in concert with each other can be enormously beneficial.

As always, experiment, play around, screw up (one day I accidentally covered myself in basil oil instead of sandalwood; I smelled like pizza all day)—and use whichever method ends up being best for you. Many of the essential oils associated with each chakra overlap,

EXPLORE THIS!

Blend a combination of oils from the above—such as the oils that promote healthy sleep—and add them to a spray bottle. Spray the mixture on your pillow and around your room before bed, or even just around the house after a busy day. You probably want to avoid spritzing your pets, your significant other, and the mail guy, but everything else is fair game!

Chakras

Essential Oils

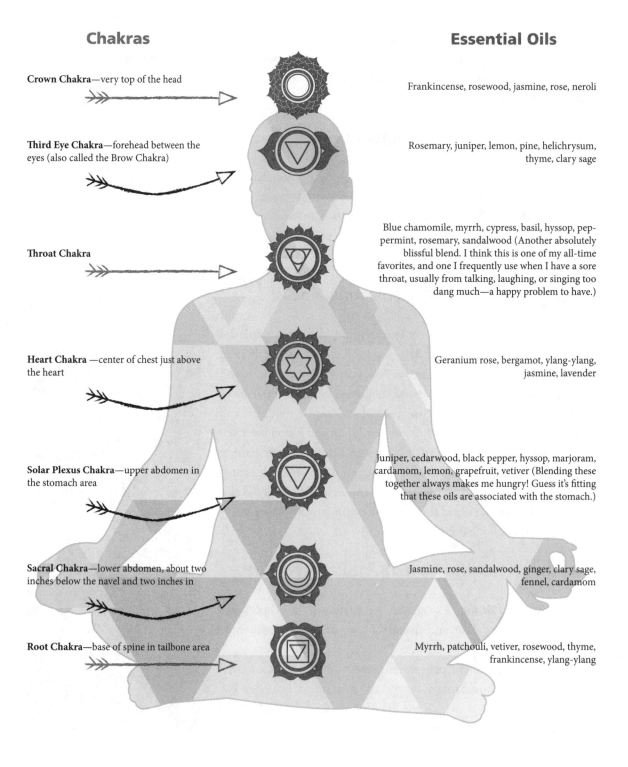

Crown Chakra—very top of the head

Frankincense, rosewood, jasmine, rose, neroli

Third Eye Chakra—forehead between the eyes (also called the Brow Chakra)

Rosemary, juniper, lemon, pine, helichrysum, thyme, clary sage

Throat Chakra

Blue chamomile, myrrh, cypress, basil, hyssop, peppermint, rosemary, sandalwood (Another absolutely blissful blend. I think this is one of my all-time favorites, and one I frequently use when I have a sore throat, usually from talking, laughing, or singing too dang much—a happy problem to have.)

Heart Chakra —center of chest just above the heart

Geranium rose, bergamot, ylang-ylang, jasmine, lavender

Solar Plexus Chakra—upper abdomen in the stomach area

Juniper, cedarwood, black pepper, hyssop, marjoram, cardamom, lemon, grapefruit, vetiver (Blending these together always makes me hungry! Guess it's fitting that these oils are associated with the stomach.)

Sacral Chakra—lower abdomen, about two inches below the navel and two inches in

Jasmine, rose, sandalwood, ginger, clary sage, fennel, cardamom

Root Chakra—base of spine in tailbone area

Myrrh, patchouli, vetiver, rosewood, thyme, frankincense, ylang-ylang so it may be a good idea to keep notes on which oils and blends you use for each one. Remember that people do react in different ways to essential oils, so it is important to use your intuition and try different blends. The chart on the preceeding page will get you going where marrying chakra energy and aromatherapy is concerned:[7]

So, why do essential oils have such an effect on us through our energy centers? Because the eyes are the window to the soul, and the nose is the front door? Well I don't know, but maybe. Essential oils are not just a combination of alcohols, phenols, and terpenes. Each oil is also considered to have its own pranic—also called chi—energy, and frequency, and these silent sounds or vibrations make our chakras "sing" again, when, otherwise, they might remain silent or mute. Think of essential oils as tuning forks for your chakras.

Essential oils change our emotional profile and can help charge our energy centers, not just because their sweet smells charm our senses, but also because their small molecules penetrate our blood-brain barrier—which otherwise keeps most everything from coming into contact with our neurons—to effortlessly target our brain on a bio-chemical level. It's almost like chocolate for the nose. By influencing our emotions through aromatherapy, we bring balance and whole-ness back to our bodies' energy centers, removing hidden blockages, fine-tuning our emotional and physical harmony, and connecting with the scents our souls crave on a deep, spiritual level. So, oil up, Soul Searcher!

EXPLORE THIS!

Incorporate aromatherapy into a chakra-balancing massage and double the energy-unblocking benefits—and come away from the massage smelling amazing too.

I hope that you have fun experiencing the world of scent and that you find take-aways from this chapter that provide you with all you need to begin to work with aromatherapy. And never forget the importance of following your nose. Just as we are drawn to certain flowers, colors, and even animals, we are also intrinsically connected to certain scents. The more you dive into the smells you are attracted to, the more clues you will get from your soul about what it craves, what serves you and what does not, and what you need more of to live in-line with your purpose. Permission to get your sniff on.

YOUR SOUL, CHAKRAS, AND AURAS

We've been talking a lot about the soul, haven't we? I've found that I can only talk about the soul in any useful way in terms of how its power manifests through our bodies and minds. I believe that your soul is your body's life source, and your soul is grounded in your body. Your emotions and gut feelings are the language of the soul, and your emotions, in turn, control your moods, attitudes, and health.

Each of our souls speaks a slightly different language. In my search, it has been both interesting and enlightening to look at all of the religious views across time, culture, and geography to come to an understanding of what the word soul means to me.

What about you? Do you, like many Buddhists and Hindus, believe in reincarnation, where one learns lessons throughout life? Do you believe that the sum of a person's actions in both this life and all previous ones and one's fate in future existences is judged through karma? What about Christianity?

Most Christians do not believe in reincarnation, but many believe that when one dies, one's soul separates from the body and goes on to be judged at the gates of Heaven. It is my understanding that, in modern Judaism, it is believed that the body and soul are one, and that the quality of one's soul is related to reaching higher levels of understanding and thus slowly becomes closer and closer to God. Islam gives two different names to the soul, *nafs* (soul) and *ruh* (spirit), and in Chinese philosophy, the symbols of balance, yin and yang, are intrinsically tied to the concept of the soul.[1]

No matter your belief system, caring for one's soul through care of one's body is essential to your soul search. Two ways to access and get to know your soul are through your chakras and your aura. We've already stuck our toes into the chakra pool in previous chapters, and now we're going to dive in completely. We'll be exploring both chakras and auras in this chapter with the goal of bringing you a little bit closer to knowing yourself from the inside out through these ancient soul-searching concepts.

Chakras

The ancient Egyptians believed the body housed seven souls called *Hathors*, named after the Egyptian goddess of fate. The belief of seven souls developed throughout Egypt and India, and today an increasing amount of people entering their spiritual awakening are becoming intrigued with the seven-chakra belief system.[2] I became extremely curious about chakras when I first began my soul search, and these days, I partake in chakra cleansing every other month.

Your energy system, or chakras, is linked to different sections of the body. Once you understand each chakra, you can begin to understand the reasons behind any ailments that might be getting you down. The essence of chakra healing is, at its most basic, healing your body's core energy centers.

Each chakra:

▷ is connected to a particular area of the body, including the bones, organs, and tissue.
▷ is represented by a particular color and vibration.
▷ represents a life theme, change, or challenge in your soul's journey.

Before we explain the chakras as an aligned energy system, we must understand how our body, mind, and soul use energy as power. If I asked you what you are made of, what would you say? Would your brain rush back to biology class and tell me you are cells or matter, or would you say you are made up of energy? Science largely echoes what thinkers like Socrates and ancient Indian philosophers posited many hundreds of years ago—that all living things are energy. Cells emit an electric energy, frequency, or vibration (there are many names for it). The idea of "good vibes" and "bad vibes" can be found in our soul's understanding of a person's energy. You can sense if someone is in a good space or not, energetically, and if it is in your best inter-est to move out of his or her space or into it. This vital energy that flows through the chakras is sometimes called *prana*, meaning the spark of life within us.

As you study each of your chakras, you'll discover how your family legacy, together with your current thoughts, feelings, and beliefs, can directly affect the health of your tissues and organs. Whether you believe in chakras as literal places in the body or as metaphoric ones, they can help you activate mind-body-soul connections to help you heal. *Chakra* is a Sanskrit word meaning "wheels or disks of energy." When I check in with my body's symptoms, I like to visualize my chakras as spinning wheels of color. Trippy, huh?

To get us started, let's take a look at this chart to help you identify your energy centers.[3]

Chakra	Body Connections
Crown Chakra or **Seventh Chakra** Represents your spirituality and connection to your life purpose. **Color:** violet or white **Location:** very top of the head	This chakra is linked to every organ in the chakra system, and it affects the brain and nervous system. People who are overly skeptical or intolerant often experience blocks in the seventh chakra. When it is unbalanced, people tend to be narrow-minded or stubborn.
Third Eye Chakra or **Sixth Chakra** Represents your creativity, intuition, and intelligence. This chakra is often called your third eye. **Color:** indigo **Location:** forehead between the eyes (also called the Brow Chakra)	This chakra is linked to our hearing, our eyes, nose, ears, and brain, and if blocked, can cause blindness, deafness, stroke, and learning disabilities. People who have difficulties listening to or accepting their reality often have problems with the sixth chakra. When it is unbalanced, people tend to exude a know-it-all personality.
Throat Chakra or **Fifth Chakra** Represents your expression and communication of your inner will. **Color:** blue or turquoise **Location:** throat	This chakra is linked to our voice, throat, words of expression, and everything in and surrounding the mouth such as the teeth, gums, lips, etc. People who do not speak the truth or suppress important thoughts instead of speaking their minds often have problems with the fifth chakra, as do people who have a hard time moderating what comes out of their mouths. When it is unbalanced, people tend to gossip a lot or dominate conversations.
Heart Chakra or **Fourth Chakra** Represents your heart center, intuition, and self-love. **Color:** green **Location:** center of chest just above heart	This chakra is linked to the heart, chest, lungs, shoulders, ribs, and breasts. People who tend to put others first at the expense of themselves often have blocks in the fourth chakra. Often blockages come in the form of weight problems, heart problems, allergies, or asthma. When it is unbalanced, people tend to feel insecure or isolated.
Solar Plexus Chakra or **Third Chakra** Represents your identity, personality, and self-esteem. **Color:** yellow **Location:** upper abdomen/stomach area	This chakra is linked to our digestive organs and can influence our whole digestive system. Blocks can be seen in ulcers, irritable bowel syndrome, heartburn, diabetes, diarrhea, indigestion, anorexia, bulimia, and hepatitis. When it is unbalanced, people are indecisive, lack confidence, and have problems following through on things.

Chakra	Body Connections
Sacral Chakra or **Second Chakra** Represents your sexuality, personal power, and relationships **Color:** orange **Location:** lower abdomen, about two inches below the navel and two inches in	This chakra is closely linked to our reproductive system and genitals. Blocks can be seen in back pain, bladder infections, urinary tract infections, and impotency. This chakra has ties to how we see our self-worth. When there is an imbalance, people often feel unstable and depressed, and experience complicated relationships with and addictions to alcohol, drugs, or sex.
Root Chakra or **First Chakra** Represents your family connection and foundations of your emotional and mental centers. **Color:** red **Location:** base of spine in tailbone area	This chakra is linked to muscles, bones, joints, and blood, and also to the first few years of a person's life and how they were positioned in their family. Blocks often are seen through stiffness, arthritis, constipation, weight problems, and hemorrhoids. When it is unbalanced, people will often experience feelings of insecurity and greed, and will lack a sense of belonging.

"Sadness gives depth. Happiness gives height. Sadness gives roots. Happiness gives branches. Happiness is like a tree going into the sky, and sadness is like the roots going down into the womb of the earth. Both are needed, and the higher a tree goes, the deeper it goes, simultaneously. The bigger the tree, the bigger will be its roots. In fact, it is always in proportion. That's its balance."

➤Osho

As mentioned above, each of our chakras emits a vibration and holds a unique energy. When one or more chakras is blocked, we often can feel it in the energy our body gives off. Have you ever felt sluggish, irritable for no apparent reason, or just plain flat, like your soul is deflated and saggy? I feel like most of us have been there, probably multiple times over. Once we learn to connect these seemingly random symptoms and triggers of our chakra imbalances, we can become more proactive about making sure we address them by balancing our energy centers from time to time.

Now, let me ask you this: Does chakra balancing sound time-consuming, weird, and generally not like something you'd find easy to incorporate into your life? If yes, no worries—it sounded pretty unsustainable to me at first too. Luckily, there are a variety of ways we can get our energy centers back in balance, and many of them are easily accessible. The good news is your soul will tell you when it is necessary to do one of these balances; it will blare at you like a spirit alarm clock. As always: mix and match, test things out, and enjoy educating yourself about this vital spiritual practice!

Chakra Cleansing

WOO–WOO SCALE: ▲▲▲▲▲▲▲▲△△
EXPLORE–IT SCALE: ▲▲▲▲▲△△△△△

Holistic healers and many massage therapists will offer chakra-cleansing sessions. To cleanse the chakras, we must first cleanse ourselves of the negative experiences, emotions, and energy our bodies are hosting and, in doing so, choose to let go, relax, and be healed. In order for a chakra cleansing to have long-lasting effects, you must also put in the mental work to clear your mind of negative thoughts so that the issue does not recur. Ask your massage therapist if they do chakra cleanses, or if they can recommend someone who does.

Chakra-Balancing Bath

WOO–WOO SCALE: ▲▲△△△△△△△△
EXPLORE–IT SCALE: ▲▲▲▲▲▲▲▲▲△

The quickest way to balance your chakras is to submerge yourself in salt water. A simple swim or surf in the ocean is a great way to achieve energy balance. Alternatively, you could have a salt bath using Epsom salts in a big bathtub—your skin absorbs the salt, leaving you feeling cleansed and centered. Make sure to grab on to something when you're getting out of an Epsom salt bath though—they turn your bathtub into a Slip'N Slide!

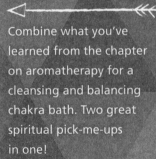

EXPLORE THIS!

Combine what you've learned from the chapter on aromatherapy for a cleansing and balancing chakra bath. Two great spiritual pick-me-ups in one!

Tension and Trauma Release Exercise (TRE)

WOO–WOO SCALE: ▲▲▲▲▲▲▲▲△△
EXPLORE–IT SCALE: ▲▲▲▲▲▲▲▲▲△

This healing experience was introduced to me when a girlfriend of mine went along to a TRE session and experienced violent tremors in her arm. After sharing with the teacher that she had never had trauma in her arm, she was left feeling uneasy and decided to go for a checkup. She was diagnosed with breast cancer next to the shaking arm. Needless to say I too gave it a go!

TRE was created by Dr. David Berceli. The exercise safely activates a natural reflex mechanism of shaking or vibrating that releases muscular tension, calming down the nervous system. When this muscular shaking/vibrating mechanism is activated in a safe and controlled environment, the body is encouraged to return back to a state of balance, releasing the tension and trauma from the body.[4]

Yoga

WOO-WOO SCALE: ▲▲▲▲▲▲▲▲▲▲
EXPLORE-IT SCALE: ▲▲▲▲▲▲▲▲▲▲

Yoga means "union" or "discipline." Practicing yoga helps us align our body, mind, and soul and is particularly effective in releasing negative energies. Through movement and stillness, the energy is pushed through the energy centers of the body and away from its point of concentration. Often, a negative issue will come to mind as this blockage is broken up. The soul plants this in your mind to let you know what caused the blockage in the first place, allowing you to mentally let it go and learn from what doesn't serve you. If you haven't already, check out chapter 1 for more on yoga. When in doubt and especially when feeling time starved, remember: simple sun salutations, Child's Pose, and Corpse Pose are your friends! Even if you can only fit ten minutes of yoga into your day, your chakras will thank you for it.

EXPLORE THIS!

Stand on a patch of grass, the beach, wherever's accessible and that feels good, with your arms at your sides and your eyes closed. (If you're a yogi, you'll recognize this as a basic Mountain Pose.) Breathing slowly and deeply, imagine roots coming out from your feet, anchoring you, centering you. Stay here, imagining your roots going farther and farther into the earth, for five to ten minutes. When you're ready, open your eyes and bask in the positive energy flowing through your chakras from the earth up. This is a great grounding exercise and will help you when you are feeling like you are losing control of life—you know, that OMG-I-am-spinning-off-into-space-like-Sandra-Bullock-in-*Gravity* feeling!

Walking in Nature

WOO-WOO SCALE: ▲▲▲▲▲▲▲▲▲▲
EXPLORE-IT SCALE: ▲▲▲▲▲▲▲▲▲▲

Let's not jump on the treadmill with an iPod blasting in your ears just yet—instead, get yourself out into nature, preferably barefoot! Even if you only manage to find a patch of grass and stand on it for five minutes, don't pass up the chance. Allow yourself to connect to Mother Earth in any way you can. This is a process of resetting by rooting yourself to the earth.

Sleep

WOO-WOO SCALE: ▲△△△△△△△△△△
EXPLORE-IT SCALE: ▲▲▲▲▲▲▲▲▲▲▲

This one's a no-brainer, but still, hardly any of us get enough rest. Whatever you can snatch—putting your feet up, meditating, taking a catnap—let your body hit the reset button and rest for as long as it tells you it needs. You'll wake up revived, reset, and most importantly, full of positive, unstuck energy!

EXPLORE THIS!

Research into the topic has shown that the amount of sleep for the optimal nap is between ten and thirty minutes, and in the afternoon (try to aim for between two and three).[5] At work during this time? Eat lunch at your desk and then use a late lunch break to grab some shut-eye in an empty office, outside on a park bench, or even under your desk. Remember my old coworker who made a little sanctuary in his cubicle? Consider giving it a try; it sure worked for him.

Heat

WOO-WOO SCALE: ▲▲▲△△△△△△△△
EXPLORE-IT SCALE: ▲▲▲▲▲▲▲▲▲△△

There is a reason why people go to tropical destinations to escape. Heat is a natural de-stressor and helps to relax the muscles, allowing negativity to flow out of the body. While a tropical vacay is great, most of us can't put our lives on hold to take one whenever we feel like it. You can also find a heat fix by visiting a sauna, spa, bathhouse, or doing a Bikram or other hot yoga class.

Detox

WOO-WOO SCALE: ▲▲△△△△△△△△△
EXPLORE-IT SCALE: ▲▲▲▲▲▲△△△△△

Master cleanse? Not necessarily, my friends. Detoxification is the process of cleansing the cells of the body and the blood that circulates through the body. One of the main aims of a detox is to remove impurities from the blood in the liver, where toxins are processed for elimination. The body also eliminates toxins through the kidneys, intestines, lungs, lymphatic system, and skin. However, when this system is compromised—when you've gone on a crappy food binge, haven't been getting enough rest, or been sick for a time—impurities aren't properly filtered and every cell in the body is adversely affected.

There are lots of different detoxes available, such as juice, green food, and raw food. Whatever sort of cleanse resonates with you, ensure you drink plenty of water to help the body to flush out any toxins and that you try and eat plenty of whole food such as organic broccoli, kale, spinach, beetroot, onion, cabbage, barley, wheatgrass, kale, spinach, spirulina, alfalfa, chard, arugula, and other organic leafy greens either during your cleanse or as you're coming out of it. Also try to incorporate garlic and green tea, both natural antioxidants (antioxidants slow down or prevent the breaking down or damage of the cells of the body). I'd also strongly recommend speaking with a nutritionist or doctor before you begin any diet plan or cleanse to make sure it's safe for your body.

EXPLORE THIS!

Experiment with these sounds as you meditate for targeted healing for each chakra.

- The sound "OO" (pronounced like the oo in food): *This sound is linked to the Root and the Sacral Chakra.*
- The sound "OH" (pronounced like the oh in coat): *This sound is linked to the Solar Plexus (inner sun) and the Sacral Chakra.*
- The sound "AH" (pronounced like the a in father): *This sound is linked to the Heart Chakra.*
- The sound "EH" (pronounced like the e in bed): *This sound is linked to the Throat Chakra.*
- The sound "EE" (pronounced like the i in machine): *This sound is connected to the Third Eye and Crown Chakra.*
- The sound "ZZZ" (like a bee!) and "MM" (pronounced like the m in mom): *These sounds are connected to the Third Eye and the Crown Chakra.*[6]

Vibration Meditation

WOO-WOO SCALE: ▲▲▲▲▲▲▲▲▲△
EXPLORE-IT SCALE: ▲▲△△△△△△△△

Given that our chakras are energy centers that operate on a vibrational frequency, incorporating humming and song into meditation can help realign our chakras through vibrations of the body. To try this out: sit comfortably, cross-legged, posture upright, and close your eyes so you can focus on the sounds and on feeding yourself energy. Each chakra has a unique frequency; therefore, each needs a unique chant.

If you just keep saying the chant in a normal voice, it will be less effective. I've found that the best way to chant is in monotone. Make your voice as deep as you can, so you can feel it deep in your body. When you chant these sounds, you should be able to physically feel the vibration of the sounds surging through your body. Don't worry if it feels silly at first! It probably will. Feel free to laugh and start over as many times as you need to until you get the hang of it.

Music

WOO-WOO SCALE: ▲▲△△△△△△△△
EXPLORE-IT SCALE: ▲▲▲▲▲▲▲▲△△

Dance party, anyone? The therapeutic properties of music have long been linked to relaxation, meditation, and healing by its ability to affect our moods. The frequency of a song can help us feel happier or calm us down depending on its beat—have you ever been in a funk and then your favorite dance song came on the radio? It's almost impossible to stay glum when that happens. Music affects us both emotionally and mentally. This is why when you go to a festival or concert, your energy can be enhanced by the beat of the music and vibrations of those around you through dancing, clapping, and singing. There are even instruments connected to each chakra! Check it out:

▷ Base Chakra or Root Chakra: The drum of the original East Indian music is considered the voice of the soul. Drums are connected to the rhythm of life and to the om mantra.
▷ Seat of the Soul Chakra: The woodwinds call the soul to the mother, as Mother Earth and the drums can help ground us to the beat of the earth.
▷ Solar Plexus Chakra: The pipe organ affects the wants of the soul and helps us to listen to our inner desires.
▷ Heart Chakra: The large harp and chimes can symbolize our attunement with the universe and sing to our souls.
▷ Throat Chakra: Brass instruments and singing represent our attunement with the universe and our choice of words and need for expression.
▷ Third Eye Chakra: The piano exemplifies the mastery of the single-eyed vision and our connection to spirituality.

▷ Crown Chakra: Stringed instruments represent the enlightenment of the mind and help with intuitive listening and communication with the soul.[7]

"To keep the body in good health is a duty . . .
otherwise, we shall not be able to keep our mind strong and clear."

>**Buddha**

Auras

WOO-WOO SCALE: ▲▲▲▲▲▲▲▲▲▲
EXPLORE-IT SCALE: ▲▲▲▲▲▲▲▲▲▲

Open your minds and hearts and boot your skepticism out the window, my friends—oh yeah, it's time to talk about auras.

Aura has long been described as an electromagnetic energy field surrounding all people, like an egg-shaped ball of energy that encompasses the body. The aura consists of seven levels/layers/auric bodies, also known as the physical, astral, lower, higher, spiritual, intuitional, and absolute planes. Each one of these subtle bodies that exists around the physical body has its own unique frequency. They are interrelated and affect one another as well as a person's feelings, emotions, thought patterns, behavior, and overall health.[8] Just like with chakras, a state of imbalance in one of the bodies leads to a state of imbalance in the others as well.

To start us off, here is a breakdown of each layer and what our body seeks and gains from that layer.

Physical Aura Plane

This is the layer closest to us and the one that decreases through our waking hours and increases while we sleep or rest. For this layer to be in balance, we need physical comfort, pleasure, and health. If our auras are in general bad health, we will have smudges in this layer. Also, people who are harboring negative emotions or who are dwelling in a negative space will have a darker physical aura plane.

Astral Aura Plane

This plane is also called the "emotional layer," as it stores our emotional history and experiences with friends and family. It is easy to tell when your Astral Aura is out of whack because you feel sensitive, unstable, and often irrational—kinda like your aura has PMS. Your Astral Aura will respond best when you amplify what it needs with your surroundings. For example, to heal negative emotions, try visualizing green. Lie on grass or spend some time under a tree. This will help to add the color to your auric space.

Lower Mental Aura Plane

This plane relates to reason, thoughts, and how we construct our own individual reality. Most people spend their waking hours in this plane. This plane expands when our minds are at work, when we are studying, and even when we're focused on something particularly hard. This is also where a person's belief systems are stored, as well as their values and ideas. When someone's lower mental aura plane is twisted and out of alignment, they will feel judgmental, down, and often agitated.

Higher Mental Aura Plane

This plane connects with our Lower Mental Aura Plane but also adds in a deeper spiritual element as well. This is where we store our higher-mind beliefs such as self-love, gratitude, selflessness, and unconditional love. Yep, your self-talk can be affecting your whole vibe—not only your confidence but also the energy you project out into the world. So regardless of what that little voice in your head is telling you, make sure your higher plane is all about how beautiful, kind, and loving you are, because even though you might think it's just an internal conversation with yourself, everyone around you can sense the conversation you're having. I invite you to take this as official permission to have a big-ass aura ego—it will only help nourish and feed the energy and environment within and around you.

EXPLORE THIS!

Our auras change as we switch moods. Just as smiling when we're not all that happy can lift our moods, similar actions can also help our auric fields perk up. So when you're feeling out of alignment, murky, or affected by other people's negative energies, sometimes it can be as simple as giving yourself healthy, positive, loving thoughts to wash away the mood from your aura. Test it out now by giving yourself an auric smile and see if you feel better.

Spiritual Aura Plane

This plane has solely to do with our spirituality and connects us to both our immediate surroundings and to the wider universe. When we are aware of this layer and connected to other people's spiritual planes, we can better sense like-minded souls. When you have a clear spiritual aura, you will find yourself connecting with other people on the same path as you, discovering the same things—basically, people you can teach, share with, and learn from. People who have yet to tap into their spiritual auric plane tend to be overly cynical, negative, judgmental, and even threatened by your spiritual growth. Don't worry. They're just jealous of your radiant aural glow. In fact when people react like this to you, that is when you know your Spiritual Aura Plane is rocking! They'll catch up to your bliss in their own time, and if they don't, it's their loss, not yours.

Intuitional Aura Plane

This plane, also known as the celestial plane, is where we store our dreams, intuition, and overall spiritual awareness. This is where we store forgiveness and acceptance as well. When you think of an enlightened person, what characteristics do you think of? I tend to go to peaceful, calm, kind, and patient. You can sense a healthy intuitional aura plane, one in complete nirvana, when you are near people like this—you also start to feel more centered in their presence. Enlightened souls, sometimes also called "indigo personalities," live in their Intuitional Aura Plane—sensitive, often eccentric, profound souls who are creative, intuitive, and gifted. When you have one of those aha moments or a massive brainwave after you've felt blocked for ages, this is your Intuitional Aura Plane clearing the runway for major spiritual growth.

Absolute Aura Plane

The absolute plane works to balance and harmonize the other layers. It houses all the experiences of a soul's journey and is the blueprint of a person's spiritual journey. Think of it as the auric big red bow—the finishing touch on top of your energy field with spiritual sprinkles on top![9]

Have you ever walked into a room and instantly gotten goosebumps—a gut feeling telling you that something was about to happen, or that the emotional temperature of the room was tense or relaxed? These experiences are your auric fields shielding you in a sense, touching other auric fields so you can intuitively pick up on different individuals' moods to help predict behaviors. Those who are good at reading people and adapting to different situations, or are quick to pick up emotional unrest in others are usually quite in tune with their body's energy system—soul, chakras, and auras combined. Some are even in tune enough to see and read auras in all their layers and colors.

> "I sometimes ask people,
> 'Can you be aware of your own presence?
> Not the thought that you're having, not the emotions that
> you're having, but the very presence of your very being?'
> You become aware of your own presence by sensing
> the entire energy field in your body that is alive.
> And that is the totality of your presence."
> **>Eckhart Tolle**

Aura Know-How

Aura colors are usually what comes to mind for Soul Searchers who've yet to learn the deeper meaning of auras and how they relate to the soul (I'll always think of the stoned groupie girl in Cameron Crowe's *Almost Famous*,[10] grabbing at Patrick Fugit and shouting gleefully, "Your aura is purple!") But like most things, there's a lot more to auras than that. So let's lift up another aura rock and see what cool stuff's wriggling underneath, shall we? On the following pages is an aura color chart with their associated color meanings.[11]

Just like we balance and cleanse our chakras, we can also cleanse and realign our auras. There are many similarities between energy cleanses and aura cleanses; however, auras respond best to the following: absorb natural light, reduce electrical exposure, and avoid mood imbalances.

EXPLORE THIS!

View your aura colors by holding your index fingers tip to tip. Standing in front of a plainly colored or white wall, hold you arms out in front of you, index fingers still touching. Slowly pull them apart, relaxing your vision to almost "zone out" mode, and you will likely see an outline surrounding your fingers of a light blue/gray light. This is your first glimpse of auric energy. The more you practice, the more you will see and the more vivid the colors will become.

EXPLORE THIS!

Peruse YouTube for clips on the meanings of your aura colors and to discover some quick tips on how to find out what your auric color is.

RED AURA

Relates to the physical body in general, the heart, and circulation. The denser the color red it creates, the more friction is happening within the aura. Red auras usually relate to financial worries, obsessions, anger, anxiety, or nervousness. However, in-balance red energy can indicate a healthy ego and a heaping dose of healthy self-love.

Deep red: grounded, realistic, active, strong willpower, or stubborn and selfish
Muddied red: anger
Clear red: powerful, passionate, energetic, sexual
Murky red: immature, dishonest, or a manipulative personality
Orange red: creative, powerful ideas

ORANGE AURA

Relates to reproductive organs and emotions. The color of vitality, good health, and excitement. Lots of energy and stamina, creativity, productivity, adventurousness, courageousness, outgoing social nature; alternately, currently experiencing stress related to addictions

Orange yellow: creative, intelligent, detail oriented, perfectionist, scientific

YELLOW AURA

Relates to the spleen and life energy; awakening, inspiration, intelligence, and action; sharing, creativity, playfulness, optimism, and easy-going nature

Light or pale yellow: Emerging psychic and spiritual awareness; optimism and hopefulness; positive excitement about new ideas
Bright lemon yellow: Struggling to maintain power and control in a personal or business relationship; fear of losing control, prestige, respect, or power
Clear gold metallic, shiny and brigh: Spiritual energy, power activated, and awakened; an inspired person
Dark brownish yellow or gold: A student, or one who is straining at studying; overly analytical to the point of feeling fatigued or stressed; trying to make up for "lost time" by learning everything all at once

WHITE AURA

White sparkles or flashes of white light: angels are nearby; can indicate that the person is pregnant or will be soon

GREEN AURA

Relates to heart and lungs. It is a very comfortable, healthy color related to nature. When seen in the aura, green usually represents growth and balance, and, most of all, something that leads to change; also it represents love of people, animals, nature; a teacher or social being.

Bright emerald green: a healer, also a love-centered person

Yellow green: creative with heart, communicative

Dark or muddy forest green: jealousy, resentment, feeling like a victim of circumstance; blaming self or others; insecurity and low self-esteem; lack of understanding personal responsibility; sensitive to perceived criticism

Turquoise: relates to the immune system; sensitive, compassionate, healer, therapist

LAVENDER AURA

This color aura is all about manifesting. Think imagination, visionary, daydreamer, etheric. Usually artists, entrepreneurs, and innovators will be surrounded by purple light be it violet or lavender.

VIOLET AURA

Relates to the crown, pineal gland (produces melatonin), and nervous system. It is the most sensitive and wisest of colors. This is the intuitive color in the aura and reveals psychic power of attunement with self. Represents someone intuitive, visionary, futuristic, idealistic, artistic, and magical.

BLUE AURA

Relates to the throat and thyroid and being cool, calm, and collected—also, caring, loving, loves to help others, sensitive, intuitive.

Soft blue: peacefulness, clarity, and communication; truthful; intuitive

Bright royal blue: clairvoyant, highly spiritual nature, generous, on the right path, new opportunities are coming

Dark or muddy blue: fear of the future, fear of self-expression, fear of facing or speaking the truth

SILVER AURA

This is the color of abundance, both spiritual and physical. Lots of bright silver can reflect plenty of money or awakening of the cosmic mind.

Bright metallic silver: receptive to new ideas, intuitive, nurturing

Dark and muddy gray: residue of fear is accumulating in the body, with a potential for health problems, especially if gray clusters are seen in specific areas of the body

GOLD AURA

The color of enlightenment and divine protection. When seen within the aura, it says that the person is being guided by their highest good. It is divine guidance and represents protection, wisdom, inner knowledge, a spiritual mind, an intuitive thinker.

DIRTY GRAY AURA

Blocking energies, guardedness

BLACK AURA

Draws or pulls energy to it and in so doing, transforms it. It captures light and consumes it. Usually indicates the inability to forgive on a long-term basis (toward others or self) collected in a specific area of the body, which can lead to health problems; past-life hurts; unreleased grief.

PASTEL AURA

A sensitive blend of light and color, more so than basic colors. Shows sensitivity and a need for serenity.

INDIGO AURA

Relates to the third eye, visual, and pituitary gland. Reflects other energy, a pure state of light. Often represents a new, not yet designated energy in the aura; spiritual, etheric, and nonphysical qualities; transcendent, higher dimensions; purity and truth; angelic qualities.

Absorb Natural Light

Spend at least one hour a day in natural light if you can. Stand outside, and if the sun is out, face it (eyes closed, of course, duh) and let the sunlight beam down on you. Think of yourself as a solar panel, soaking up the rays for future use.

Reduce Electric Exposure

Being around computers, cell phones, TVs, and radio frequencies can interfere with our natural frequencies. This is most commonly felt when we cannot sleep, and sleep is one of the best ways to cleanse the chakras and auras. Any chance you get to spend some time away from electronic devices, take it. Turn off, unplug, and pack up your gadgets for a span of time each day, or if you can't afford to do it each day, try a couple of hours on the weekend.

Avoid Mood Imbalances

That is a polite way of saying no drinks or drugs for you, buddy. Anything you use to artificially alter your mood will work against the natural alignment of your energy centers and auras. My dirty habit is chocolate when really I should use music, rest, or exercise to pick me up. Don't worry, a martini or a Kit Kat every once in a while isn't going to shatter your aura into a million pieces—but take it easy.

EXPLORE THIS!

Think you need your iPhone in dreamland? Nah. Unplug and turn off all your electronic devices at night before you go to sleep if possible. Don't just unplug your phone from the charger; unplug the chord from the wall too! Give your auras a much-needed electronic-buzz break.

If I'm honest, the aura and chakra stuff was the hardest to crack on my spiritual soul search. There were times my self-talk would convince me I was totally batshit crazy for staring at my fingertips, waiting for my colors to reveal themselves or envisioning seven brightly hued spinning wheels churning away in my body. The trick is to keep at it, because when you relax and adopt a fun, give-it-a-go attitude, you'll find that's when the magic happens.

Can't seem to make magic happen? I hear ya. I also had an auric visionary block, and it was super frustrating. I'd advise you to go get an auric reading and enlist an auric expert to help give you insight into color clues or even teach you what to look for step-by-step. Alternately, if the whole chakra thing still seems weird or daunting, seriously, hit up your local massage therapist or holistic healer—I'd bet my prettiest crystal pendulum that they'll be there for you to help you along the way to understanding, proficiency, and yes, even (hopefully especially!) fun. Promise yourself one thing when dealing with your auras and chakras: stay positive and open, and let that divine energy flow.

YOUR FENG SHUI

The first time someone said "Feng Shui" to me, I was insulted. Um, why was this person swearing at me? What did I ever do to them? Whoops.

Turns out it's not a swear word, but rather a powerful way to balance out the energy in your surroundings, much like we can balance our chakras and energy centers. During the process of writing this chapter, I drove my partner mad—engaging in torture by furniture shifting, I managed to completely rearrange the house. Multiple times. I think Feng Shui *is* now considered a swear word in our house as far as my partner's concerned.

This chapter takes a look at the energy that surrounds us in our daily lives, both in our environment—including our homes, workspaces, and more—to understand how we impact the earth, use energy, and create spaces that serve our highest selves.

The idea of Feng Shui has been used in many cultures for years, from Indian Feng Shui, called *Vastu Shastra*, which was used throughout the ancient Vedic era and in which every element of living was looked at as an art; to the ancient Chinese, who recognized that everything in your environment had an energy, a symbolism, and a connection to you.[1]

While most people are familiar with Chinese Feng Shui, it is worth looking into different cultures' energies and environmental traditions if Feng Shui tickles your oh-my-god-I-can't-stop-shifting-furniture fancy. For example, in Hindu culture, sleeping with the head facing north or west is an epic fail. They strongly believe that the direction your head faces while sleeping has a strong effect on your physical and mental well-being as well as what you attract into your waking life.

The words *Feng Shui* (pronounced feng-shooee or fung-shway) are a combination of two elements in Chinese: wind and water. The two elements are vital to our survival—wind or air to breathe, and water to drink and cleanse. Combined, these two elements determine the climate and can create either a beautiful, placid day or a severe storm, depending how they come together. These two elements have long dictated how humans live and evolve and still play a central role in balancing out the energy of any environment. Feng Shui as understood through the lens of Chinese philosophy is a method of using *chi* (energy) to dictate the overall energy of a space, like a home, workplace, or public space. Just like water or wind can flow freely, the same needs to occur as chi moves through a space. You can focus a room's chi to attract different aspects of life such as success, romance, or abundance.

Try this on for size: think about your surrounding sanctuary acting in the same way your body acts for your soul—housing essential energy. Just as it is important that your body is in balance for your soul to flourish, the energy of the spaces we inhabit must be in order for us to feel happy, grounded, alive, and at peace. When you transform a space into a sanctuary—whether through the simple addition of a potted plant or through an entire redecoration overhaul—you really do feel like you have a way to escape from the world, where you can go when you need to tap out of your hectic day.

A Soul Searcher's sanctuary is the key to their sanity in a world where sanity's thin on the ground, so don't underestimate the power of surrounding yourself with happy chi. Once you shift the energy in a home, you'll be like, "chi-whiz (sorry, sorry, I couldn't help myself with an energy pun), why didn't I do this months ago?" So roll up your sleeves and warn your housemate, partner, or family that some shit's about to shift!

How does Feng Shui actually work? Let's start with some familiar territory from the previous chapter: colors. Colors represent the five key Feng Shui elements of fire, earth, metal, water, and wood. Next, Bagua maps, also known as energy maps, can be used to help Feng Shui (yep, it's a verb and a noun!) a room to focus on the needs of the resident such as fame, fortune, family—whatever it is you desire. The nine sections of the Bagua map are outlined on the following page.

When a Bagua grid[2] is placed over the floor plan of a building, it pinpoints the specific areas that influence the nine key aspects of life. You can then place symbolic items in the relevant locations to enhance those areas of your life, almost transporting your home into a shrine of energy that attracts positive elements into your career, love life, home life, and more.

Bagua maps can reveal if money is going down the toilet, doors are closed and blocking off new opportunities, or if developments and blockages in love are on

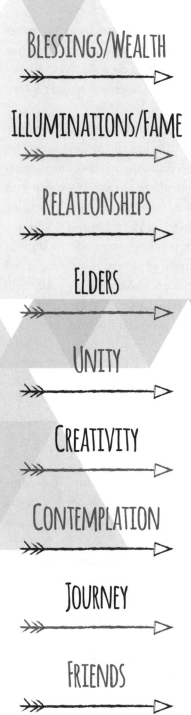

BLESSINGS/WEALTH

This section relates to our financial situation and level of prosperity. *Cha-ching!*

ILLUMINATIONS/FAME

This section relates to popularity, reputation, and status in our community or industry. Think of it as your personal celebrity corner.

RELATIONSHIPS

This section relates to the state of our personal lives, business lives, and relationships, both personal and professional.

ELDERS

This section reflects our light council, otherwise known as our key mentors, influences, and guides. It's the cool kids club, basically.

UNITY

This section symbolizes the center of the room and generally needs to be kept free from anything that can burden, distract, or handicap us. You know how people will often fill the middle of a big room with an area rug and nothing else? That's a rockin' unity space decision.

CREATIVITY

This section reflects our source of inspiration and attraction of new thoughts and ideas. This is your lightbulb-moment spot.

CONTEMPLATION

This section relates to our areas of relaxation or meditation where it's best to clear our heads and reflect. This is your chill-out space. *Ahhhh.*

JOURNEY

This section reflects our destiny, path in life, or soul's purpose.

FRIENDS

This section relates to our friends and mentors, who we surround our self with for relaxation, fun, or motivation. This is your social space—a place to unwind, let loose, and shake it out with the peeps you love.

the horizon by looking at the layout of a house and the flow and focus of energy therein. Energy can be blocked, introduced, or pushed out of an environment for a variety of reasons and through a variety of channels, including doors, windows, water, mirrors, and even that massive pile of clothes on the floor you haven't folded from last week!

Good Feng Shui, or as I like to call it "good chi'it," can be achieved by simply incorporating the right elements into a space and removing the wrong ones. This could include changing colors, adding crystals (weeeeee, more crystals), clocks, mirrors, or it could even be as simple as shifting your furniture around. Have you ever shifted the couch, then felt you needed to shift the coffee table, then something else, then something else again because it just didn't feel right anymore? You, my friend, were practicing the art of Feng Shui whether you knew it or not. As Buddha said, "When you dig a well, there's no sign of water until you reach it, only rocks and dirt to move out of the way. You have removed enough: soon the pure water will flow."[3] The same works for Feng Shui—you'll move trinkets, junk, old clothes, paperwork. Trash anything that you know is blocking energy (always listen to that gut of yours!), and when you hit a clear flow, you will know.

Feng Shui in the Bedroom

WOO-WOO SCALE: ▲▲▲△△△△△△△
EXPLORE-IT SCALE: ▲▲▲▲▲▲▲▲▲▲

Calm down, Casanova, we're talking Feng Shui right now, not Kama Sutra. In all honesty though, the bedroom should be all about the two big S's—sleep and sex (if you're having it/want to be having it, that is)—and bringing Feng Shui into the bedroom should support and augment these two primary purposes.

Do you feel like your bedroom or home is an oasis? Do you walk into it and instantly feel like you are safe, warm, sheltered, clean, and inspired? What word comes to mind right now when you think of your bedroom? If your mind gets too chatty answering this question, feel free to say, "Shut up, mind. I am talking to my soul, here!" What does your soul think about your sanctuary?

Because we spend most of our time in our bedrooms sleeping, it is important to start in your bedroom if you are going to apply Feng Shui to any element of your life, in particular your bed. Below is a list of Feng Shui tips for your bed and bedroom. Keep in mind that unless you hire a Feng Shui architect-cum-interior-designer guru to build your house, don't sweat the small stuff. What's our Soul Searcher mantra? Do what you can and what works for you, and don't sweat the rest.

Headboard

Make sure you have a solid headboard, either wooden or textile. Think of it as your crown while you sleep, your halo, your turban—whatever resonates most with you. You need something that supports and protects you while your body rests, repairs, and recharges.

Solid Wall

Similar to the headboard, a solid wall behind your bed is important to protect your energy. Check that your bed is not under or right next to any windows.

EXPLORE THIS!

Add, shift, or remove one thing from that table over there and see if it changes how you feel about the room. Move your bed from one wall to another. Do you sleep better? Worse? Over time, you will look at your bedroom as a shrine constructed just for you and set it up to serve you and your soul's needs. If you share a room with a partner, make sure to get them involved and check if they are okay with you changing their space (learn from my mistakes here, people!)—after all, there are two souls in your particular habitat rearrangement, not just one.

New, Clean Mattress

Starting to feel like the Princess and the Pea on that old, musty thing you've lugged along with you ever since college? I really dig those Jackson Pollock stains your mattress has too—they really add to the chi in the room. Ew. Two simple rules when it comes to a mattress: it needs to be comfortable so you can get the best sleep possible, and make sure it's clear of any previous attached energy, so preferably new.

Above the Floor

Energy needs to circulate freely under your bed, so clear any clutter out from under the bed (yeah, even that box of embarrassing pics from your bachelorette party and that bag of clothes you've been meaning to donate for the past, oh, ten years or so), and more importantly, do not store anything under the bed if possible, unless you live in a very small space and that's one of your only storage options. Also, if your bed is not lifted off the floor, grab some bed legs or even cinder blocks to elevate it. Sleeping a little closer to the sky's never a bad thing; plus it allows energy to flow freely under you while you sleep.

Door Distance

Position your bed as far away from the main entrance door as possible, trying not to align the bed with a wardrobe, other large piece of furniture, or visible doors. It is beneficial, however, to have clear sight of the door for when you wake up—for example, if your bed is diagonally aligned to the door, an easy view should happen naturally. With a clear view to the door, we tend to feel more in control of our lives. Clear entrance, clear exit, right?

Balance It Out

Make sure that everything next to your bed is as balanced as possible on each side of the bed. For example, replicate on both sides bedside tables, lampshades, and photo frames. The more even they are, the more balanced you will feel. This may feel a *liiittle* bit anal to you at first (it did to me—I was even straightening my picture frames so that the angles mirrored each other exactly on either side), but the visual balance will soon begin to strike you as calming and centering instead of goofily exact.

Decoration

Some key rules to decorating the walls of your room that I've found to work like a dream are:

▷ Focus on inspiring artwork that calms or motivates you.
▷ Try to stay away from anything with water painted in it. (Feng Shui tradition maintains that keeping water-related imagery in your bedroom invites financial troubles.)
▷ Experiment with having pictures of family members or religious figures watching over you while you sleep and then with taking these pictures away. Which feels better energetically? In my experience, keeping lots of photos of loved ones in the bedroom impacts different people in different ways.

Focus on Rest

Make sure your bedroom's key focus is rest (and also sex if sex is currently a part of your life), so take away any distractions . . . yep, the computer and TV need to go, lady; it's just a Feng Shui fact. Trust me, once you're not distracted by late-night reruns of *Real Housewives*, the quality of both your dream life and your sex life will skyrocket.

Remove Negative Energy

Mirrors are a key factor in sleepless nights and restless dreams, and are believed to even open the door to infidelity if you share your room with your partner. (Don't worry. They were the first element of Feng Shui to get my attention too.) If you have a fixed mirror, drape fabric over it before you go to bed. Otherwise, if you can move it to another room (I moved mine to our bathroom door), I recommend it.

Water-Free Zone

The bedroom should not have any pictures of water-related imagery, fish tanks, or even things associated with water in it, as this is said to promote bad finances and even invite robbery. I am such a worrywart that I don't even like glasses of water in my room! I know that I'm a little extreme there, so I feel like a glass of water on your bedside table is probably fine for most folks.

Plant-Free Zone

Plants can have too much yang energy, which can also imbalance your sleeping space. Take them out of the bedroom, or if there is nowhere else to keep them, keep them out of sight while you are in bed.

Don't Be a Slob

How many times did your mom yell at you to clean your room when you were growing up? It was a constant refrain in my house when I was a kid. Well, our moms were right—no one wants to live with a slob, including your chi! Clutter or a messy room prevents the circulation of energy and, if you share a room with a partner, can even leave one person in the relationship feeling trapped and unhappy in the space. Give yourself and your partner or roommate, if you have one, a break by devoting one day a week to tidying up.

Pick Your Color

Yep, we're back to colors! Think back to the chapter on crystals and gemstones, and to which colors resonated most with you. Let those colors influence which hues you surround yourself with in your home, office, and any other space you occupy on a regular basis. Specific color families are particularly advantageous when highlighted in different rooms and spaces as well. Here's what these color families can mean for your bedroom:

Fire: Red, orange, purple, pink, bold yellow
Fire colors represent passion and energy—they can help your career flow more easily and help you get more recognition in your professional endeavors. Fire colors can also ignite passion in the bedroom with a loved one. I keep a few key accents in fiery red and orange around to remind me to never let passion slip from the bedroom.

Earth: Beige, neutrals, soft yellows
Earth colors symbolize grounding and stability and are great colors for structure, protection, and strong foundations. Neutrals are the colors of the walls, floor, and doors in my bedroom.

Metal Colors: whites, grays
Metal colors symbolize lightness, clarity, and efficiency. Metal colors are perfect in a room where you unwind from your day or where you need to focus and relax. I like this color family to be represented in my bed linens and in and around the desk in my bedroom.

Pastel Colors: light green, light blue, light purple, light pink
Soft, gentle colors like light or pastel colors can help to create a quiet, calm, and serene environment—perfect for rest and recharging. For example, my bedroom curtains are light blue.[4]

"We live as ripples of energy in the vast ocean of energy."

>**Deepak Chopra**

Feng Shui in the Home

WOO-WOO SCALE: ▲▲▲▲▲▲▲▲▲▲

EXPLORE-IT SCALE: ▲▲▲▲▲▲▲▲▲▲

Bangin' energy flow isn't just for the bedroom, of course. Below are some general house rules to follow as you continue to learn and explore:

Entrance of the Home

The front door is considered the mouth of the chi—where energy enters the home—so make sure it is inviting. What is your front entranceway's message to the world: come in; welcome; we're proud, clean, tidy, beautiful? By adding in potted plants, laying down a welcome mat, and tidying up the garden by your front door, you will find more positive energy flowing up to and into the front door— and into your life.

Remove Unfriendly Furniture and Furnishings

That table you always stub your damn toe on or chair that just doesn't sit right is a sign it is blocking chi or welcoming in negative chi. Move it or get rid of it! Can you say "garage sale"?

Bring in Natural Elements

Reintroduce nature into your home by adding plants, water, crystals or gemstone rocks, natural light, and airflow wherever possible—except for water and plants in the bedroom; that's a Feng Shui faux pas, as mentioned above.

Put Out the Fire in the Kitchen

The kitchen is full of fire energy elements, so it is important to not add to the fire energy with power lighting or spotlights. Use as much natural light as possible in your kitchen.

Place Water by Your Front Door

Placing flowing water in a foundation or water feature of some sort by your front door represents the flow of wealth into the home, and by positioning it by your entry-way door, you are welcoming in new financial opportunity.

Close Off Drains

By closing the door to the bathroom, you are blocking off any drains that might, well, drain positive energy or material wealth from your life.[5]

Add a Wind Chime

A wind chime hung in the right-front area of your home will attract more help and assistance in your life. Who doesn't need a little help from their friends now and again?

Feng Shui in the Workplace

WOO-WOO SCALE: ▲▲▲▲△△△△△▲▲
EXPLORE-IT SCALE: ▲▲▲▲▲▲▲△△△△

Most of us spend a significant amount of time at our jobs, so why shouldn't our work-spaces be just as harmoniously constructed as our home ones? Here are some tips for optimizing your workspace using the principles and practices of Feng Shui:

Positivity on the Walls

Surround yourself with motivating, inspiring, and uplifting artwork, images, colors, and messages. Try not to keep anything in your workspace that reminds you of obligation or hindrances. I know, I know: *But it's* work, I can hear you thinking. There's no way to make our workspaces 100 percent perfect in this regard, but there are things you can do to make your space a little more welcoming and less hostile to positive energy. Have a wall clock that ticks loudly away all day, constantly reminding you of how much time you still have to go before you can go home? Take it down and use your phone's clock instead when you need to check the time. Drape strings of bright beads and swaths of multicolored cloth across the doorway or windows to bring some more color and vibrancy into your surroundings. Play with your space—it's yours, after all!

Face the Entrance

Move your desk or workstation so that you are facing the entrance rather than having your back to the door. By doing this you remove any feelings of vulnerability and are prepared to face people who come to do business with you.

Introduce Plants

Add easy-to-maintain plants to your workplace—succulents or bamboo can help clean the air, helping you to breathe easier, relax more, and balance out the energy in the room. I have a friend who has a collection of small succulents in her office that she swears lower her blood pressure. They're like a cute little plant army of positivity!

Live by a Mantra

Frame, paint, or post your mantra onto the wall in plain view of your desk, pick one that inspires, motivates, and grounds you. Another great way to incorporate a mantra into your work is by sticking a Post-it note to your computer screen that has a mantra for the month, week, or day.[6] Fun fact: My boss actually has a mantra Post-it on his computer screen that reads "Don't be a dick," for real!

Feng Shui and the Environment

WOO-WOO SCALE: ▲▲▲▲▲▲▲▲▲▲
EXPLORE-IT SCALE: ▲▲▲▲▲▲▲▲▲▲

While we cannot control the natural world, we have the ability to influence how we interact with its energies, both positive and negative. Our use of fuel, power, lighting, food, and what businesses we choose to purchase goods from all stem from a growing public awareness of corporate social responsibility to not be greedy users and abusers of the environment.

It's easy for us to point the finger at big oil companies or overseas sweatshops, but have you ever taken a good look at your own day-to-day consumption? Do you recycle? Compost? Take public transport if it's available? Plant trees? The fact is that everyone's contribution—no matter the size—has an impact on the earth.

> "As people alive today, we must consider future generations: a clean environment is a human right like any other. It is therefore part of our responsibility toward others to ensure that the world we pass on is as healthy as when we found it, if not healthier."
> **>His Holiness the Dalai Lama**

Chi, after all, is based off the natural elements of wind and water, two key ways that energy is generated in the world. When we think of yin and yang, we think of balance—energy in, energy out—a cosmic scale that reflects energy given and taken. When you look at the resources you consume, would you say there is a balance in how you take and give back to the earth? We take food, water, and energy from the land, but do we balance the scales and give what we can back? This too is Feng Shui.

Below is a list of small but powerful ways you can incorporate green initiatives into your daily lifestyle as an environmentally conscious Soul Searcher:

Recycle More

When we waste less, we instantly lower our negative environmental impact. How we treat our waste can then improve how our impact is measured. Having separate bins for different waste can make recycling easier. Separate your waste into three separate bins so one can go to the garden, one to recycling, and the other to the trash.

Switch It Off

Lessen your wasted energy use by switching lights off when you leave a room, and switching off unused appliances at the wall and unplugging them. Not only will you save money, but you are also reducing your environmental impact. Win-win!

Plant Your Impact

Make a garden or plant trees to help contribute to cleaner air. If you live in a dense urban area, you can make the most of potted plants and hanging pots, or hop on Pinterest and learn how to construct your own urban terrain or recycled crate indoor oasis. If you've got the space, a garden—even a small one—is also a great spot to compost your organic food scraps—not to mention you'll benefit like crazy from living in a space that has cleaner air. Again, win-win.

Change the Way You Travel

Traffic is getting worse across the globe; more cars join the roads every year, and that equals more pollution. You still need to get from *A* to *B*, but try to rethink how you travel: carpool, take public transport, or even walk or ride a bike if you can. Not only will you possibly get to your destination faster if you're traveling during nasty rush hours, but sometimes it may even be cheaper! Hate to sound like a broken record here, but it really is a win-win.

Make Better Choices

As a consumer, you have the choice to purchase products and, in doing so, endorse companies. Try to choose companies that are local, that will have less distribution impacts from how the food traveled to you. Try to pick companies that take responsibility for their global impact, and in particular, research the egg brands, fisheries, meat products, and clothing labels you buy. You can have a big impact by supporting companies that do right by the environment.

Change Your Work Environment, Change the Environment

Many of us have little to no direct choice in how the companies we work for impact the environment, but if you have the freedom to choose, pick a company that reflects your environmental goals, one that is open to listening to ideas about how to change their global impact for the better. Take the chance!

Switch Out Your Lights

Making better choices in lighting can be the quickest way to reduce your power bill and energy usage. Try to replace blown light bulbs with energy efficient bulbs—not only will you save on power, but you'll also find yourself with some extra cash at the end of the month. (*Must not buy more crystals, must not buy more crystals, must not*—oh hell, who am I kidding?)

Reduce Your Plastic Usage

Use reusable tote bags or shopping bags when you do the grocery shopping, so you stop contributing to plastic waste altogether.

Feng Shui Your Car

Make sure your tires are inflated to the correct pressure and remove any excess weight from your trunk. This will lower your fuel usage and save you some coin. By driving more smoothly, you can also reduce your fuel costs, so try not to accelerate and break so often, instead moving slowly and smoothly so you don't overtax your engine.

Insulate Your Home

Cheap insulation can come in the form of a big throw rug or perhaps in adding carpet to your home to prevent cold air from entering and heat from escaping. By insulating the ceiling, walls, and floors, your house can stay warmer for longer, meaning you will have to spend less time and money heating it.

Cleaning Your Car

If you can, track down a car wash that utilizes recycled water. Craving some vitamin D? Why not get your outdoor fix and wash your car at the same time by using a bucket, hose, and nontoxic, biodegradable soap on a lawn so that the water gets absorbed by the grass?

Reduce Water Usage

Try to not let the water run continuously, like when you brush your teeth. Take shorter showers, and don't defrost food by running water over it. Make sure the dishwasher or washing machine is full before running a cycle to ensure you make the most of the energy and water being used.

Pick Nontoxic Products

Pick products that are natural or nontoxic to not only you but also to the environment. There are a wide variety of eco-friendly cleaning products now available that don't place undue strain on the earth.

Water Bottles

Try not to purchase plastic water bottles—instead, use a cute, reusable water bottle or jug to help lower your plastic usage. Many plastic water bottles cannot be broken down, which is a huge, huge bummer for planet Earth, to say the least.

Go Digital

Get your bank statements, power bills, and news digitally. There are some great apps that give you instant access to all these resources at a swipe or click of your phone, rather than wasting paper and resources to get stuff by mail.

Recycle This Book

Seriously: when you're done reading, either regift it to a friend to read and pass on, give it to a library, or literally recycle it! Even better—read an eBook next time!

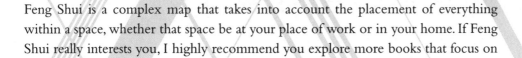

Feng Shui is a complex map that takes into account the placement of everything within a space, whether that space be at your place of work or in your home. If Feng Shui really interests you, I highly recommend you explore more books that focus on

Feng Shui and that can give you more knowledge, tips, and recommend Feng Shui professionals to work with. There are even Feng Shui classes you can take at some colleges and cultural centers.

In the meantime, keep moving things around, experimenting, and always listening to what your soul's telling you about the ways in which it feels most comfortable in each space. Your soul's got this whole living-inside-the-perfect-house thing down with your body, so it knows what's up when it comes to what your body needs from the space that surrounds it.

PART II

▲

AWAKENED MIND

Have you ever heard somebody say something like, "Don't worry, honey, it's all in your head," or "It's just your mind playing tricks on you!" I hear that kind of thing in passing almost daily. *Erm*, so what *if it's all in our heads*? I want to ask. Does that somehow make what someone is thinking, feeling, or believing any less important or real?

We're so used to dividing our minds, bodies, and souls into separate containers—never brushing up against each other, never reaching out to each other, never even allowed to exist in harmony— we often forget that, just as biological organisms work in symbiosis with the world around them, so do the core components that make us, well, us. (Your foot bone wouldn't work for you if it wasn't connected to your anklebone that is connected to your leg bone . . . you with me?)

Our minds need nurturing just as much as our bodies and souls do. Our minds are how we take in, process, and then use all the information life throws at us. Our minds store our memories and dreams and our knowledge, and are the seat of how we view both our internal and external worlds. Mental health is just like physical health, because—news flash—the mind is part of the body, y'all! You just have to look at studies on how different mental and spiritual states influence disease and recovery to witness how powerful the mind's influence can be over our overall physical, emotional, and spiritual wellness—for example, according to the American Cancer Society, some proponents of spirituality in the context of health claim that prayer can decrease the negative effects of disease, speed recovery, and increase the effectiveness of medical treatments.[1]

I pray, even though I am not religious. People ask me who I am praying to and I tell them, "Anyone who is listening." I see it as that "energy in, energy out" thing, yin-yang, balance. It is me sending out positivity, well wishes, and hope to any god, any guide, anyone in the universe that can heal or help me. To me, sending a prayer is like putting in my universal takeout order. Supersize my health, wealth, and well-being please!

Now, do I think that this means that you should run out and convert? No—not unless that's the path that's calling to your soul. The point I want to make is that when your mind's thinking good thoughts that are in-line with your body's health and soul's purpose, good things are probably gonna happen more than if your mind's been relegated to the sidelines. Good vibes attract good shit! Simple.

A huge part of caring for and honoring your mind as a part of the whole package is recognizing the processes that happen in it and live there every day: your dreams and memories, your sense of self, and your belief systems. In this section, we'll be exploring some of the mind's spiritual territory, learning about both the mundane and the fantastical significance of your dreams, peeking into your self-image through the meaning behind your name, and examining which universal value systems ring the truest for you. Grab your thinking cap—we're about to open your mind's eye. Or as a wise man, Blissologist Eoin Finn, once told me: we are going to "take a ride with the wise guide inside."

YOUR DREAMS

Remember how John Lennon sang about being not the only dreamer out there in his world-renowned 1971 song "Imagine"? He certainly got the "I'm not the only one"[1] part right. Most people dream, whether we're talking about the dreams that come to us in our sleep, daydreams, or dreams of a broader, more goal-oriented nature, like dreaming about our "dream house" or "dream job" or perhaps dreaming about going on a grand adventure.

Many of us experience prophetic and vitally important dreams in which we feel we've been handed down some form of ancient, transcendental wisdom from beyond while we slumber—just like most of us have those bizarre, naked-standing-in-front-of-a-crowd-and-accompanied-by-an-old-coworker-your-dead-grandma-and-a-quartet-of-banjo-playing-sloths dreams too.

Whether prophetic or mundane, dreams often hold the keys to a variety of spiritual truths, and can have very practical ramifications for our everyday lives. I personally feel like most of us don't even have the time to think in any deep or meaningful way about our dreams and what they might mean—especially since the average person gets fewer than eight hours of sleep a night (sometimes way fewer) and sleep-related disorders are on the rise. Between 1993 and 2006, for example, the number of times a year that a U.S. doctor gave a diagnosis of insomnia rose from fewer than a million to more than five million.[2] No wonder the world is turning into a pretty grouchy place—peeps need some pillow time! On top of our many issues with sleep and sleeplessness across the globe, easily accessible resources that could help us understand and unlock what goes on in our heads when our conscious minds shut off and our dreaming selves take over are pretty thin on the ground.

For most Soul Searchers, just getting a good night's rest is a challenge, let alone seeking meaning and enlightenment through dreams. But learning about one's dreams and their importance to one's soul and overall spiritual health is just like anything else on your spiritual journey: it's a one-step-at-a-time kind of thing. Ready to grab that lavender-scented sleep mask and some industrial-grade earplugs and drift off into a dream world of discovery?

Disclaimer: It is highly likely that this section will actually get you amped about sleeping and excited about bedtime. Why? Because while you are sleeping, you are resting, resetting, regrouping, and downloading new information, which makes sleep very important work. Side note: I did check on your behalf and apparently supervisors do not accept doing "sleep work" as a valid part of a productive workday.

Types of Dreams

To get us started on unlocking the importance of dreams and dreaming in the modern-day Soul Searcher's life, let's take a peek at some of the many forms and functions of dreams, including some types of dreams you might never have paid attention to until this moment.

Lucid Dreams

Pinch me, I'm dreaming. Lucid dreams are quite simply that: you're lucid—aware that you're dreaming. Have you ever had one of those "Hold on a second . . . this is only a dream!" moments just before you wake up? Well, most dreamers do wake themselves up once they realize they are "only" dreaming—a natural end to the deep sleep cycle they have just experienced. Some dreamers, however, have mastered the skill of remaining asleep in the lucid state of dreaming. They become an active participant in their own dreams, making decisions and influencing the dream's outcome without waking up. Now, if only I could point my dreams in the general direction of Ryan Gosling . . .

Nightmares

A nightmare is a dream that usually causes the dreamer to stir and wake up feeling anxious and frightened. Often triggered by trauma, stress, or conflict in the dreamer's waking life, nightmares can be recurring or not, but are united in their unsettling nature that often bleeds over into waking life. Nightmares may also occur because the dreamer refuses to acknowledge or accept a particular situation he or she is experiencing. Studies by the University of Colorado medical school have found that most dreamers who have regular nightmares also have a family history of psychiatric problems or suffer from mental illness themselves, have had negative recreational drug experiences, or are in rocky and unstable relationships.[3] The studies also showed that many people who identify as creative souls are prone to nightmares. I can personally vouch for that last bit; I've had some pretty twisted stuff happen in my dreams. No matter what the stressor in one's life is, we store emotional baggage in our chakras and energy centers, which can spill over into our dreaming states and cause—you guessed it—even more flippin' stress. Nightmares are often an indication of a fear or hurt that needs to be acknowledged, confronted, and healed. Dreams are ways for our souls to make us take note of lessons that need to be learned and issues that need to be resolved.

Recurring Dreams

Recurring dreams repeat themselves almost identically again and again. These dreams may be positive, but most often they are nightmarish in content. Dreams may recur because a conflict depicted in the dream remains unresolved or ignored in waking life. Once you have found a resolution to the problem, your recurring dreams will likely go the way of the dodo as well.

Healing Dreams

I have experienced a roller coaster of healing dreams. Over time, they transformed from nightmare-like experiences to teaching moments that I could not only glean knowledge from, but also gain acceptance and healing as well. For example, when I was sixteen, my mother passed away from cancer. Anyone who has watched a parent fall ill or sat by their bedside as they passed can tell you it can be a very emotional and traumatic experience. After she passed, my mother would often cry, vomit, moan, and sigh sadly in my dreams, and I would constantly wake to a terrible feeling of helplessness. Over time, however, the dreams changed—she would smile, sit quietly with me, observing and just being present. I gradually started to feel more at ease, more accepting of the ordeal the disease had put us through, and more at peace knowing my mother was no longer suffering. I felt like I could check in on her through my dreams. What had begun as dread of falling asleep for fear of getting a visit from my sick mother quickly turned into excitement in the hopes she might pay me a healing visit.

Healing dreams are messages from the soul about our health and well-being. Many dream experts believe that dreams like these can help us avoid potential health problems and help us heal when we are ill. Dreams of this nature may be telling us that we need to go to the dentist or doctor, that we have an imbalance in one of our energy centers, that we need to start eating more healthfully, or that we just need to generally take better care of ourselves.

Prophetic Dreams

Prophetic dreams, also called precognitive or psychic dreams, are dreams that seemingly foretell the future. One theory to explain this phenomenon—one that particularly resonates with me too—is that our dreaming minds are able to piece together bits of information by simply making logical connections and observations from our waking life that our conscious minds can't or won't while we're awake. In other words, our unconscious mind knows what is coming before we consciously piece together the same information. It connects the dots for us!

EXPLORE THIS!

Paul Coelho said, "We must never stop dreaming. Dreams provide nourishment for the soul, just as a meal does for the body."[4] You can begin to train the mind to recall dreams rather than instantly deleting them as soon as you open your eyes in the morning. The best way to do this is to imagine yourself remembering your dream before you fall asleep. Consider keeping some paper and a pen next to the bed so you can quickly jot down the things you remember. The key things that come to mind will be the most important. Think color, mood, objects, people, animals, and actions.

Signal Dreams

Like prophetic dreams and healing dreams, signal dreams help you solve problems or make decisions in your waking life. Many of us are guilty of not paying attention to our subconscious—or more likely just wake up to the sound of a beeping iPhone and instantly forget our souls' adventure-filled nights. However, our subconscious is always talking to us—in fact, you've probably noticed that it just won't stuff a sock in it even when you want it to!—helping us connect our thoughts and emotions to situations in our lives through symbols, clues, and signs of guidance. We just have to learn to listen and then learn how to understand what we hear.

Dream Symbolism

Now that we're familiar with a number of different kinds of dreams, the next logical step to unraveling the knot of what happens between when we shut our eyes and when we open them again is to investigate what our dreams could mean to us. Have you ever dreamed your were flying, falling, or fighting? How about repeating the same task over and over again? What about that one that everyone seems to have had at one point or another with your teeth falling out? Yuck.

No matter how gorgeous or gross, how interesting or boring, every emotion, thought, and action in a dream holds keys that will unlock important information about your waking life. The texture of our subconscious, which is expressed through our dreams, is a direct reflection of our soul's health. When we awaken to our subconscious mind through the symbolism of our dreams, we begin to be able to take closer note of our conscious life. Take a look at some common dreams and their meanings below.[5]

Ten Common Dreams and Their Meanings

Animals

You are channeling your animal side, the primal pieces of yourself that connect you to nature and survival. The animal kingdom is all about survival of the fittest. Being chased by a predator suggests you're holding back repressed emotions, like fear, instead of confronting whatever situation you are looking to escape or hide from. Pay attention to the animals you see in your dreams, think about the people or situations they may represent, and ask yourself how the animals

EXPLORE THIS!

Take the paper and pen one step further: start keeping a dream journal. It's supercool how well you start to remember your dreams when you write them down. Keep your journal and a pen or pencil on your bedside table, and when you wake and remember a dream you've just had—even if it's just incoherent bits and pieces—write it down! You'll never know what your subconscious is trying to communicate to your soul if you don't remember what it said in your dreams when you wake up. I recently looked back at my first attempts to write my dreams down—"Ferris wheel," "too many tomatoes to pick," and "MERYL STREET [I'm pretty sure I meant Streep] WAS THERE" are some of my favorite scribblings from those early days. Now, I'm so used to writing down my dreams that my records more closely resemble little stories than the almost undecipherable psychedelic grocery lists at the start of my journal.

make you feel. Think about your waking life and how this might connect to the animal or animals you tend to dream about. Every animal has a unique meaning—similar to the concept of spirit animals—so consider doing some research into dream symbolism, either online or at your local library.

Babies

Dreaming about babies is usually less about your own offspring (though it certainly can be) and more rooted in your own inner child. They represent a need for unconditional love, nurturing, and support. Babies can also represent the birth of new ideas and new beginnings—a new chapter in life, whether it be a relationship, career move, or experience.

Being Chased

Talk to anybody about dreams and nearly everyone will admit to experiencing at least one dream about being chased. They're super-freaky! Dreams in which we're being chased by someone or something are rooted in our fight-or-flight instincts, which sometimes bleed over into our dreams. It can mean that you are feeling under threat by someone or something. Reflect on whom or what is chasing you in your dream, and how your pursuer could be a possible threat in real life.

Death

Death in dreams, ironically, can actually represent birth in your waking life. A death of a friend or loved one represents change—the transition between an end and a new beginning. If you have recently lost a loved one, dreaming of death may be your subconscious mind's attempt to come to terms with your grief through your dreams, so you can achieve release in your waking life as well. Like my dreams about my mother, these dreams can be very healing.

Falling

Ever woken yourself up with a jolt, like you suddenly crashed down onto your bed? I bet these are always a hit with your bedmate, that's for sure. Falling is a common dream that connects to our anxieties and fears about letting go in our waking life. We may feel like we are losing control over a situation, a person, or a long-held belief or prejudice, and we experience this letting go as falling in our dreams.

Food

Whether you dream about stuffing your face or wandering the empty desert longing for dessert, dreaming of food (or the lack of it) symbolizes a craving for knowledge, because it nourishes the body just as information nourishes the brain. Food for thought?

Killing

Killing in your dreams does not make you a closet murderer; it represents your desire to kill part of your own personality. Chances are you have become aware of something about yourself that you're not a huge fan of and are working toward killing off that piece of yourself. It can also symbolize hostility toward a particular person and the desire to see them suffer or struggle.

Sex

When most people think about sex dreams, they think of them being largely the territory of guys, but girls totally have them too! The meaning behind sex dreams for both men and women is about as straightforward as you can get: you seek intimacy and are experiencing a literal desire for sex through your dreams. Dreams that feature sex or erotic imagery could point to a desire to explore new experiences in your waking life as well.

Teeth

Have you ever had all of your teeth fall out in your dream and woken up only to race to the bathroom and check that they're all still in your head? Gah! Loose, wiggly, or broken teeth are a very common dream event that points to general anxiety of losing control in your everyday life, and can point to hidden fears of getting old and being unattractive to sexual partners.

Water

Dreaming of water can symbolize the overall state of your subconscious mind. Calm pools of water reflect inner peace, while a choppy ocean suggests unease and upheaval. The night before I first went to study transcendental meditation, I had a dream that I was out in the middle of an ocean in the middle of the night. The ocean was gently rolling along when suddenly a huge wave formed in front of me. I took a deep breath and dove down deep, digging my hands into the sand to anchor myself as the wave went over me. I resurfaced to a perfectly calm ocean once more. The next day, the teacher drew a picture of a wavy ocean, and then explained to us that as we go deeper into transcendental meditation, the process would resemble diving deeper into the ocean—it gets quieter and calmer as you delve to its depths, finding peace and stability there. The dream was bang on the money in terms of forecasting the swell of inner peace about to flood my subconscious.

EXPLORE THIS!

Be sure to note common themes (colors, objects, people) as you record your dreams in your dream journal. After a while—a week or two, a month, it's up to you—read back over your entries (even if they're ridiculous, near incomprehensible, or embarrassing) and see if you notice any patterns emerging. What might these patterns mean? Take this one step further and get a fellow soul-searching friend to start a dream journal too and then compare notes!

Common Colors in Dreams and Their Meanings

Just like the symbols above, colors can have a tremendously important story to tell you when you drift off for a catnap or a full night's sleep. Do you constantly dream about a field or red flowers, or the blue of the deep ocean? Maybe you find yourself lost in the snowy tundra night after night, or dream about a child with bright green eyes forever asking to be picked up and carried? Some of the answers lie ahead.[6]

Black

Black symbolizes the unknown, the unconscious, danger, mystery, darkness, death, mourning, rejection, and even hate. Blackness invites you to dive deeper into your unconscious in order to gain a better understanding of yourself. It can give us clues about a lack of love or support in your life. More positively, black represents potential and possibilities. It is like a blank slate. If the feeling in the dream is one of joy, then blackness could imply hidden spirituality and divine qualities. Like my deep-ocean dream, you have a deepness to you. Darkness isn't always about evil—it can also be about the light.

Blue

Blue represents truth, wisdom, heaven, eternity, devotion, tranquility, loyalty, and openness—pretty nice, yeah? Perhaps you are expressing an itch to soul search, to escape and explore new lands or take on a new experience. The presence of this color in your dream may symbolize connections with your spiritual guides and your optimism about the future. You have clarity of mind, like a cloudless clear sky or a still, calm lake.

Brown

Brown in your dreams represents that you have a sense of worldliness, practicality, domestic bliss, physical comfort, or conservatism. Brown also represents the earth, and may be a sign that you need to get back to your roots. Women in particular who see a lot of brown in their dreams—think the ground beneath your feet as you walk along a forest path or the brown of a lover's eyes—could be experiencing nesting feelings and getting ready to begin a family and focus on their domestic life.

Fuchsia

My favorite color! Despite its exuberant hue, the color fuchsia represents meditation and your connection to your spirituality. If you're dreaming in fuchsia, you are most likely letting go of old, stale thoughts and teachings from your upbringing that you may no longer agree with, and welcoming a new change. This color is also associated with emotional stability.

Gray

Gray indicates fear, fright, depression, ill health, ambivalence, and confusion—yikes! You may simply be feeling a bit gray—flat and out of sync—in your day-to-day life if you're dreaming in shades of gray. You may feel emotionally distant, isolated, or detached. On the positive side of things, the color gray can symbolize your individualism, and can signify a crossroads in your life having to do with who you are, who you want to become, and where you want to go.

Green

Green signifies a positive change, good health, growth, fertility, healing, hope, vigor, vitality, peace, and serenity. The appearance of the color may also be a way of telling you to just go ahead and *do* something. Alternatively, green is a metaphor for a lack of experience in some area of your life. Green is also symbolic of a struggle to gain recognition and establish your independence. On the darker side, this color is often associated with greed and jealousy. Dark green indicates materialism, cheating, deceit, or difficulties with sharing. Watch out for how you're spending and who and what you're coveting if you're dreaming in dark green.

Pink

Pink dreams represent love, joy, sweetness, happiness, affection, and kindness. Being in love or healing through love is also implied with this color. Alternatively, the color implies immaturity or weakness, especially when it comes to love. Waking unsettled from dreams full of the color pink may indicated that you are struggling with issues of dependency or problems with your parents.

Red

Red is an indication of raw energy, force, vigor, aggression, power, courage, impulsiveness, and intense passion—sounds like a bit of a high-octane recipe for disaster doesn't it? The color red has deep emotional and spiritual connotations, both positive and negative—it all depends on the context. Are you dreaming about a red sea tossing and turning in a storm? Perhaps you've got some deeply embedded anger issues to sort through. How about the rolling waves of red satin sheets billowing across your skin? Whoa there, your significant other better get ready to be pounced on the minute they get home from work tonight. Alternatively, the color red in your dream can indicate a lack of energy, that you are feeling tired or lethargic. One thing's for sure: when you're seeing red in your slumber, it's time to take a moment and really process what these dreams might mean before moving forward.

Yellow

The color yellow, like most colors, has both positive and negative connotations. If the dream is a pleasant one, then the color yellow is symbolic of intellect, energy, agility, happiness, harmony, and wisdom. On the other hand, if the dream is unpleasant, then the color represents deceit, disgrace, betrayal, cowardice, and sickness. You might have a fear of making decisions or find it hard to take action in your waking life. Your desire to please others means you put others' needs in front of your own needs and happiness. As a result, you may be experiencing setbacks. To dream of a yellow room suggests that you need to use your mind to solve a problem. Yellow is the color of creativity, so there may be an idea or creative project in you waiting to come out.

"Sleep is the best meditation."
>His Holiness the Dalai Lama

How We Sleep, How We Dream

Even the way we sleep says something about our waking life; different positions can reflect our personalities, conflicts, and relationships with our bedmates if we have them. The position we sleep in can also have a direct impact on our bodies, and can hinder or benefit us.

What kind of sleeper are you? Fetal roller-upper? Flailing starfish (. . . that kinda sounds like a fancy sushi roll)? Sacked out on your stomach? Check out the chart on the following page to find out what each position can tell you about the state of your sleeping mind and its impact on your waking self.[7]

Sleep to Dream

I actually really look forward to bedtime. Sure, call me lame—I'm 100 percent okay with that. I love sleeping because my soul always finds a way to get into an adventure; I learn things, experience things, and get clues about waking-life situations I may not have had a deep understanding of otherwise. I have woken up my past partners with mischievous giggles and loud laughter in my sleep because of one grand adventure or another. I've even connected with loved ones who've died and souls that are about to come into my waking life. They say our souls' guides teach us through our dreams.

Position	Effect on the Body	Reflection on Self
Fetal Position Sleeping on your side with your knees tucked up toward your chest, placing your body into a ball-like shape.	This position restricts our airways and can be stressful for our breathing and lungs. It also puts stress on the back and neck. It's said to contribute to the formation of wrinkles as well. On the plus side, this position is ideal for pregnancy and for people who snore.	People who like this position tend to be people who like to be in control of their lives at all times; they like planning and for things to be in order, and often fall prey to overthinking, worrying, and being too sensitive. Fetal side sleepers are also kind and thoughtful people. Often people under stress or pressure will sleep in this position as it feels protected and reflects a child in the womb.
Log Position Sleeping on your side with your legs and arms stretched out in a long line (like, well, a log).	Sleeping on your side stretched out like this is the best natural resting position for your spine, and thus can assist in back and neck pain relief. However, sleeping on your side can result in speeding up gravity's impact on your body, including sagging breasts and wrinkles.	These types of people tend to be inflexible and rigid; they like rules and can often come across as bossy, headstrong, or stubborn. However, log sleepers also enjoy a challenge and aren't afraid to take control in any situation.
Yearning Position Sleeping on your side with your legs and arms stretched out in front of you.	This position holds the same pros and cons as the log position.	The yearning position is for the dream chasers—they are opportunists and like to be challenged in life. They can be their own worst critics too, and tend to be quite hard on themselves.
Soldier Position Sleeping on your back, arms by your sides, legs outstretched (like a soldier standing at attention).	Sleeping on your back is considered one of the best positions for the natural flow of blood to your organs, and can also help people with digestion problems. This position can be a bad idea if you are a snorer though!	People who sleep in this position tend to put on a confident front for the outside world, even when they're not feeling that way. They can suffer from narrow-mindedness; however, on the positive side, they are driven, focused, and tend to be loyal people. They stand tall in waking life.
Starfish Sleeping on your back, arms stretched up and legs stretched out so that your body shapes a star.	This position holds the same pros and cons of the soldier position. Additionally, sleeping on your back can also benefit your skin and help work against the aging process.	People who rock the starfish position are open, liberated, free-thinking, and vibrant types. They are confident and open to all walks of life and all ways of thinking.
Stomach Position Sleeping on your stomach with your head facing into the pillow or with the neck twisted to either side.	This position can also aid digestion; however, because it is common to twist the neck so you can breathe clearly, it can be stressful on your spinal chord, as it works against the natural curve of your back.	Stomach sleepers tend to be confident, sociable, and friendly people who are in their element in crowds or in the spotlight, and also tend to be more sensitive to the thoughts and opinions of others behind closed doors.

We'll learn more about guides and how they interact with us both through our waking and dreaming states in chapter 10, but for now, the central question that must be asked before we continue to appreciate the many things our dreams give us is this: If you can't get to sleep, what's the point in knowing anything about dreaming?

As I brought up earlier, for some of us, living in this frantic, modern-day world, sleep doesn't come easily. In fact, the Center for Disease Control has gone so far as to call insufficient sleep a "public health epidemic,"[9] and anyone who's ever gone without a normal sleep schedule knows that without sleep, the mind and body do not function at their full potential—stressing and polluting the soul's overall health, as well. Since mind, body, and soul are intricately connected, and we can't suffer the pain of one while enjoying the health of the others, here are some tips and tricks to help your body support a healthy, quiet mind and, in turn, pave the path for a soul that's ready to receive all the many benefits of sleep and dreaming.

EXPLORE THIS!

When you're in dreamland, do you have a partner in your bed? There are also meanings behind how you and your partner sleep that reflect your relationship. Check in with our old guru Google and look up what your couple sleeping position reflects about your relationship.

Eat Earlier and Lighter

Giving your body less to digest can help it relax and rest more easily. Trying not to eat after seven or so in the evening can help, as your body and digestive system will be more rested by the time you go to sleep. I try not to consume caffeine, soda, or other drinks high in sugar in the evening either—I fail at this at times, but a Coke with spicy Mexican food's a life-giving necessity sometimes, am I right? Herbal teas such as chamomile are great to relax the senses and are an excellent coffee substitute for nighttime too.

Make Your Room Dark and Quiet

Peace out, world! Ensuring your room is as dark and quiet as possible clears the space of distractions. It is natural for us to sleep in darkness and wake to light. If you have quite a light room and have issues sleeping because of it, buy some blackout curtains or a soft, comfy sleep mask. If you live by a busy street or other source of noise, consider picking up some fancy earplugs. If total silence freaks you out (I have a friend who can't stand the sound of her own heartbeat in her ears when she wears earplugs), invest in a white noise machine to provide a soothing background hum to lull you off to dreamland.

> "Sleep is just like darkness. It is not accidental that you find it difficult to sleep when there is light. Darkness has an affinity with sleep. That's why it's easy to sleep at night. Darkness all around creates the milieu in which you can fall asleep very easily."
>
> >Osho

Dream Crystals

WOO-WOO SCALE: ▲▲▲▲▲△△△△△
EXPLORE-IT SCALE: ▲▲▲▲▲▲▲△△△△

Did you know that in almost every computer, wristwatch, and radio, even in your cell phone, there is a crystal?[10] It is a programed crystal set to work on a certain frequency. Crystals can be programed to assist with any element of your life, including dreams. Expanding on what we learned in chapter 2 about crystals interacting with one's chakras and certain crystals inviting different kinds of energy into our lives, crystals can be used to facilitate healthy sleep and productive dreaming.

EXPLORE THIS!

Just before you plan on going to bed, select a crystal that resonates with you (and also one that's relatively small and smooth—you don't want a giant hunk of pointy amethyst jabbing you in the skull all night) and hold the crystal in your hands for a few moments, focusing until you can feel a gentle pulse between your hands. Visualize the crystal surrounded by light, and then state your intention for what your crystal will bring you—a healing dream that you will remember and understand on waking, a peaceful night's rest, a visit from a guide—then ask for the ability to receive this thing while you sleep. Now place the crystal under your pillow, and don't forget to have your dream journal on hand for when you wake!

Crystals to aid dreaming:

▷ Red and yellow jasper are great if you are bad at remembering your dreams.

▷ Bloodstone stimulates dreaming and awakens your subconscious when you are relaxed and in a dream state, opening the door for dreams to come to you.

▷ Amethyst helps with communication and connection, and can aid intuitive dreams. An amethyst under your pillow can also protect you from negative thoughts or nightmares.

Hot Water

WOO-WOO SCALE: ▲▲▲▲▲▲▲▲▲▲▲
EXPLORE-IT SCALE: ▲▲▲▲▲▲▲▲▲▲▲

A hot bath in particular helps to reduce blood pressure and is a natural muscle relaxant. Incorporating relaxing scents such as lavender and ylang-ylang can also help promote relaxation before bedtime. More aromatherapy tips can be found in chapter 3.

Free Your Mind

WOO-WOO SCALE: ▲▲▲▲▲▲▲▲▲▲▲
EXPLORE-IT SCALE: ▲▲▲▲▲▲▲▲▲▲▲

Think about your favorite bedtime story growing up. You know the one—it probably ended with a happily ever after, yeah? Now think of the last thought that runs through your head before you go to sleep now—bills . . . relationship woes . . . work worries . . . family drama . . . Our brains are a veritable playground of unicorns, fairies, miracles, love, and happy endings, aren't they? Yeah, I didn't think so.

While it's almost second nature for most of us to fall asleep with negative emotions swirling in our minds, like stress, worry, and fear, if you can commit to putting in the extra

EXPLORE THIS!

Too worked up to sleep? Lower and align your vibe with this ancient vibrational scale. The Solfeggio Chakra Scale uses varying hertz frequencies to balance the chakras and flushes out a range of negative vibrations, starting with guilt and fear and then moving into facilitating change and growth, then finally onward into transformation. Lie in bed resting and listening to the scale, and allow your vibration to gently change as you rest.[8]

effort to shift yourself to a positive, happy, grateful frame of mind, your whole life can change. Most people spend between six to eight hours asleep a night—enough time to completely recharge your body, mind, and soul. Doesn't it then stand to reason to give yourself five minutes to help put yourself in the best mood possible before you recharge your entire being for the next day? Think of it as giving yourself a motivational pep talk before you send your body off into a dimension of dreams and relaxation.

Live to Dream

While everything we've just covered can be enormously helpful to drifting off, and thus opening the door to dreams of all sorts, your pursuit of a healthy and active dream life shouldn't just be confined to the bedroom. Here are some tips to try out during the daytime that I have learned along my journey toward having peaceful, tranquil, and spiritually enlightening sleep—sleep that makes soul-nurturing and enlivening dreams welcome each time my head hits the pillow.

Daydream

WOO-WOO SCALE: ▲▲▲▲▲▲▲▲▲▲

EXPLORE-IT SCALE: ▲▲▲▲▲▲▲▲▲▲

Daydreams are one of the best ways to relax your mind and think about the positive things you would like to welcome into your life. So let your mind loose! Fantasize about things you find beautiful, about your goals, the life you are pursuing, and all the things you will achieve. Build yourself your dream existence in your head. And hell, if you'd rather fantasize about Hugh Jackman teaching you to surf or Jennifer Lawrence tripping on her Oscars' gown and tumbling right into your arms, go for it. Falling asleep while fantasizing is a great way to not only manifest positive things into your life, but also to get positive energy flowing, no matter if the things you fantasize about are realistic or not.

Daydreamers are usually creative, imaginative, intuitive, and visionary—they spend hours of their lives imagining and role-playing things they wish for and enter another

EXPLORE THIS!

Flip back to chapter 1 and try out five minutes (yes, just five is fine, but do more if you'd like to, of course) of relaxing yoga or meditation. I've found that simply focusing on the way my breath moves in and out of my body for a few minutes is enough to calm my heart rate, clear my mind, and prep my soul to receive whatever sleep has to offer.

dimension of their own personal enchantment on a daily basis. In doing so, these dreamers are, in fact, welcoming all the things they desire into their lives, even if those things aren't concrete in their daydreams. By focusing their energy and thoughts in this way, the subconscious begins to make their dreams into reality. The art of visualizing and receiving things such as love, wealth, and health is a powerful support activity to actively pursuing these things in practical ways.

Affirmations

WOO-WOO SCALE: ▲▲▲▲▲▲▲△△△△
EXPLORE-IT SCALE: ▲▲▲▲▲▲▲▲▲△△

Before you go to bed at night, make sure to remind yourself of everything that is special about you and that you are proud of. Give yourself some props! It may be something you achieved that day, a way you reacted, an action you took, even a single thought or feeling that you are proud of. When we tell ourselves how nice, loving, smart, and successful we are before we sleep, it locks that message into our subconscious, helping us believe it more and more and feed our positive self-image. Some people choose to fall sleep listening to affirmations in audiobook form, others choose to fall asleep thinking positive things about themselves, and others write them down and read them before they sleep. Do whatever resonates most with you.

> ## EXPLORE THIS!
> ◁————————≪
>
> Make a daydream playlist. I find music really helps me to daydream; however, I am also very sensitive to how music affects me, so I make a playlist with feel-good music that inspires me or reminds me of fun times. When making yours, look for lyrics, hooks, and musical themes that resonate with you specifically. Perhaps try making a couple of playlists: one for when you want to daydream about being an ass-kicking adventurer or when you want to visualize specific goals or actions, and one for when you want to drift off on a calmer sea of endless possibilities and pleasures.

Fairytales

WOO-WOO SCALE: ▲△△△△△△△△△△
EXPLORE-IT SCALE: ▲▲▲▲▲▲▲▲▲▲

Read your favorite childhood book or watch your favorite movie from when you were young. I'm serious! Stories fill our hearts, enliven our minds, and feed our spirits. Walt Disney knew this secret to the soul . . . and so did you when you were a little squirt! Allow yourself time to connect with your inner child and be inspired, carefree, and happy while enjoying this little portal into your past. This is particularly a positive pre-sleep exercise to do if you house emotional baggage from a negative childhood.

Nailed-It List

WOO-WOO SCALE: ▲▲▲▲▲▲▲▲▲▲
EXPLORE-IT SCALE: ▲▲▲▲▲▲▲▲▲▲

Make a list of things you love, things you are proud of, things you have achieved, and things you are going to achieve. By making a list, you can more clearly focus your energies on the things you want to attract in your life, rather than the things you want to get rid of. Keep this list by your bed or tack it up on your mirror in your bathroom, so you see it when you brush your teeth before you go to bed.

Send out Good Vibes

WOO-WOO SCALE: ▲▲▲▲▲▲▲▲▲▲
EXPLORE-IT SCALE: ▲▲▲▲▲▲▲▲▲▲

Send someone a positive text or email, or write them a letter telling them all the things you admire about them. If you're feeling shy, you don't have to physically hit send or pass the message on to the recipient—the universe will deliver the message for you. I challenge you to be brave and send it anyway though. You never know when someone in your life might need exactly that type of kindness out of the blue.

Happy Times Training

WOO-WOO SCALE: ▲▲▲▲▲▲▲▲▲▲
EXPLORE-IT SCALE: ▲▲▲▲▲▲▲▲▲▲

You know how when you're feeling low, your brain seems to barf up all the little things you're embarrassed about from your past, like a cat with a hairball? That crappy thing you did to a friend in middle school, the bitchy remark about a coworker that he overheard, that white lie you told your hubby that you knew you shouldn't have that one time . . . It's basically the worst, right? Makes you feel like a huge jerk.

I challenge you to put your brain in reverse and try the opposite—kind of like your life flashing before your eyes, but only highlighting the positive bits. Imagine you're seeing your life as a movie trailer, running a quick-cut edit of your happiest moments. Sit back and let your soul guide you through your life's highlights. Enjoy it after all, you're this movie's writer, director, and star!

EXPLORE THIS!

Instead of waiting to see what tomorrow will bring, tell yourself what sort of day it's going to be instead. And believe it. Most importantly, be excited about it. You'll be amazed how much this can influence how you'll feel when you go to sleep that night and how you feel upon waking.

Tap into Your Inner G

WOO–WOO SCALE: ▲△△△△△△△△△

EXPLORE–IT SCALE: ▲▲▲▲▲▲▲▲▲▲

Gratitude. Close your eyes and think about all the people, lessons, and life experiences you are grateful for. Give thanks to the good and bad lessons, the positive and negative people who have crossed your path. See the lessons in the actions you've taken and in the actions of others. Forgive anyone who has upset you, accept the things about yourself that upset you, and give thanks to your soul for its love and guidance. If you end each day with this simple exercise in gratitude, acceptance, and love, you prep your soul to receive the wonders of sleep and dreaming.

The art of sleep and the mystery of dreams has interested Soul Searchers of all backgrounds throughout history, with records of dream analysis dating back to approximately 3500 BCE and records of it being studied in ancient Egypt, Greece, Babylonia, Phoenicia, Japan, and the Americas, to name just a few.[11]

One symbol of sleep and dreaming that I've always been captivated by is the dream catcher. *Bawaajige nagwaagan* in Ojibwe, meaning "dream snare," the dream catcher has been a longstanding symbol in soul-searching culture, and endures today across many cultures in addition to its Native American roots.

Storytellers throughout Ojibwe history have spoken of a "spider women" called *Asibikaashi*, who was a guide and protector for the tribe. As the Ojibwe nation spread wider across the land, her reach and influence shrank. To help protect the people (and its sleeping, and therefore defenseless, children), the mothers and grandmothers weaved magical webs using willow hoops and sinew to make dream catchers that watched over their children's beds and filtered out bad dreams, only allowing positive thoughts to enter their developing minds. When the sun would rise, the sunrays would hit the dream catcher's web, vaporizing the bad dreams and negative thoughts caught there. Perhaps, with all the challenges we face as a species in this remarkable but challenging modern life we lead, a little protection to keep the bad dreams at bay is just what we all need.

EXPLORE THIS!

>>>>————————————>

It is important to respect the origins of the dream catcher and be careful in picking a dream catcher for your home that is not meaningless due to being made for mass commercialism. If you choose to make your own (there are many excellent online tutorials available), I recommend making one using colors and beads that resonate with you, and while you are doing so, ask for protection from whatever spiritual guides you believe in, whether they be your ancestors, a deity or spirit, or the earth itself. Think about your positive dreams and picture the shield you are making blocking out any thoughts or dreams that may work against you in both your dreaming and waking states.

"Who looks outside, dreams;
Who looks inside, awakes."
>Carl Jung

Just like how the dream catcher trapped nightmares, it is now your job to start snatching up all your dreams, good and bad alike, and decode them. Many people sleep through their day-to-day lives, unaware of the many enlightening opportunities to seek more from what happens in between closing and opening their eyes. But not you. Spiritually speaking, you're as wide-awake and as wired as a three-year-old fueled on red food coloring and sprinkle cupcakes. You are awake to both your waking and dreaming lives, and are moving forward with a new language that will aid you in interpreting the signs and symptoms of your talkative spirit. As a Soul Searcher, the aim of the game is to connect the dots, follow the signs, and sniff out the spiritual crumb trails laid out by your soul. So don't forget to make the most of the clues given to you when you're dreaming. The path may get rough sometimes, but don't worry—you're not the only one.

7

YOUR NUMEROLOGY AND NAME

Labels. They're not just for jars in your pantry or tags on your clothes.

We start making sense of the world around us when we are little partly with the help of labels: Mom, Dad, cat, dog, good, bad. As we grow up, labels start to define us: our age, our sex, our job title, our religious affiliation. When our children point to a rose and curiously ask what it's called, should we say it's a rose? Or should we say that it's *called* a rose? As Juliet says to Romeo, "a rose by any other name would smell as sweet." While this may have been true enough for Juliet to show that she'd love Romeo just as much no matter what his last name was, we can't deny that the names and labels we carry through life have meanings of their own, and these meanings have broad ramifications on the way we live our lives.

We make a lot of assumptions—both positive and negative—about each other based on these labels. But how often do we make these assump-

tions about people's actual names? Our name is treated as just another label for many of us—it might mean something to us, it might not, but usually a name just serves as an identifier to set us apart from the next person. Some of us have never really given our names much thought at all. Have you ever taken time to investigate the meaning behind your name or the numerology connected to the letters in your name and your date of birth? I definitely hadn't until recently. Our names are one of the first clues about both our past lives and future destinies. We hear our names every day, answer to them, sign them, but how much do we really understand about our most common label?

Numerologists believe we all have the "perfect" name, and that our birth name reflects our personalities and inner selves. Our name breaks down into numbers that tell us even more about who we truly are. Numerology is also based on the belief of reincarnation, that we have existed before the lifetime we are experiencing in the present. Our numbers are chosen for this lifetime, for the life path set out for us by the larger cosmic order of things, and to serve this life's lessons and experiences.

EXPLORE THIS!

Do you know the meaning, alternate forms, and origins of your name? Get googling and have a peek into your name's etymological origins and symbolic meanings.

Consider numerology its own kind of spiritual science. It's like astrology in that it can help you to figure out more about your inner self through an outer system—for astrology, that system is the stars; for numerology, it's numbers. In numerology, each letter in your name is associated with a number value. When we add these values together with our birthdate or the current date, we can see patterns of numbers that dictate different stages of our lives known as life path numbers, soul numbers, personal year numbers, and so on.

While many people change their names for a variety of reasons, the trick to mastering numerology and the true meaning behind your name is to focus on the name given to you at birth. For example, when I was born, my birth family gave me the beautiful name Renee, meaning "rebirth." When I was adopted, my adoptive parents believed that this name was important to me and my story, and so they chose to keep it as my middle name and gave me the first name of Emma, making my full name on my birth certificate Emma Renee Mildon. Emma has numerous meanings and translations. Originally a short form of a Germanic name that began with the element *ermen*, meaning "whole, entire, all, or universal."[1] From this, I take my name to mean wholeness through rebirth—the combination of my two names and my two origins.

People who use numerology believe that numbers and letters govern much of what happens in relationships, health, finances, and life in general. Many names hold clues to professions, past lives, and passions. By understanding your numerology, you can work with your numbers instead of against them. Incorporating simple numerological practices into one's life is actually really practical and fun, and can easily be integrated into day-to-day life without much muss or fuss. Numerology can help you focus on things that are meant to be; then you can watch things flow freely and organically into your life, instead of fighting against the natural order of things. Like many spiritual pursuits, there is no scientific proof that any of these claims are true, but that shouldn't stop us curious Soul Searchers from taking interest in the insights that numerology can give us. Let's start exploring!

Philosophers have studied the relationship between numbers, letters, and the natural and spiritual worlds for thousands of years. Many cultures developed different scales and formulas to study a person's numbers, but all essentially used numerology to better understand the journey of life. Pythagoras, the Greek philosopher and mathematician, is perhaps the most famous numerologist, and the ancient Chinese, Egyptians, Indians, and Babylonians saw a powerful connection with numbers and destiny as well. Across the globe, civilizations have been studying the connections between letters, numbers, and the universe for many years, and Soul Searchers the world over continue to do so today. Even though numerology's gotten a bit of a wacky rap of late, you can bet that in the time of Pythagoras, number talk was not considered the babblings of a number-crazed hippie but rather a universal language through which some of existence's most intriguing mysteries could be explored. Put aside your calculators, grab some scratch paper, and get ready to carry the 2, add the 1 . . .

Chinese and Vedic Numerological Systems: A Quick Peek

Chinese numerology focuses on the sound of a number and what word that sound is connected to. This is the deciding factor in whether a number is auspicious (likely to bring good fortune) or inauspicious (likely to bring misfortune or at least not encourage good fortune). There are also various lucky and unlucky numbers in Chinese numerology, as well as lucky and unlucky combinations of numbers.[2]

Indian—or Vedic—numerology believes numbers possess certain vibrational significances that connect to the material world and the nine planets (well technically Pluto's planet status is still in debate, but for astrology purposes it is), linking this form of numerology closely to astrology. Ancient Indian Soul Searchers sought to combine all wisdom and knowledge to create a holistic approach to living. They used elements of astrology, numerology, Feng Shui, and natural healing (Ayurveda) in their day-to-day lives to achieve this goal.

When a child was born in Vedic society, all available clues were used from the get-go in order to divine the child's likely path in life, including the date and time of the child's birth and even the placement of planets. Next, letters were carefully taken into consideration, ensuring a child's given name aligned with their destiny, physical characteristics, and name numbers. In Hindu tradition, the elders would offer the family a selection of letters that reflected the vibration of that child's birth date, and then these letters had to be incorporated into the child's name.[3] Vedic numerology also used a person's numbers and astrology to create a *yantra*, a visual tool (to help the energy of the body), while a mantra, for example, helps to focus the energy of the mind. As a name takes all elements of a person's vibration and existence into consideration, a yantra is designed for a person by taking their number vibration and transforming it into a geometric symbol.

Western Numerology: The Basics

As explored above, there are many different numerological traditions across the globe. Today, one of the most widely used types of numerology is what's often referred to as Western numerology. Western numerology is based on Pythagoras's theory that numbers link to the alphabet, and that these links can be examined in various ways to glean meaning. It also takes into account the energy vibrations that link time, space, and living and nonliving matter to find a person's life purpose number and to decode the meanings behind their birth names. For our purposes, we'll be focusing mostly on Western numerology from here on; however, it is important to use the scale and method of numerology that resonates with you best to get the best results, so be open to all forms of numerology when you are learning and then follow the formula that connects with you best.

Below are some forms to get us started.[4]

Western Numerology Chart

1	2	3	4	5	6	7	8	9
A	B	C	D	E	F	G	H	I
J	K	L	M	N	O	P	Q	R
S	T	U	V	W	X	Y	Z	

Use the name on your birth certificate for best results, rather than names you've taken later in life or nicknames. If you are married and you've taken your partner's name, you can do your maiden name and your married name.

Add your numbers together. If you end up with a double number, add it together. For example, if you end up with 34, your number will be 7, (3 + 4), and if your number is 26, your number is 8, (2 + 6). The only exceptions are 11, 22, and 33, as these are master numbers (we'll check those out a little later) and should remain double digits.

Below is an example of my full name added up through the system above:

EMMA RENEE MILDON

$$5 + 4 + 4 + 1 +$$
$$9 + 5 + 5 + 5 + 5 +$$
$$4 + 9 + 3 + 4 + 6 + 5 = 74$$
$$7 + 4 = 11$$

Because I land on a master number, 11, I do not continue to add my numbers together.

It is important to look at any repetitive numbers within your name. For example, when you look at my name, you can see I have a lot of repeating 5s. Fives symbolize change—usually a change in the home, work, or relationships. Also, any master number is often linked to obstacles and a hard childhood. When you compare the numbers to my life of adoption and then the death of my mother as a teenager, it is easy to see the link. What about you? What do the numbers reflect about your life? Any adventures or hardships coming your way?

Now that we've touched on the basics of Western numerology, let's dig deeper. Here are some simple meanings behind your numbers.[5] Every number has a unique vibration and brings different elements to your life.

EXPLORE THIS!

Just as there are professional astrologers, aromatherapists, and yoga instructors, there are professional numerologists. If numerology is something you find yourself especially attracted to, consider seeking out a professional numerologist to help you take your interest further. I've studied under Peter Vaughan, a numerology expert and creator of the Vaughan Process, and it was a very enlightening experience for me.

Individual Number Meanings

1 Independence, leadership, beginnings—ones are self-starters, proactive, and courageous. However, they can also be selfish and excessively strong-willed.

2 Cooperation, harmony, emotions—twos are peacemakers and sensitive souls who enjoy a balanced life.

3 Expression, creativity, communication—threes are imaginative and inspired and often live creative, artistic lives.

4 Hard work, process, stability—fours are the disciplined, dependable, and trustworthy workers.

5 Change, freedom, experience—fives are the socialites; they are adaptable and worldly.

6 Love, responsibility, service—sixes are the guardians and protectors, and are most often healers or teachers.

7 Contemplation, wisdom, metaphysics—this is the Soul Searcher's number; they seek knowledge, answers, and experiences.

8 Power, money, business—eights hold the success number; they are a great judge of character and are street smart, which makes for great business leaders or politicians.

9 Humanitarian, transformation, endings—nines are the lovers of the world; they are caring, nurturing, and charitable.

Master Number Meanings

11 Inspiration, intuition, awareness—elevens are most often connected to physics, clairvoyants, or prophets.

22 Ambition, discipline, power—twenty-twos are manifesters, doers, and believers.

33 Teacher, humanitarian, and nurturer—thirty-threes are the movers and shakers, combining the attributes of both the 11 and 22 master numbers.

Your Life Path Number

WOO-WOO SCALE: ▲▲▲▲▲▲▲▲▲△△

EXPLORE-IT SCALE: ▲▲▲▲▲▲▲▲▲▲▲

Your life path number is calculated from your birthdate and holds keys to your personality as well as to the lessons, challenges, and opportunities that may be presented to you throughout your life. For example, the Dalai Lama's life path is 22, indicating spiritual leadership, and Gandhi's life path is 9, pointing toward humanitarianism.

To get started, first write down your date of birth. I've included mine below for an example. Next, add them together like we did our birth name above. Repeat the addition if you are left with a double digit. The exception is again master numbers, which do not get added together and are 11, 22, and 33.

$$2 + 7 \,\text{(day)} + 3 \,\text{(month)} + 1 + 9 + 8 + 6 \,\text{(year)} = 36$$
$$3 + 6 = 9$$

My life path number is therefore 9—I am destined to walk the path of the humanitarian. (I don't think I can live up to Gandhi, but hey, a girl can try, right?) What does your life path number say about you? Find out below.[6]

1 Hardworking, natural leaders, a strong desire to be number one—due to your determination and self-motivation, you won't let anything stand in your way of accomplishing a goal. The best careers are ones where you can be your own boss.

2 Harmony, peace, cooperation, a natural peacemaker—you'll be an excellent diplomat or counselor and enjoy creative endeavors, whether they're musical, artistic, or even gardening and farming.

3 High level of creativity and self-expression—you communicate well which means you can become a poet, actor, writer, artist, or musician. In fact, many writers, radio broadcasters, actors, singers, performers, and counselors share this life path number.

4 The worker bees of society—determined, hardworking, and practical. Careers include building or construction, law, a mechanic, engineer, or accountant.

5 An adventurer, seeking change and variety in life—you could do something as dramatic as being a photographer for *National Geographic* or as straightforward as being a flight attendant. Whatever you choose, ensure it offers you flexibility and flavor.

6 Incredible nurturers of any gender—aim for a career that rewards your responsibility. You'll do much better as a manager than as a worker. If it means more education, then get it. Be proud of yourself for being capable and driven!

7 Intellectual, analytical, intuitive, reserved, and a thinker—seven represents spiritual focus, analysis, being original, independent. If you have this number, people often feel like they don't know you; you are a mystery, and some may see you as eccentric—but that doesn't worry you much. You know you rock it.

8 You long to establish financial security; you're ambitious and also goal driven. You are a natural executive and excellent in the business or political arena. You have a need for success and a strong desire to be recognized for your achievements; you would also excel as a counselor, historian, and history teacher. Move over, Indiana Jones!

9 Nines are humanitarians, through and through. You often feel unloved or abandoned in a sense, and thus responsible for making others happy, and fixing or healing others. You would benefit from a career that sees you giving something back—helping or healing people would fulfill you.

11 You are sensitive, understanding, and intuitive. You might not be a leader, but you are a visionary and a very talented idea person. Your ability to quickly and accurately analyze a situation is a real strength in the business world. You're probably your friend group's go-to advice guru.

22 Those with a life path number 22 have great spiritual understanding and ability to apply knowledge in a practical way and achieve enormous success. You are here to teach others.

33 This number is the Master Teacher. Your focus is on reaching the world and uplifting the loving energy of mankind. You are not concerned with personal ambition, and you have great devotion to a cause or mission. You, kid? You're gonna change the world.

EXPLORE THIS!

There are many more numbers you can calculate about yourself, right down to the number meanings for this year, this month, and even this very day. You can calculate your connection with a friend or partner and compare numbers. You can dip into different paths and practices as the interest strikes you or simply figure out your numerological basics and leave it at that. However numerology resonates with you, I suggest you make it part of your education—grab ten or fifteen minutes and hop on Google and Amazon to find some books, courses, and online communities having to do with numerology that resonate with you. As a topic, it can be quite complex and take some brainpower to learn, and it seems to spark interest in the analyzing, logical, and calculating Soul Searchers. One more tip: Don't get down on yourself if numerology takes a bit of time to master. Start slowly with the starters in this chapter and go from there.

Your Birthday Number

WOO–WOO SCALE: ▲▲▲▲▲▲▲▲▲▲△△
EXPLORE–IT SCALE: ▲▲▲▲▲▲▲▲△△△

For those Soul Searchers who like to keep things simple, you will be happy to hear you don't need to add anything together for this one! Your birthday number is one of your core numbers and is simply the day you choose to enter the world. Check out yours on pages 135 and 136. A quick note: some of these will read very similarly to the life path numbers above, as there is a fair amount of numerical overlap between the two.

Your Daily Number

The more numbers you explore, the more you understand about your life. For instance, if you want to know what kind of day you're going to have on a specific date, then the below is the numerological math for you.

1. Add all numbers from your birthday together. For example, March 27, 1986 would be: $2 + 7 + 3 + 1 + 9 + 8 + 6 = 1 + 8 = 9$. My birth number is 9.

2. Using the Western numerology alphabet number chart, add together your name number. For example, my name:

EMMA RENEE MILDON

$$5 + 4 + 4 + 1 +$$
$$9 + 5 + 5 + 5 + 5 +$$
$$4 + 9 + 3 + 4 + 6 + 5 = 74$$
$$7 + 4 = 11$$

3. Next, add together the date you're interested in. For example, October 6, 2015 is $6 + 1 + 0 + 2 + 0 + 1 + 5 = 15$, then $1 + 5 = 6$.

4. Now, add all of your numbers together. Here we go: birth number 9 + name number 11 + special date 6 = 26, then 2 + 6 = 8. Eight is a good day for business ventures, financial returns, and is a day for general success.[8]

Find out your date number meaning below:

Day 1:

Action Day—today is a day to get shit done! If you are a procrastinator, then day 1 is a good day to allocate as a work or organizing day.

Day 2:

Balance Day—today is all about order and reflection. Take time to review decisions, evaluate, and plan ahead. You will be able to predict and foresee challenges better than usual on these days.

Day 3:

Ease Day—today everything just clicks, flows, and works. It is a great day to plan social engagements such as parties or networking events.

Day 4:

Chore Day—today is all about ticking things off your list and getting on top of your chores. You will find day 4s are productive and satisfying days.

Day 5:

Danger Day—this is your caution day. Try not to jump out of a plane or dive with sharks! This is a day to be aware that you may be caught off guard or surprised, so keep on your toes on day 5s.

Day 6:

Rest Day—this is your chill day and is a time not to try and work against the flow. You need to rest, relax, and recharge on any day 6s, whenever and however you can. Try to avoid stressful encounters.

Day 7:

Wisdom Day—today you will find that new information finds its way to you whether you meditate, study, or expose yourself to new situations or experiences. Day 7s are days of expanding your mind and spirit alike.

Day 8:

Abundance Day—today is your day to win at life! It is a good day to kickstart new ideas, ventures, and partnerships of all sorts.

Day 9:

Announcement Day—today is all about achievements. The bells are chiming; the crowds are cheering for you. It is a great day for marriages, announcements, and general celebrations. Day 9s are days of triumph.

> "Mathematics expresses values that reflect the cosmos, including orderliness, balance, harmony, logic, and abstract beauty."
> **>Deepak Chopra**

The beauty of numerology is it can be applied to any and every date, which means you can use it to forecast everything from personal conundrums to business decisions to greater life challenges. Essentially, if you have a number, you can learn something from it. As with most things, the more you practice, the better you'll become, so crunch some numbers for your friends, colleagues, or family members—this will help you become more familiar with the characteristics of each number and number combination's energy. Don't lose sight of the fun behind the math, and remember to reach out for help through further research or professional guidance if you feel lost or confused.

Now that you know your numbers, you'll always count your blessings.

EXPLORE THIS!

Not number savvy? I have a brain fart whenever I try to add two numbers together and totally rely on my iPhone calculator. My advice? Download one of the great numerology calculator apps available to you—some are even free—and they can be great pocket guides to help you work out your friends' or families' numbers and date days to help you quickly and easily incorporate numerology into your daily life without giving you headache of exponential proportions.

Your Birthday Number

First
People born on the first are the first in the group—leaders. You are born to succeed and are always on the go, looking for your next challenge, invention, and experience. You have creative gifts and are determined—a born entrepreneur!

Second
Harmony, peace, cooperation, a natural peacemaker—you'll be an excellent diplomat or counselor and enjoy creative endeavors, whether they're musical, artistic, or even gardening and farming. That is, if you can deal with all those barnyard smells. If you can, you're a braver soul than me!

Third
High level of creativity and self-expression—you communicate well, which means you can become a poet, actor, writer, artist, or musician. A number for many writers, radio broadcasters, actors, singers, performers, and counselors.

Fourth
The worker bees of society—determined, hardworking, and practical.

Careers include building or construction, law, a mechanic, engineer, or accountant.

Fifth
An adventurer, seeking change and variety in life—whatever your adventurous calling may be, ensure it offers you flexibility and flavor.

Sixth
Incredible nurturers. Aim for a career that rewards your responsibility. You're more of a leader than a team member. If being that leader means more education, then go get it. Be proud of yourself for being capable and driven!

Seventh
Intellectual, analytical, intuitive, reserved, and a thinker—seven represents spiritual focus, analysis, and being original, independent. If you have this number, people often feel like they don't know you; you are a mystery, and some may see you as eccentric—don't listen to the haters though. Rock your eccentric self.

Eighth
You long to establish financial security, and you're ambitious and goal driven. You are a natural executive and excellent in the business or political arena. You have a need for success and a strong desire to be recognized for your achievements. You would also excel as a counselor, historian, and history teacher.

Ninth
The humanitarians, nines often feel unloved or abandoned in a sense, and thus feel responsible for making others happy, and fixing or healing others. You may benefit from a career that sees you giving something back, as helping or healing people would fulfill you.

Tenth
You are a dreamer and a doer combined into one! This means you have big ambitions and work hard to see them transform into reality. You know how to plan out success and how to action the plan—the perfect combo.

Eleventh
Similar to those with their birth name numerology adding to 11, you are intuitive and inspiring and are best suited to serve as a healer, messenger, or teacher. You are a visionary and an idealist that can lead, touch, and motivate others.

Twelfth
You have a creative, artistic talent for adding flare to every element of your life. You are a social butterfly; people are attracted and drawn to your open, warm, and fun sense of humor.

Thirteenth
You are grounded, stable, and have a strong loyalty to your friends and family who are your top priority in life. You have great discipline in your work, and everyone in your proximity can sense your high morals, good work ethic, and core values.

Fourteenth
You have a taste for adventure; you are flexible and adaptable, and you love change. The idea of packing up and going into the unknown excites you. You love to travel and have a knack for attracting good luck.

Fifteenth
You are a kind soul, generous, understanding, and thoughtful, and a great listener. Because of this, you are also a natural healer; people tend to share their problems with you and leave conversations with you feeling lighter.

Sixteenth
The ultimate seeker—you have a deep need to understand the unseen in life, knowing there is more, and you curiously question everything. At times, you will be drawn to the higher world more than the real world, so your mission in life is to stay grounded and keep in mind you are an earth angel, not an actual one!

Your Birthday Number

Seventeenth

You have a knack for success in your career and will naturally be followed with abundance. You will have the finer things and will savor that lifestyle, enjoying life to the fullest. You see the big picture and like what you see.

Eighteenth

The peacemaker and a natural humanitarian, you want to improve the condition of life. You generously give your knowledge and energy to others and feel most satisfied when you are helping others. In fact, the more you do for others, the more you will receive.

Nineteenth

You are a pioneer and take pride in your independent, self-confident, and original take on life. You approach everything in your stride and believe in yourself so much you are not afraid to take a risk. You have your own back—and that is very cool.

Twentieth

You are a sensitive soul that is hugely affected by your environment so it is important that you surround yourself with bright, positive, loving people, and allow yourself a lot of self-love.

Twenty-First

You have a sparkle, both for socializing and for creating. Your imagination runs wild, which makes you an excellent story-teller, visionary, and thinker. You think outside the box and always seem to be the life of the party.

Twenty-Second

Your mission is to build a foundation. You have a vision as well as the skill set to build an organization, practice, or business and function as the driving, stable, and founding force ensuring it is built strong from the ground up.

Twenty-Third

Life is for living, and you want to be sure to experience all that life has to offer. You are adaptive, which allows you to chop and change your surroundings—all part of your journey. You are empathetic and sensitive, which means you easily plug into others. You may think you find it hard to make friends when actually you are often too on the go to realize you make friends quite easily.

Twenty-Fourth

You are very down-to-earth and grounded, and your roots are very important to you. You put your family and friends first and foremost, and enjoy living life in balance—working hard and playing hard.

Twenty-Fifth

You are a logical, practical person who follows their gut feelings about things and is able to look at the big picture in life. You like the facts, so are very good at researching and problem solving, and you always look to the solution rather than the problem.

Twenty-Sixth

Money comes naturally to you, and you attract good business and live a nice lifestyle as a result of these successes. You are realistic and at times can be too hard on yourself—look at what you've achieved and give yourself more credit sometimes.

Twenty-Seventh

A born leader, your purpose is to lead and inspire people. You are highly creative and have a great connection to creating and humanity that combine to make writing, speaking, or performing all great professions for you.

Twenty-Eighth

You are ambitious and like to push things forward, always pushing the people in your life to be the best versions of themselves. While you are confident, you also need encouragement and like to lead a supportive and grateful team.

Twenty-Ninth

You are very insightful and think in a more creative and imaginative way than most people. You like color and pictures, and are an excellent visualizer, which also means you can predict, see, and read situations very intuitively.

Thirtieth

You make life more beautiful; you dress well, take pride in your appearance and home, and in the work you do. You are charismatic, inspiring, and charming in your whole presentation and persona.

Thirty-First

The grounded, stable, strong type, your roots are important to you—you value your friends and family and are very loyal and logical when it comes to your priorities in life.

YOUR ASTROLOGY

Some people reach for the sky. You and I, dear Soul Searcher, we reach for the stars—in fact, we are guided by them. Dating back to at least the second millennium BCE and practiced by the Mayans, Chinese, Babylonians, Greeks, Romans, Indians, and many other cultures and peoples, astrology is one of the most ancient of soul-searching traditions. Astrology is the study of connections between cosmic and earthly events, and for many years, astrology was treated as a science—it even laid the groundwork for the field of astronomy.[1] When Alexander the Great led his conquest of Asia, the Greeks were exposed to ideas from Syria, Babylon, Persia, and central Asia. Astrological concepts and practices continued to spread across cultures and centuries, eventually resulting in what we understand as Western astrology today.[2] Before astrology faded into the background to make room for astronomy, it was widely employed to forecast the weather

and life events, and to help guide important political figures through their reigns.

Today, astrology is largely considered—you guessed it—kind of woo-woo. If you asked anyone in the general public "What is astrology?" they would probably tell you their star sign, whether they believe in it or not, and maybe tell you they read their horoscope in the paper each week. What many people don't realize is how influenced they are by the planets and stars on a daily basis.

Take, for example, the very real and tangible effects of the tides and the seasons. These aspects of daily life on our planet may seem very ordinary and earthbound, but are in fact also largely influenced by the movement of the planets and stars around us. Our days start and end by the light of the sun and moon. The moon's cycles can even directly influence our moods, behaviors, and sleep patterns.

For thousands of years, the sun has represented male energy and the moon female energy, a yin and yang of celestial balance. Throughout spiritual history, gods and goddesses alongside ordinary mortals have worshiped or found a kinship with the moon, the sun, the planets, and the stars. My mind is immediately drawn to images of the Virgin Mary that I've seen time and time again, portrayed with a new moon, symbolizing fertility, birth, purity, and peace. Take the Egyptian god Thoth as another example; he was said to use the moon for magical power and wisdom. Guan Yin, the Chinese goddess of kindness and purity, aids conception and protects wandering souls and travelers on their journey. The Druids, ancient Egyptians, Mayans, Essenes, and Romans positioned their sacred sites to align with the summer sun, to celebrate the role of light in growth, both terrestrial and spiritual.[3]

At the Great Pyramids of Egypt, the sun on the summer solstice crowns the head of the Sphinx; the Druids celebrated the marriage of heaven and earth and the defeat of the dark god at the summer solstice, just as the Egyptians celebrated the defeat of the dark god Seth by Horus, the sun; and in Rome, the cleansing festival of Vestalia is a Roman tradition associated with the goddess Vesta. The word *solstice* actually means "stationary sun" and is a time of great spiritual energy indicating when the sun is at its highest (summer) and lowest (winter) points in the sky.[4]

The winter solstice is also a celebration of light and has had a huge impact on spiritual history with ancient pagan, Celtic, Roman, and even Christian connections to the birth of Christ and the "holy month." The spring and fall equinoxes also have ties to Islamic and Hebrew calendars. The word *equinox* translates to "balance" or "light and dark," and dates back to 45 BCE when Julius Caesar established the spring equinox on his calendar. In Christianity, the spring equinox is a time of the passion, crucifixion, and resurrection through the Bible's telling of Jesus's trials and journey. In ancient Egypt, it is the time of the ancient Egyptian god Osiris's resurrection, and the resurrection of the Mayan maize god Hun Hunahpu. The Great Sphinx of Giza in Egypt is a symbol of resurrection and gazes precisely at the rising of the sun on the spring equinox. (Come on Soul Searcher, you should be good at sniffing out a spiritual trend by now! Resurrection—the sun rising up everyday. Everyday we are reborn. We season. We blossom.)

The temple of Angkor Wat in Cambodia aligns with the spring equinox and depicts the scene of the "churning of the milky ocean"—the struggle between the forces of light and darkness.[5] At the temple of the feathered serpent in Mexico at Chichen Itza, the feathered serpent Quetzalcoatl ascends the nine terraces of the pyramid on the spring equinox.

Throughout history, the autumnal equinox has often been misinterpreted because of its associations to darkness; people tend to jump to conclusions and consider it a negative or evil time. However, everything must be balanced, and we cannot have light without darkness—this goes not just for the order of nature, but also for our spiritual growth.[6] The autumnal equinox is traditionally connected with harvesting, but it also represents a time of growing darkness, as after the equinox is over, the sun continues to descend and diminish (as it does after the summer solstice), so that the nights are longer than the days, bringing the change of seasons and the cold and death of winter, which in turn gives birth to spring again.

> "Even a happy life cannot be without a measure of darkness,
> and the word 'happy' would lose its meaning if it were not balanced by
> sadness. It is far better to take things as they come along with
> patience and equanimity."
>
> **>Carl Jung**

The traditions of the solstices and equinoxes are always about balance, light and dark, and the earthly and celestial order of nature and life, birth and death, beginnings and endings. Human and divine representations of the sun (Apollo, Ra, even Jesus) and the moon (Artemis, Diana, the Virgin Mary), and figures representing both earthly and celestial forces and patterns, are part of how humans understand their place in the universe. They all represent our part in the greater design of existence, marking our path through the stars as we journey together.

Today, it is easy to write off ancient spiritualists and acolytes of the stars and seasons as simple-minded nature worshippers. But there is a reason why natural principles are consistently found throughout many sacred texts, ancient sites, and cultural and religious practices—it is because we are ruled by the natural forces of the universe and the celestial motion that unites us all as we effortlessly spin through the cosmos.

The Solstices, Equinoxes, Moon Phases, and You

So, how do things like the solstices and equinoxes affect you? Mankind has been aware of the moon's effects on the earth as well as the human body, soul, and mind for many years. For example, the moon pulls more than just the rise and fall of our ocean's tides—as we are made up largely of water, our bodies too experience a shift, a pull, a rise and fall similar to the tides, so it is natural for us to feel the effects of the lunar phases. In fact, it is an age-old practice to rest, restore, or even detoxify the body when it coincides with the moon's movements.

Try to stay in tune with these calendars and check in to see what is happening in your life during the moon cycle and at each equinox and solstice.[7] Take note of times when you may feel overwhelmed, times when things flow effortlessly, or times when you just want to fly solo and reflect.

Here is an embarrassing confession of mine—I try not to go out on a full moon. Not because I morph into a werewolf or something, but because I become so sensitive that I tend to emotionally explode like a pressure cooker that's been left on high for too long. When I am in a relationship with someone, I tend to keep a conscious eye on the full moon and watch how we both behave or what our souls crave. When both people are aware of the influence of the celestial bodies that surround them, they can make sure they work with them, rather than against them.

Check out the charts on the following pages for insights into how each solstice, equinox, and moon cycle can influence your life.

Solstices and Equinoxes

WOO-WOO SCALE: ▲▲▲▲▲▲△△△△
EXPLORE-IT SCALE: ▲▲▲▲▲▲▲▲△△

See chart on page 141.

Moon Cycles

WOO-WOO SCALE: ▲▲▲△△△△△△△
EXPLORE-IT SCALE: ▲▲▲▲▲▲▲▲▲△

See chart on page 142.

Your Astrological Identity and Destiny

As Soul Searchers, we love unearthing new things about ourselves, our journeys, and our purposes. Astrology can be a fantastic tool to do just that. Your astrology and position within the zodiac is your spiritual energy signature made from the exact date and time of your arrival into the world, and can track your identity, values, family, lovers, experiences, networks, skills, and gifts. Your astrology is a blueprint for your life, and it

An end of a cycle reflecting organic closure, death, and making way for new beginnings. This is often a time of sacrifice, conflict, and confrontation to help drive the natural end of things that no longer serve us on our spiritual journey.

Northern Hemisphere
September
Southern Hemisphere
March

You will feel more passionate during the summer solstice; it is a good time to ignite ideas. This is also a time of awakening, so focus on something you want to achieve or connect with. It is also a time to give birth to new ideas, as well as for fertility.

AUTUMNAL EQUINOX

WINTER SOLSTICE

SUMMER SOLSTICE

Northern Hemisphere
December 21/22
Southern Hemisphere
June 21/22

Northern Hemisphere
June 21/22
Southern Hemisphere
December 21/22

VERNAL EQUINOX

The yin/yang of light and dark, good and bad, this is a time to reflect, rest, and embrace the darker side of life as we are reminded that the light always comes back. It is a time of sanctuary and hibernation, like a child in a womb preparing to be born and rebirthed into the next phase of life and light.

Northern Hemisphere
March
Southern Hemisphere
September

This is seen as a time of challenge and growth through lessons—often hard ones. It is a time of struggle and is usually a time we are under pressure or stress, or are confronted with something that will result in spiritual growth.

Waning Moon: A time to let go, forgive, and reflect. This is a good time to operate in solitude and meditate. Make time for you during this cycle.

New Moon: This signifies a new chapter and new beginnings; you will have newfound energy. This is a good time to start projects or pursue new opportunities.

Waxing Moon: Time to work on your vision board—this is a growth phase, so make sure you focus on what you want to come next. This is a time to focus on your goals and your direction in life. It is a good time to store energy or begin a cleanse.

Full Moon: You will be more sensitive and intuitive than normal, as this is a time of full power and energy—sleepless nights or an overly active mind are common. Try to surround yourself with like-minded souls and positive influences. It is an excellent time to flush toxins from the body, rest, and restore.

NEW

WANING CRESCENT

WAXING CRESCENT

THIRD QUARTER

FIRST QUARTER

WANING GIBBOUS

WAXING GIBBOUS

FULL

holds clues to help guide you, showing you what your true purpose is and how you are going to best embody it. Astrology can help you better understand challenges, warn you of approaching obstacles in your life, and even guide you to find your soul mate.

For example, there is a huge chance you are reading this chapter in either your late twenties or late fifties. These times in our lives are called our Saturn Return—transit times when your life will have huge shifts and you will experience a zoom-out moment with everything you have achieved or not achieved in life up until your twenty-ninth or fifty-ninth year. These times are so you can reflect, analyze, make choices, and move forward into the new phase of your life, and it can often be a stressful or challenging year for people as they make changes and implement the shift. Think of Saturn as a wise old man who has the ability to see through your excuses—try your best to live by your truth during this time, cull what doesn't serve you, change, grow, and don't be afraid to let go of your old habits.

Astrology and You

Astrology uses combinations of the solar system, energy points, the stars, planets, moons, your birth time, location, and date to create a map to pinpoint your place in the universe. Astrology goes a lot deeper than the star signs many of us read in the gossip mags and newspapers.

For those of you who have an affinity for stargazing, find you are more emotional during a full moon, or generally like guessing people's star signs: you are about to tap into a whole new astrological level of knowledge!

EXPLORE THIS!

There is a lot of information out there on the Saturn Return, so if you are already experiencing this or are about to dive headfirst into your twenty-ninth or fifty-ninth year, I recommend finding a book that resonates with you and allowing it to guide you through this phase. When I got my astrology reading done while writing this book, I was on the edge of tipping into my Saturn Return, and boy, is it a ride!

"Three things cannot be long hidden: the sun, the moon, and the truth."
>**Buddha**

When stargazing, there are times the human eye can only see a handful of twinkling lights in the night sky, especially when we're in cities or suburbs. At other times and in different locations—generally when we are in a quieter spot in nature with less light pollution—the complexity of the constellations can keep our busy eyes occupied for hours spotting shooting stars, planets, and other astral bodies.

Astrology is complex and takes into consideration that your soul passes through different transits and energy points throughout your life on this pale blue dot.[8] Astrology is a great tool to unearth the complexities of the soul, and a good reminder of how influenced we are by the push and pull of our solar system. After all, we live by the sky day by day, even if we're stuck inside working all day or too busy to even take a peek at the stars from time to time. Even if we don't believe in anything else but the simple existence of the stars, moon, and sun, we can still choose how much wisdom we take from them. You can use the sun to tell the time . . . or you can use the whole solar system to tell your life.

"Traditional science assumes, for the most part, that an objective observer independent reality exists; the universe, stars, galaxies, sun, moon and earth would still be there if no one was looking."

>Deepak Chopra

As with many of the other chapters in this book, when I began to write this chapter, a master crossed my path to help light the way. My guiding guru for this section was astrologer and author Philip Young, PhD, whose words and teachings are now being passed on to you, little stargazer. Philip was kind enough to make a personal chart for me and walk me through my own personal life journey using astrological principles. A kind, intuitive, open man who passed on his wisdom selflessly to help benefit both my and now your journeys, his reading astounded me and reflected the same things that my numerology and Tarot readings did. Any doubts I had about astrology quickly disappeared as he shared more and more with me about the Saturn Return, my life's purpose, and even finding love. Who wouldn't want to know about all these things and get a teaser about how it all works out? Like you, finding out more clues about my life's journey only fueled my desire to continue my search.

As we said at the beginning of our time together, a journey always begins with a single step. Our first step here is to discover more about your sign. Keep in mind that if you fall on a cusp—a date close to the change of a sign—it is not uncommon to exhibit traits of both neighboring star signs.

Astrological Signs[9]

WOO-WOO SCALE: ▲▲▲▲▲▲▲▲▲▲
EXPLORE-IT SCALE: ▲▲▲▲▲▲▲▲▲▲

Zodiac Sign	Dates	Element/Planet	Sign Traits
Aries	March 21–April 19	**Fire** Mars, Lilith	Independent, driven, determined, leader, and ambitious
Taurus	April 20–May 20	**Earth** Venus, Vulcan, Vesta	Patient, strong, reliable, humble, and stable
Gemini	May 21–June 20	**Air** Mercury, Urania	Social, curious, good communicator, and flexible
Cancer	June 21–July 22	**Water** The moon	Sensitive, nurturing, diplomatic, emotional, and impulsive
Leo	July 23–August 22	**Fire** The sun	Loyal, warm, creative, romantic, and generous
Virgo	August 23–September 22	**Earth** Mercury, Chiron, Hygeia	Logical, reflective, organized, meticulous, and practical
Libra	September 23–October 22	**Air** Venus, Zeus, Pallas	Balanced, justice-oriented, natural, diplomatic, and orderly
Scorpio	October 23–November 21	**Water** Pluto, Eris	Strong, stable, intense, and purposeful
Sagittarius	November 22–December 21	**Fire** Jupiter, Juno	Forward thinking, positive, exploratory, and worldly
Capricorn	December 22–January 19	**Earth** Saturn, Ceres	Determined, strong willed, responsible, and accomplished
Aquarius	January 20–February 18	**Air** Uranus, Astraea	Focused, insightful, idealistic, original, and wise
Pisces	February 19–March 20	**Water** Neptune, Venus	Indecisive, spiritual, imaginative, and sensitive

A lesser-known but just as important element in astrology that many Soul Searchers who are familiar with the twelve zodiac signs may wish to explore is that of the twelve astrological houses. Each house has its own characteristics and influences over a person's experiences, challenges, and lessons. See the chart on the next page for a description of each house.[10] Using the time and date of your birth, you can look at your house in the stars, effectively helping you map out your soul-search journey. To discover how each house influences you personally, consider having your horoscope drawn up by a professional astrologer.

Astrological Houses

WOO-WOO SCALE: ▲▲▲▲▲▲▲△△△△
EXPLORE-IT SCALE: ▲▲▲▲▲▲▲▲△△△

Beyond this point is where the complexity kicks in, so hold on to your shooting stars, lady. Moving forward, you have two options: connect with a professional astrologer who will make you a chart and talk you through your houses, energy points, and rulerships, or you can reach for the stars on your own by reading books or enrolling in a course. However you choose to search, follow your instincts on what would best serve your soul at this point in your life. Don't have time to take a course? Order a couple of books on Amazon or check them out at your local library. Don't know where to start in finding a professional astrologer? Google is your friend, my dear, just be sure anyone you find is legit.

Something to note before we move on: all of the glyphs, tables, lines, and numbers on a personal chart can blow your mind a bit; I was lucky enough to have someone to personally guide me through my astrology charts, which I would highly recommend if you can swing it. Save yourself an astronomical headache!

Let's start with the outer layer of the circle and work our way in. The outermost ring on the chart holds the symbols from the zodiac (such as Aries, Taurus, and so on). The second layer holds numbers that represent the twelve houses. Inside each house you have different glyphs that represent different astrological bodies and energy points that correspond to your life and the events within it. Still with me? Don't worry. This was about the time my mind started filling with white-noise static, kind of like when the teacher in Charlie Brown talks. From here on in, you generally need an expert who can train you on the meaning of glyphs, how to read astrological data, and how to intuitively unlock the meaning behind your star signs, planets, houses, and life

Eleventh House

The eleventh house is about friends and community, and is driven by a vision that we are all one. The eleventh house drives you to bring your dreams to reality and sets you to work.

Tenth House

The tenth house brings clarity surrounding career and purpose, and results in success, popularity, and even sometimes fame. The tenth house also has a strong influence on your mother's role in your life.

Ninth House

The ninth house is a goody! It is all about long journeys, adventure, soul searching, and an awareness of spirituality and religion.

Eighth House

The eighth house influences new beginnings, transformation, and the shift from letting go to beginning new. This house is all about growth.

Twelfth House

The twelfth house is about the journey to achieving our life goals, including the challenges and sacrifices. The twelfth house can commonly be coupled with solitude.

Seventh House

This house influences all partnerships including marriage, business partnerships, and friendships. Oh, and yoga. Yes! Yoga means union, and people who have the seventh house as an influence tend to be spiritually open. Get bendy, people.

First House

Ascendant/Rising Sign

This house influences your personality and how you project yourself to others. The first house amplifies our true self, and the impression we leave those in our company.

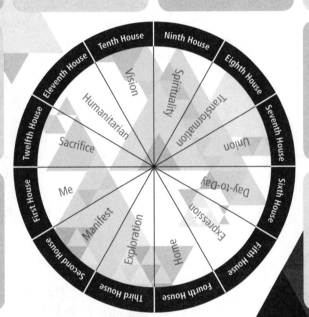

Sixth House

This house influences your day-to-day life including your health, work, and lifestyle. Influences in the sixth house may include an interest in exercise and nutrition. This is the self-love house.

Second House

This house rules how well we secure ourselves with money, success, and possessions. Those influenced by the second house are heavily driven by universal laws, such as the laws of attraction.

Third House

This house influences those in your immediate company including your family, siblings, work colleagues, and friends. The third house influences love and relationships, especially the lessons we learn from those relationships. (Sound familiar? Hint: that's you, Soul Searcher!)

Fourth House

This house influences your roots, upbringing, home, and parents. Influences in this house are all about settling— letting the ready know they have learned all their lessons, and are not going to become more grounded and settled.

Fifth House

This house influences all elements of expression including love, children, creativity, and animals. The influences of the fifth house tend to be about a sense of direction from ownership.

experiences, which is a complex journey and something that must be learned over time. Consider this your jumping-off point, whether it leads you to other books that go into more exhaustive detail, online courses, or to astrology experts.

It is up to you how high you reach to touch the stars and widen your understanding of signs, houses, solstices and equinoxes, the sun, the moon, and where your world spins among them. Remember, this is just another clue to help you connect with your soul's life lessons and unearth your purpose. Your answers are written in the stars—go reach for 'em!

"Men should take their knowledge from the Sun, the Moon, and the Stars."
>**Ralph Waldo Emerson**

YOUR UNIVERSAL LAWS

"The meaning of life is to find your gift; the purpose of life is to give it away."
>**Proverb**

We all live our lives by certain sets of laws. We might not call them laws, but that's sure what they are. Do you wake up at a certain time each day? Do you only allow yourself dessert on the weekends? Do you make sure you're out of the office by a certain time each night, no matter how much work might still need to be done? These are all examples of the many little laws we set for ourselves in our lives. But what about the big ones? The ones that everyone has, if not lived by, they have at least heard of? These are the laws that shape and govern the living, breathing entity that is humanity—the laws of life—whether through religion, philosophy, or society, or a combination of all of the above.

Why should we Soul Searchers care? What do universal laws have to do with our chakras and astrological signs and Feng Shui? Short answer: everything.

Let me set it up this way: we're in the section of this book that's focusing on *mind* in our body-mind-spirit soul-searching journey (remember that it is all intersecting and connected). The mind is where everything the body and the soul experience and learn comes together and you form opinions about yourself and how you see the world. Our universal laws—the Ten Commandments in Christianity, the laws of physics, karma, the law of attraction—are the result of our minds synthesizing all the experiences of our bodies and our spirits and making sense of them universally. We may not all subscribe to the same universal laws, but that's not really what "universal" means in this context. It means that, no matter your background or belief system, there's at least a kernel of universal truth to be found in all of these systems that we all can relate to and make use of. And as Soul Searchers, this is important for us to recognize, cherish, and make our own in whatever way we see fit. After all, our home is within the universe—we're all going to be here for a while, so it makes sense to work with it rather than against it, right?

Take the world's religions for example. No matter their sometimes-significant differences, all religions more or less promote one thing: kindness. They all collectively seek to help provide faith, hope, and direction in life. Kindness, goodness, love—whatever word you want to assign to it, this is the one core universal element no matter what religion you may or may not believe in. Regardless of your god, culture, background, or history, the one fundamental necessity, the driving force behind our lives is that universal need we all see: belonging, kindness, love.

The Ten Commandments? Sure, some of them are pretty restrictive—"thou shalt have no other gods before me"—and a little trivial in the big picture of things, like "thou shalt not covet thy neighbor's wife"—solid advice, but maybe not absolutely vital to your spiritual well-being like certain other commandments, like "thou shalt not kill" and "thou shalt honor thy mother and father." There's a reason why some commandments are more recognizable and more widely adopted than others—the ones that matter the most to people of all faiths are the ones that have to do with kindness toward ourselves and our fellow humans. These are the laws that speak to us from our minds, bodies, and souls, the ones that deep down were preprogrammed prior to any religious and cultural upbringing or digestion of spiritual wisdom.

How about Hinduism? Both a religion and a way of life, Hinduism is one of the foundations of Indian culture and is made up of many traditions, one of them being the concept of karma. Karma, which can also be found in Taoism, Jainism, and other world religions and spiritual paths, is the belief that one's actions have consequences both in this life and in future lives—at its most basic, it means that negative actions will have negative consequences, and positive ones will lead to positive outcomes. This concept thus dictates how a person moves through life—will they create negative energy and thus a negative imprint on the world, and their soul, by being a jerk, or will they work to make the world (and their soul) a better place, both in this lifetime and in all the lifetimes to come? Again, it comes back down to our central point as Soul Searchers: goodness. This is the law we abide by.

So what are your life laws? What philosophy do you ascribe to? Philosophical beliefs can vary drastically across cultures, continents, and centuries, but many world philosophies also converge on certain central points, or laws, and those laws often have to do with the pursuit of balance, wholeness, and happiness. Take utilitarianism, for example.[1] It's a form of ethical philosophy that theorizes that our actions should always be undertaken with the goal of bringing about the maximum good for as many people as possible. A universal law of stopping to think before you act, of asking, "Is this just benefiting me, or is this going to benefit others?" A view of the world as a whole, of all the people as a single tribe, and how to bring the best to as many people as possible, not just our own. A similar philosophy is deontology, which centers on a moral obligation to live and act from a place of duty to one's self and one's fellow humans, regardless of whether the consequences are good or bad, and a focus on how these choices may affect others. Immanuel Kant's theories are believed to be of a deontological nature in that they speak of acting out of duty and hold that true ethics lie in the motivation of someone's actions, not in the consequences.[2]

And science? Science is often painted in a kind of cold and dispassionate light because it's all about the facts (and rightly so), but that doesn't mean that there's not serious spiritual gold to be found within the disciplines of biology, physics, mathematics, astronomy, you name it. Have you ever looked at a human iris up close and noticed the breathtaking similarities it has with a constellation or nebula? The precise beauty of the Fibonacci sequence; the "miraculous spirals" reflected in both the arms of distant galaxies and things like hurricanes and the shells of some sea-dwelling creatures here on earth, like the Nautilus; and the poetry (yes, it's poetic!) of the first law of thermodynamics (all the energy in the universe can change into different forms, but it can't be created or destroyed)—these things speak to us on a deep spiritual level across the borders of language and culture and time.[3]

What about the so-called "New Thought" movements, like the law of attraction? Although very à la mode today, the law of attraction has actually been around for a long, long time and discussed by some of the world's most venerated thinkers, from Plato and Einstein to authors Esther Hicks and Rhonda Byrne. The idea that there is a universal law in which "like attracts like"—in other words, what you think, wish for, put out into the world all returns to you in kind—is one that straddles philosophical, scientific, and experiential planes. Take the concept of a "vision board" from Rhonda Byrne's bestselling book *The Secret*, in which readers are tasked with creating a collage of some sort that represents everything they would like to welcome into their lives, from relationships to career goals to personal desires and beyond.[4] This, simply put, is a visual representation of the law of attraction; it is saying, "I welcome these things/people/ideas into my life by actively envisioning them in front of me as if I already possessed them." What your soul desires most, what the mind thinks about most, what the body craves in nourishment, is what you will attract into your life in turn. Esther Hicks says it this way: "If you want it and expect it, it will be yours very soon."[5]

What universal laws do you live by? Do you believe in karma? How about a god or other form of spiritual higher being? Whatever laws you live your life by, there is no going back now! Even if you've just begun your journey as a Soul Searcher, you are already wiser, more loving, and more aware than you were pre-soaking up this information.

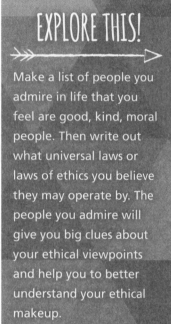

EXPLORE THIS!

Make a list of people you admire in life that you feel are good, kind, moral people. Then write out what universal laws or laws of ethics you believe they may operate by. The people you admire will give you big clues about your ethical viewpoints and help you to better understand your ethical makeup.

Here's my challenge to you: Find little ways to recognize and incorporate your universal laws and beliefs into your daily routine. Take a moment to look up at the sky and give thanks to the cosmic chaos for allowing you to exist on this little rock whirling through space against all probability. Do something nice for someone you don't know—pay for the coffee of the person behind you in line or compliment or joke with someone on the subway—and watch the positive karmic energy boomerang back your way. How you make your universal laws matter is up to you—just make sure you do.

As you go, you will be shifting through states of intolerance and tolerance as you experience others' views on spirituality. Just remember that you do not have to take on what they think and what they believe, nor do they have to take on what you think and what you believe. In this way, we allow for the idea that everyone's journey is their own.

> "Knowing our personal mission further enhances the flow of mysterious coincidences as we are guided toward our destinies. First we have a question, then dreams, daydreams, and intuitions lead us toward the answers, which usually are synchronistically provided by the wisdom of another human being."
> **>James Redfield**

For myself, I feel a responsibility to share and learn about wisdom, thoughts, and inspiration with other like-minded souls, and have always found that these people flow into my life at perfect times. For those who are simply curious, I often think of myself as a messenger, pointing out different potential paths, introducing teachers or guides, and lending them books, objects, and bits and pieces of philosophy I feel will resonate with them. The thing I avoid the most is being preacher-esque in any way, shape, or form. I consider myself more like a promoter with a tendency to customize and recommend different elements of spirituality and universal laws to people when they seem open and ready.

Few listen to their soul and even fewer learn from it. Dear friend, live by your soul; it makes you more enlightened than most. You operate by a universal law, one seen in all religions, practiced by all great leaders, so go through life with a mantra of acceptance, understanding, kindness, and love; smile at strangers; give your energy away by listening, helping, and loving those around you.

"Yeah, yeah, Emma," you might say. "Kindness is all well and good, but I'm only human!" Well, of course. We all are. Being human means that you'll slip from your spiritual path sometimes. But being a Soul Searcher means that you are also aware when you snap or get moody, angry, or resentful (basically, when you act like you're the lead baton twirler of the dick parade), but you have the tools and knowledge to work through and release your negative energy and move back to a place of oneness and positivity.

> "Put your heart, mind, and soul into even your smallest acts. This is the secret of success."
> **>Swami Sivananda**

If I could offer up one more universal law before we move on, it would be this: laugh, daily and preferably loudly. You'll be happier for it and happiness attracts magic so go on, have a laugh! When it comes to nourishing the soul, our buddy Buddha has some valuable lessons for us—that dude knew how to laugh! Joy was his jam. Think of how many smiling, laughing Buddha statues or figurines you have seen in your lifetime. What a great way to be remembered. As you move forward into Part III, I want to challenge you to be your own version of a joyful Buddha. This means you need to find your joy. Joy is the best fuel for your soul. Now, I won't get all bossy about joy here—only you know what speaks to your soul and what you find joyful. It might be spending time with your family or around children; it might be spending time in nature; it might be reading or laughing or watching your favorite television show. Whatever it is, seek it regularly, prioritize it, make time for it— put yourself and your soul first. Think about it this way: when your stomach grumbles, you typically feed yourself, so when you feel low and your soul screams out to you, feed it—feed it joy and laughter. That's a law I think we all can get behind.

EXPLORE THIS!

Grab some paper or put in some calendar notifications that sum up your universal laws and serve as reminders throughout your day. They can be as simple as something like "Be kind," "Act from love," or "Strive to understand before judging." Let them act as gentle touchstones, especially during your most hectic days, when your ethical code can sometimes slip from your list of priorities.

Part III

VIBRANT SPIRIT

Well, friends, here we are: the "soul" part of this whole soul-searching shebang! The buildup has been great, and now you can prepare for a soul-gasm. A soul-gasm is that joyous, free-flowing feeling that hits you when your mind, heart, and soul click into alignment.

As we touched on at the beginning of our journey together, there are lots of different ways to define *soul*. Some people call it a life essence; others define it as a manifestation of a higher power within us; for others still, *soul* is merely the closest we can come to describing what it means to be truly alive. Some believe that the soul lives on after death, or that the soul is transferred to different bodies over and over again until it finally ascends to enlightenment. Practically every culture on the planet and throughout recordable history maintains some form of belief in what we call the soul—it's a pervasive and undeniable part of being human.

This section is definitely about the soul, yes, but it's also about the spirit. Sometimes *spirit* is used interchangeably with *soul*, and I think that makes sense. But *spirit* in this context also means inquisitiveness, fun, and vibrancy—it's an invitation to explore beyond the boundaries of the mind and the body to embrace the ethereal side of existence.

This means that you're probably going to have to stretch that woo-woo muscle just a liiittle bit more. Set your skepticism on the back burner and open your heart to the weird and wonderful world of spiritual guides and past-life regression as well as dipping your toes into what may be more comfortable territory too, like astrology and soul mates and even just the simple joy of throwing your hands up in the air at a concert and singing along. All of these things are spiritual, and all of them can contribute to the health and well-being of your soul—so read on, Soul Searcher. Your search continues.

10

YOUR GUIDES

You wouldn't go blundering off into the wilderness without at least a map, would you? I'm hoping this is true because I, of course, did that once—seven hours, countless bramble scratches and bug bites, and an empty water bottle and stomach later, I stumbled back to my camp a lot crankier and somewhat wiser . . . I hope.

Just like a map, a guide can be the difference between a great adventure and a serious bummer when exploring the great wide world and learning about spiritual guides, angels, elders, and ancestors. On my soul search, it was singlehandedly one of the most comforting experiences of my life. I know, I know, a little out there, right? I understand. But remember, exploration and an open mind, heart, and soul is just as healthy as a healthy dose of skepticism. With that in mind, let me tell you a few stories about guides.

I had developed huge abandonment and trust issues as a child that only worsened when my adoptive mother passed away of cancer in my early teens. I was entering womanhood without a mother figure and I felt lost, angry, ripped off, and more alone than ever before. It was then, in my emptiest days, that I began to notice certain things around me. I experienced recurring signs, messages, and coincidences that left me feeling like someone or something was with me. To this day, I see dandelions whenever I miss my mother, and every time I see one, I smile and thank her for stopping by.

I have no idea why dandelions—I have no memory of dandelions associated with my mother, and they have no symbolic meaning that I know of, though they remind me of blowing the seeds and making a wish. I like to think that maybe they represent the journey of me finding my way to my mother again. Like a dandelion seed, my adoption saw me land in a loving home where I could grow and where my mother's wishes for a family could be fulfilled.

I didn't grow up a believer. My father was from a Catholic upbringing, and my mother an atheist. From an early age, I was curious about things I had never been taught about, like Tarot, candles, and dream catchers. I collected little angel figurines. I felt a familiarity with things that should have been entirely new to me. Like my spirituality today, I did not align the things I was interested in with any one religion, but rather to a deeper spiritual truth or truths I didn't yet understand. This is one of the reasons why I think I have an affinity for angels, because in many ways, they do not have a strict connection with any religion either. Angels are spoken of in many religions, and even people who do not classify themselves as religious or spiritual believe in angels. In fact, in a 2011 poll conducted by CBS, eight out of ten Americans stated that they believed in angels.[1]

Many Soul Searchers have different labels for their guides—some are gods; some are angels; some call them elders, ancestors, spirit guides; and some are even animals. We also connect with guides through different mediums—some follow guided meditations, others use angel or Tarot cards, some use crystal pendulums, and some just look for everyday signs, like my dandelions. I also always get messages in songs—when this happens, the lyrics are always so resonant, it is deafening. When I do guided meditations that connect me with my guides, I get shivers, goose bumps, and such an overwhelming feeling of love that it brings me to tears. Where my guides are concerned, I like to use a combo of the above, because then I feel like I am likely to hear the message loud and clear, no matter what's being communicated—and a lot of the time my guides have to practically shout to get their points across to me!

That's the thing about guides—while they are always with us, they will not speak up unless invited to. You know those times you've been in dire straits, at your wit's end, and desperate for some help from the universe, maybe yelling, "Really?!" up at the sky? And then maybe, just maybe, when you've asked for some help or a sign or a solution, you've gotten one? Those were moments when your guides were bailing you out. Because you dialed the emergency spiritual hotline, they knew you were welcoming their assistance. One of the most revolutionary things I have learned in my ongoing soul search is to ask for help. Put it out there. And also thank them for it when they deliver. Most important, keep an eye out for signs from your guides so you don't walk straight past the lifeline they're throwing you.

EXPLORE THIS!

There are no rules when connecting with your guides. Whatever you picture, whatever sits best with you, go with that. It is said that spirit guides will usually connect with you on a level you are comfortable with, so open yourself to anything that speaks to your soul.

"You don't need a formal prayer or invocation to call the Angels to your side. Simply think, 'Angels, please surround me,' and there they are."
>**Doreen Virtue**

I once had a connection with my guides that left me startled and amazed. It blew any lingering doubt right out the window. To this day, it is still the most powerful message I have ever received from my guides.

I had returned home to New Zealand after living overseas in Spain and America, and was feeling uprooted and a bit lost (root chakra issues, ha!). I had decided to invest what little disposable income I had into a life coach to help me clarify the direction I wanted to head and kick-start me. The universe pointed me to Jasmine Platt, a spiritual life coach who not only pumped my life full of inspiration, but also shared her spiritual wisdom with me. We connected right away, and before long, I was using spiritual methods to protect myself from energy vampires, surrounding myself with other light workers, and beginning to communicate with my guides and spirits. I often left her feeling refreshed, like I had just finished a juice cleanse, had a makeover, and woken from a ten-hour sleep!

One evening, I arrived back home from a two-hour teaching with Jasmine to an empty house; my partner at the time was out. My amazing feeling of stability and calmness was left behind as I walked toward the dark, empty house, and with each step, I got more and more irritated. My partner was great at having fun, letting his hair down and getting rowdy. I was a bit more lame, "a yawn," some would say. I loved people and having a laugh but hated not having a plan, and things not running to a schedule drove me wild. So him not being home and me not knowing where he was really put my panties in a twist.

I could still feel all of this amazing energy in me from my lesson with Jasmine, but now it was tainted with frustration, anxiety, and stress. I walked into the house, threw my bag down, and stomped down the hallway to the phone. I angrily punched in his cell number, only to slam the phone back down with no response. I lifted my arms up making a circle around me, practicing my newly learnt skill of energy protection, finishing with my hands above my head, palms facing together, closing the protective seal. (We explore protection further in chapter 13.)

In that moment, all of the lights blew in the house and I was left standing in complete darkness. I hung up the phone and froze. I walked toward the window to see if the streetlights were still on, to see if the whole neighborhood had lost power. The streetlights were still shining bright; I looked out another window to check the neighbors to see all the other houses on the street still lit up. I stood still, silent, and calm in the dark for a few moments. It was a strange feeling—I didn't feel scared, but I felt like I was being made to stop and refocus.

The front door creaked and in walked my partner. I was still a little pissed. Giving me a weird look for standing in the doorway in the dark, he tried to flick the light switch, and then used his phone as a flashlight and headed to the fuse box. I, on the other hand, reached for my iPod, jumped into bed, and blindly scrolled through my songs, all the while asking my guides to please pick a song for me to listen to. I put my iPod on random. Loud bass suddenly pulsed through my headphones and into my ears as I heard Britney Spears start singing the lyrics of "I Wanna Go," telling me to "blow out" "when the light's out."[2]

I had to laugh; clearly my guides had a sense of humor. Firstly, they had picked the only Britney Spears song on my whole iPod—hilarious in itself. Well played, guides. I mean, what guide thinks, *Hey, let's send her a Britney song*? Apparently mine do. Secondly, they were telling me to take a step back, shake it off, and have fun—to get my knickers out of their twist and loosen up. They were right. Spirituality is an adventure. Soul searching is meant to be fun, and your guides are often playful, so remember to be playful back!

After I heard that song and it changed my perspective on a frustrating moment, I became more aware of many more little signs like it, and even traced some other guided messages through songs that had played at some of the biggest milestones of my life. I felt so comforted to know that my guides had been there with me through those memories. For example, there was one that happened when I was sixteen years old and my mother was terminally ill. She was bedridden and so exhausted she could no longer talk; she was using every ounce of energy she had to not fall asleep. I remember thinking it was because she was afraid she would never wake up again, and maybe I was right. She spoke to me with her eyes—her eyes could laugh, and boy, did they still have the power to tell me off too! On the morning before she said good-bye to us, I sat next to her, holding her hand, and asked her, "You love me, don't you, Mom?"

Her eyes replied with a quick eye roll and a hearty glare as if to say, "What do you think? Of course I do!" My mom passed away only hours later. Everybody left the room, and I stayed sitting with her. I felt guilty for needing her to tell me she loved me when she physically couldn't. I was angry at myself, not to mention very upset to have just witnessed her death. I leaned into my mom to give her a hug good-bye and told her I was sorry. As I stood up to leave, a song came on the radio. I hadn't even noticed it was on until then. The song was "More Than Words" by Extreme, and it reminded and reassured me in that moment that love is so much more than words. It is actions, it is feelings, and it does not need to be spoken to be heard.

It wasn't until a year later that I shared this with my sister, who is quite a skeptic when it comes to spirituality. The next time my sister, father, and I were all together, the song came on again, and my sister looked over at me and smiled. I believe it was my guides, including my mom, letting us know that they were with us. After all, a loved one who has passed over is simply another spirit guide, only you know this guide by name.

As evidenced above, guides don't always speak directly to you when they have a message for you—although sometimes they do! Guides come in many forms. This chapter will cover some of the most common guides people encounter, and the most common ways that your guides tend to get in touch. As you go, I invite you to take in whatever information resonates most clearly and strongly with you, and then to follow up on that by seeking out the guides that you feel the strongest affinity for. Trust me, they'll notice and get in touch.

Types of Guides

There is so much to learn and discover about our guides. It's definitely an ongoing process for me. You can call upon different types of guides when you need them most, and each of us has different forms of spirit guides. Some may feel closer affinities to animal guides, and others may feel more connected to certain angels or spirits of relatives who have passed away. As always, the best way to find out which guides call to you the strongest is to ask them. Open yourself up to the possibility of making contact, and you will.

Angels

WOO-WOO SCALE: ▲▲▲▲▲▲▲▲▲▲▲
EXPLORE-IT SCALE: ▲▲▲▲▲▲▲▲▲▲▲

The following chart outlines a few earthly elements the angels are connected to.[3] This can help you call upon whatever angel you feel best suits your needs.

Archangel Michael	**Archangel Gabriel**	**Archangel Raphael**	**Archangel Uriel**
Angel of protection	Angel of birth, parenting, and communication	Angel of healing and protector of travelers	Archangel of sinners and music
Represents: Love **Element:** Fire **Direction:** South **Season:** Autumn **Color:** Red (although a lot of people also associate this angel with blue) **Zodiac signs:** Aries, Leo, and Sagittarius	**Represents:** Overcoming doubts and fears **Element:** Water **Direction:** West **Season:** Winter **Color:** Emerald **Zodiac signs:** Cancer, Scorpio, and Pisces	**Represents:** Healing **Element:** Air **Direction:** East **Season:** Spring **Color:** Blue (lots of people also associate green with Raphael's healing) **Zodiac signs:** Gemini, Libra, and Aquarius	**Represents:** Clear thinking **Element:** Earth **Direction:** North **Season:** Summer **Color:** White **Zodiac signs:** Taurus, Virgo, and Capricorn

"Angels light the way. Angels do not begrudge anyone anything, angels do not tear down, angels do not compete, angels do not constrict their hearts, angels do not fear. That's why they sing and that's how they fly. We, of course, are only angels in disguise."

>**Marianne Williamson**

Spirit Animals

WOO–WOO SCALE: ▲▲▲▲▲▲▲▲▲△
EXPLORE–IT SCALE: ▲▲▲▲▲▲△△△△

Spirit animals are another form of guide that resonates with some Soul Searchers. It's not uncommon for a Soul Searcher to feel an affinity to an animal—a connection, something that draws them in. It may have been your favorite animal from childhood, a favorite pet, or perhaps an animal you have had repeated sightings or have dreamed of. Our guides present themselves to us how we are willing to see them, and it is natural for many Soul Searchers to connect with their guides through the face of an animal. Pay close attention to the animals in your life, as this may well be the way your guides trying to connect with, protect, and lead you through trouble. Below is a list of some common animal spirit guides and what they symbolize.[4]

Bear

The bear is one of the most powerful animals in the spirit-guide realm. This guide is in tune with emotional and physical healing and likely to be connected with Soul Searchers who feel a deep connection to the earth and the outdoors.

Butterfly

The butterfly is a symbol of transformation. The butterfly guide will appear throughout times of life change and development, and with the guidance of the butterfly, transition through these changes will come with more ease and grace.

Cat

The cat spirit animal is the symbol of curiosity, adventure, and independence. The cat can also represent the art of patience and wholeness.

Deer

The deer spirit guide is generally seen by sensitive, highly intuitive Soul Searchers who are extremely spiritual. People connected to this animal are confident and successful while also being gentle and graceful.

Dove

The dove represents peace and, as a spirit guide, symbolizes blessings and new beginnings to help the worried or stressed mind find peace.

Dolphin

The dolphin spirit guide represents playful wisdom. Often dolphins are spiritual teachers or help communicate as messengers for other guides.

Elephant

The elephant (my spirit animal) symbolizes wisdom, gentleness, and spiritual understanding. Quite often Soul Searchers that are set to work in a humanitarian capacity connect with the elephant spirit guide.

Frog

The frog is the spirit guide of healing, representing the process of healing both emotional and physical wounds. The frog usually connects with Soul Searchers who are on the journey to finding peace from suffering.

Fox

The fox is the guide of camouflage and symbolizes the art of detachment and living from our gut instincts to adapt and grow with our surroundings.

Horse

The horse is the guide of passion, drive, and an appetite for freedom and expression. The meaning of the horse can vary depending on how you see your horse, from tame to wild, working horse to racehorse.

Hawk

The hawk spirit guide represents perspective and the ability for you to see things from all sides—the perfect view for spiritual development.

Lion

The lion spirit guide represents heart and courage and connects with Soul Searchers who have a deep sense of authority and are born leaders.

Mouse

The mouse represents the art of detail and symbolizes scrutiny. The mouse guide reminds us not to overlook the smaller details in life.

Owl

The owl is the spirit guide that has the ability to see what others miss. Owls help Soul Searchers to see the deeper meaning of things and discover the hidden treasures in life.

Peacock

The peacock represents resurrection and connects with Soul Searchers who are in the process of transforming or reinventing themselves.

Turtle

The turtle is a highly spiritual guide that represents the journey toward wisdom, truth, understanding, and peace. The turtle also symbolizes a need to take a break, self-reflect, and check our grounding and connectedness to our spiritual path. Turtle spirit guides often connect with teachers.

Tiger

The tiger guide represents raw feelings and emotions. Tiger guides connect with Soul Searchers who are intuitive and good at following their instincts.

Wolf

The wolf is connected to intelligence, instinct, and freedom. The wolf may appear when you have mistrust in social situations and be a reminder for you to follow your primal instincts.

Ways Guides Communicate

Your guides will communicate with you by using something that gets your attention or makes sense to you. You may experience any number of the communication methods below, or something entirely unique to you and your personal guides. My guess is that at least a few of these methods will ring true to an experience or memory you have, and will serve as a jumping-off point to explore more.

Messengers

WOO–WOO SCALE: ▲▲▲▲▲▲▲▲△△△
EXPLORE–IT SCALE: ▲▲▲▲▲△△△△△△

Have you ever had someone come up to you out of the blue and say something quite deep and profound? Messengers can be friends or strangers bearing messages that are often exactly what you need to hear, when you need to hear it. These profound comments can be reassurances or clues from your guides. So if your Uncle Joe, who usually is sipping bourbon and sucking on a cigarette and is never comprehendible, ever, suddenly pipes up with an earth-shattering moment of clarity, making a comment that resonates deeply with you. I say take a moment to contemplate his heretofore unknown wisdom because who knows? Maybe it isn't Uncle Joe speaking . . . or even his bourbon. Just sayin'.

EXPLORE THIS!

The key benefit to connecting with a spirit animal is applying the wisdom and nature of this animal to your day-to-day life. Try to honor that animal through your behaviors and actions. Not to be Captain Obvious here, but try to focus on the positive attributes of the animal as much as you can. For example, if your spirit animal is a cat, channel that tenacious hunter's energy and independence…not its habit of sleeping on keyboards!

Numbers

WOO-WOO SCALE: ▲▲▲△△△△△△△△
EXPLORE-IT SCALE: ▲▲▲▲▲▲▲△△△

Have you ever looked at your watch at an exact time two or three days in a row? Or seen lots of the same repeating numbers seemingly everywhere you look? That's because each number has a different meaning behind it—a message from your guides. Begin to pay closer attention whenever you see a series of numbers. Somebody might be trying to tell you something. Some common recurring numbers and their messages are[5]:

1:11, 11:11

Known as the wishing hour, this is the time when your guides want you to focus on what you want rather than on what's in your way. Repeating ones often mean that you are manifesting quickly, and seek to remind you to be careful what you wish for.

2:22

You are worrying over spilled milk. You need to see that the things you are worrying about are in perfect order, so let go of all your stress and doubts and trust the process.

3:33

A group of threes symbolizes all of your guides surrounding you. They want to reassure you that you are not alone and that they are by your side, protecting and walking next to you.

4:44

Earth angels are prone to spotting fours, as this is the angels' number letting you know that they are walking with you—or reminding you that you are an earth angel yourself!

5:55

Fives symbolize change or a shift in your energy that can bring new opportunity and growth. Be open and aware of these shifts so you do not miss out on any opportunities that are unfolding ahead of you.

6:66

These numbers are a reflection that you are out of balance and possibly not following your soul's purpose. When all you see are sixes, it's time to refocus your goals and priorities, and check that you are always operating from a loving place—not out of greed, jealousy, or fear.

7:77

This is a high five from your guides! They are letting you know you are on the right path and that you should start to see rewards for following your soul's purpose.

8:88

Your guides show eights to let you know that the worst is over and that you are entering a new chapter of your life. In order to enter this new phase, you may have to let go of a few things you have been holding on to in order to progress.

9:99

Nine is a master number and reflects that you have a great skill, talent, or gift to share with the world. When you see nines, it is your guides' way of letting you know it is time to share yourself with those around you.

Just like we explored in the chapter on numerology, different combinations of numbers can also have different meanings. If you tend to see lots of number combinations and feel that this is one of the chosen channels through which your guides speak to you, then I recommend exploring different numerology books and angel number books. Some of my favorite numerology books are Michelle Buchanan's *The Numerology Guidebook* and Doreen Virtue's *Angel Numbers 101*. Get thee to thy local library or bookstore!

Angel Cards

WOO-WOO SCALE: ▲▲▲▲△△△△△△
EXPLORE-IT SCALE: ▲▲▲▲▲▲▲▲▲▲

These card decks are an excellent introduction to connecting with guides, as they are straightforward, easy to interpret (most coming with a how-to guide), and can be easily ordered online by doing a quick Google search. Pick a pack of angel cards by simply going to the pack that speaks to you the loudest. It may be the name of the deck, the pictures, the color—whatever it is, don't overthink it. Let the deck grab you!

Tarot Cards

WOO-WOO SCALE: ▲▲▲▲▲▲△△△△
EXPLORE-IT SCALE: ▲▲▲▲▲▲▲△△△

Most of us have at least heard of Tarot, right? Dating back to the fifteenth century, Tarot is the practice of reading a deck of cards (usually seventy-eight in number) for messages about one's life and future. The cards are generally divided into two categories: the Minor Arcana (cups, pentacles, swords, and wands) and Major Arcana (characters and identities such as The Fool, The Lovers, and The Hanged Man—these cards are also called the trumps). There are many different types and styles of Tarot cards, from old fashioned to modern, colorful to simple. Start with a simple deck and teach yourself the basics. If you're feeling ambitious or already have a background in Tarot, more traditional decks often intrigue older souls that have a deeper understanding or a closer connection to their spirituality. These cards tend to call for much more training, an ability to understand and interpret the cards, and they require openness when trying to understand the messages hidden within them. If you are drawn to the traditional Tarot, then I'd recommend learning more about them, as over time, you may find Angel Cards to be too simplistic for your communications with the spiritual realm.

> **EXPLORE THIS!**
> ≫———▷
> Always place a clear quartz in the box with your cards to cleanse them of any lingering energies, especially if other people touch them.

Crystal Pendulums

WOO-WOO SCALE: ▲▲▲▲▲▲▲▲△△
EXPLORE-IT SCALE: ▲▲▲▲▲▲△△△△

Yep, more crystals, y'all. A crystal hanging from a long string, also known as dowsing, can be used to connect with spirit guides. Almost any crystal can work, as long as it's a crystal that resonates with you. To begin, you need to "program" the crystal by letting it know your intent and clearly letting both the crystal and your guides know how to communicate—which way to swing for yes, which way for no, and so on. Many

Soul Searchers are surprised by crystal pendulums, thinking they will bring little communication from their guides, but then, with patience and clarity, finding the crystals swing in response to their questions.

Guided Meditations

WOO–WOO SCALE: ▲▲▲▲▲▲▲▲▲▲
EXPLORE–IT SCALE: ▲▲▲▲▲▲▲▲▲▲▲

These blew me away. It took me almost a year to really connect to guided meditations due to a mix of being time poor and having a constantly wandering mind, but man, was it worth the effort once I finally settled down long enough to give it a shot. Guided meditations are best experienced with headphones to completely block out any outside interference and to help quiet and soothe the mind. Also, do these without any potential distractions, so the cat and the kids should not be in the room with you. Believe me, it is super-frustrating when you are midway through a guided meditation and Whiskers jumps onto your lap and starts meowing at you. (And no, that does not mean your cat is automatically your spirit guide . . . though most cats, I'm pretty sure, would like you to think so.)

In most guided meditations (on CD, DVD, or online), a calming voice will talk you through relaxing your body and your breathing, and then on an adventure into your inner world. Whatever you see, feel, hear, smell, and taste (yes, even the last two) are clues from your guides. I get shivers and often a few simple words gifted to me from my guides, for example. Once, I even heard two children giggling and saying, "Hello, Mommy" to me! If you are patient, relaxed to the point that you come out of the meditation and don't know if it was a dream or not, and you invite your guides in to speak with you while you are in this state—sometimes with something as

EXPLORE THIS!

Head back to chapter 2 and read up on crystals and gemstones. Make sure you identify which ones resonate with you the most; then get online or go to your local mystical menagerie shop and pick up a couple.

EXPLORE THIS!

There is a wide range of free guided meditations available if you do some poking around. The key is finding a voice that makes you feel settled and connected—definitely not one that irritates you—which can be harder than it sounds. Hunting high and low for one that works for you is worth the effort. If you need a starting point, check out the Soul Searching Extras at the end of this book for some recommended meditations from my own library.

simple as a hello—I promise you that you will feel some level of deeper spiritual satisfaction upon reemerging from your guided meditations.

EXPLORE THIS!

⟫⟫⟫————————⟶

Take a peek at your smart-phone's app store and search for angel or Tarot apps—they're out there! Remember, we modern-day Soul Searchers can make all the distracting, ever-present technology work for our minds, bod-ies, and souls in tangible ways. While you're at it, check out some medita-tion apps too, so you can squeeze a guided medi-tation session into your lunch break or in right before you go to bed. Your guides are waiting for you to tune in.

Electronics

WOO-WOO SCALE: ▲▲▲▲▲△△△△△△
EXPLORE-IT SCALE: ▲▲▲▲▲▲▲△△△

Yep, your guides can tap into power sources—they are, after all, made up of energy. Ever notice a flickering light in your home or as you drive down a quiet street, or a particular song that pops on the radio, or something on TV you just happen to see and it seems super-serendipitous? These are your guides personalizing your pro-graming from the spirit realm.

> "We build our energy and center ourselves in our situations, in the questions we have, then we receive some form of intuitive guidance, an idea of where to go or what to do, and then coincidences occur to allow us to move in that direction."
> **❯James Redfield[6]**

The plainest and most effective way I can recommend think-ing about your angel or spirit guides is quite simply this: change out your shadow for your spirit. Your shadow already follows you wherever you go—it's with you every step of the way; even when you forget it's there or turn your back on it, no matter what, it will always be right there with you, on your soul-searching journey, whether you choose to acknowledge it or not. So stop and say hi once in a while. Start a conversation. See what speaks to you. As with many things in life, a simple hello is always a good start.

"WE DO HAVE THE ABILITY TO MANIFEST THINGS, BUT OUR PURPOSE, OUR END, OUR LEGACY IS ALSO CONTROLLED BY OUR DESTINY. SO FOCUS ON WHAT COMES EASY—THAT IS YOUR DESTINED LIFE."

YOUR AKASHIC RECORDS AND PAST LIVES

Ever had a matrix moment? A moment where you felt like you have cracked the code of life, clocked time, or entered into a wormhole to the past. A bit too dramatic for you? How about just a déjavu? This, dear soul, is yet another sign of your spiritual awakening.

Akashic Records and Past Lives

WOO-WOO SCALE: ▲▲▲▲▲▲▲▲▲▲△△
EXPLORE-IT SCALE: ▲▲▲▲▲△△△△△

The Akashic Records, also known as "The Book of Life,"[1] are something I stumbled across when I was traveling—or as we like to call it, soul searching. I was living in Spain and overheard two English women talking about the records of our souls. I leaned in. Feeling homesick, just hearing English had initially drawn my attention, but now I leaned in to eavesdrop in spite of myself. The more

I listened, the more curious I grew, and I was left wanting more information to better understand these so-called "records." I hurried home along the cobblestone footpaths of Mallorca, Spain—a small Mediterranean island I was calling home mid-soul search—so frantically that I almost bowled over a tiny Spanish nun, so eager was I to find out more about what I'd heard.

> "Something deeply hidden had to be behind things."
> **>Albert Einstein**

Once back in my lodgings, I consulted the source, the oracle, knower of all things, the one guide we all collectively have in common—Google, our omnipresent digital guru. (Side note: Google does *not* hold your Akashic Records. I'm sure it's on their to-do list because, hey, it is Google). What I discovered when I began researching was it was not the self-help or religious theory I had originally assumed but rather an ancient spiritual belief centered on our energy or *prana* (the Sanskrit word for "energy of life.")

The term *Akashic*[2] is tied to the Sanskrit word meaning—depending on who you ask—sky, ether, or essence, and for the context of this chapter, dates back to the eighteen hundreds and the theosophical inquiries of philosopher and occultist Helena Blavatsky.[3] The broader concept itself, however, dates back thousands of years. References in the Old Testament and beyond to a celestial recording of sorts of all life gave birth to the theory that there is a collective hub of knowledge—reference points to our souls' journeys through the universe. The Akashic Records are ledgers of our every action, reaction, thought, and belief—not just in this lifetime but every lifetime.[4] Think of these records as something that blossoms, welters, regrows, flowers, and seeds again differently every lifetime as we learn to grow through different cultures, experiences, journeys, lovers, and friends. This reflects the energy that makes up everything in the universe.

The Akashic Records are a cosmic recording of existence that is on another plane from us altogether, often called the astral plane—but that doesn't mean we can't access them here on little ole earth.[5] We'll get to that a little later on in the chapter.

Something else I found interesting when researching the Akashic Records is the concept of soul vows, or contracts.[6] It is said that, with each incarnation, we enter into certain agreements with the universe in order to experience different things on Earth. For example, in one life, you might be a carefree partier in order to truly understand the meaning of joy and excess. In another existence, you might live an opposite lifestyle, such as that of a monk or simply an introvert, in order to learn the nature of sacrifice or simplicity. As we reincarnate over and over again, our souls learn from each experience, and these experiences are written down in our Akashic Records.

According to this philosophy, we also have a number of exit points written into each lifetime.[7] These can be illnesses, accidents, or a number of other scenarios that result in us leaving that lifetime. In addition to mapping out our life's blueprints and exit points before we are reincarnated, we also make sacred contracts with entities on the other side to watch over us, protect us, help us, and advise us through our soul's earthly

EXPLORE THIS!

To get yourself thinking about the possibilities of what you may have experienced in a previous life, try an online past-life regression quiz for a bit of fun. Online quizzes are by no means always exhaustive or accurate, but can be an interesting starting point. If you'd like to learn more, I would advise you participate in a past-life regression with a professional.

journey. These entities are our guides that walk with us every step of the way through our journeys, helping teach, support, and care for us.

Some might call this destiny. I don't think that means we have no power over the choices we make in our lives, however. I think of the Akashic Records more as a handy cheat sheet for your life, instead of a set of predestined, rigid rules set down by the universe that you must follow.

Okay, enough about what they are—let's check out how to access and make sense of them. But wait a second, because here's a cool trick: You have already accessed them. You have, do, and will continue to do so whenever you want to because you know how to tap into this past-life knowledge already.

I can hear you thinking, *That's great, Emma, but, um, how . . . ?* Don't worry, friends, we're getting there. That flash of intuition, that familiar déjà vu, that gut feeling—whatever you want to call it, those little blips in your spiritual radar are all clues that you are connected to your divine wisdom, which is stored in the Akashic Records. Think of it like a direct link to your spiritual server.

People tend to access their Akashic Records through prayer, meditation, and even random flashes of insight. Many of us experience these glimpses of the Akashic Records on a daily basis. Some of us experience visions through daydreams, sights, sounds, thoughts, dreams, and meditation, through which we get a glimpse of an experience we haven't personally had before, a peek into a past life, or a strong feeling of connection to something, someone, or somewhere. There are often clues in your personality to your Akashic Record. I, for example, am a total water baby. I surf, dive, and have even worked on boats all over the world—basically, I feel most at home on the water. This gives me ties to Viking past lives and even to Atlantis. I love reading about these cultures and time periods, and feel a deep connection to them. By learning more about your past lives through your Akashic Records, you can learn to do it more proactively and become more aware of unexplained connections you have with people, places, and things in your life.

EXPLORE THIS!

Channel a wormhole to the past online—search for videos or audio of guided meditations for past-life regressions and find a voice or audio track that resonates with you. Lie comfortably on a couch or bed and listen to the track, your mind open, receptive, and judgment free, and your heart, mind, and body open to any smells, sounds, or visions that arise that may hold clues to a past life.

To get started, think about countries you have always had an affinity with, times in history that interest you, and the types of people you are attracted to, to help tap into clues about your past lives. If you feel like you are not connecting with anything in particular, I highly recommend a past-life regression. I got one done in Miami by a master hypnotist named Eli. Back then, I was curious but a total skeptic. I told Eli that I doubted his ability to hypnotize me, but the experience shocked me to the core—almost literally. Listening to Eli talk, relax me, and guide me through one of my past lives, I could feel my body being shaken as I transported back to a life I had never seen or connected with before. I could hear people speaking another language—it sounded Yugoslavian, from what I could recognize . . . and I could understand what they were saying! I was in a body; I could see my feet walking, smell what they smelled, hear what they heard. I wore tatty brown leather boots that barely kept my feet warm as I tried not to slip on the icy cobblestones. The streets were caked with dirty ice from sleet, and the sounds of horses and carts against the old road echoed in my ears. I could hear Eli whispering in the distant background the whole time, reminding me to pay attention to the people I saw and look in their eyes.

The memory jumped forward, and I was putting dinner on a bare, worn-down kitchen table. I had big, strong hands, and I was male. Sitting at the table were two little boys who sat patiently, quietly, clearly almost scared to speak or move. I grunted and pointed to the meal—a simple bowl of lumpy mashed potatoes. I felt guilty for being so cold, so loveless.

The memory jumped again, and this time I was leaning against a counter talking with a friend fluently in a foreign language that my waking mind still could not comprehend. I spoke of my deceased wife, and I spoke of running away. I shared that I hated what was left of my life and that I had no love to give my children or myself. I felt guilty for being so cold, so loveless.

The final jump took me back to the house. My hands were older, and the house was eerily silent. I gazed at pictures of my two boys, all grown up with families of their own now. I felt alone, and I felt like I *deserved* to be alone. I felt guilty for being so cold, so loveless . . .

When I woke, I was disappointed that I had been such a nincompoop of a man, a grumpy sort that I despise in this lifetime. I shared this with Eli, who explained and reminded me that I was a younger soul then, that we all have good and bad past lives that we learn different things from, and that I was shown those memories to help me with my purpose in this lifetime. "Later on in life, other memories will come through to serve you at that time," he said. "Don't be disappointed. Just look for the lessons." After a long silence, I shared the lesson I thought I'd learned: even when you have nothing left to give, there is always love to share. Since then I have smiled, tried to understand, and loved every grumpy old man that has grumbled or grunted at me, remembering, *Love them anyway, for you've never walked a mile in their shoes.*

So, again: What can *you* learn from lessons you have already experienced in past lives? Lots. And why should you care? Well, consider this, my fellow Soul Searcher: If we have the ability to access these experiences, why wouldn't we? Why wouldn't we be on the lookout for messages that might save us from making the same dumb mistakes over and over again, or signs that might shed light onto certain mysteries and questions that keep cropping up in our day-to-day existence? We can access, process, and make use of this divine knowledge base in two ways: through our instincts and through our intuition.

The things we learn through our experiences and that we come preprogrammed with because of evolution make up our instincts, like the reason the hairs on the back of your neck stand up when you're walking down a dark alley. Intuition's a bit fuzzier, but no less important. You know how you can sometimes just *feel* if someone's a good person or not just by shaking their hand? That's intuition. Both are influenced by our past lives.

Instinct is our ancestral knowledge handed down through evolution. It is our natural ability to know what is good and bad—we instinctively sense danger by the subtlest change in our environment. We can feel when things are not right. Our bodies are programed to go into fight-or-flight mode at the twitch of an eyelid. Think back to the age of the caveman—food, shelter, and safety were not givens, and we often had to fight to survive. Some of us still live in fight-or-flight mode all the time, regardless of whether we need to or not. This is often the mark of a young soul. Don't worry. That's not a bad thing! It just means that your soul's instincts haven't let your body and mind get off the express train for long enough to process and grow from your soul's caveman days. How do you help your soul transition from relying solely on instinct? Learn from your past lives and from the habits of older souls.

EXPLORE THIS!

Make a life map. Start with things you loved as a child—from trains to princesses—countries you have always wanted to travel to, and languages that have always interested you. Also take into consideration the types of people you may not like for any reason at all, and the things those people may have in common with each other. List your fears, your favorite animal, your favorite foods from different cultures, what you love doing in your spare time—whichever of your interests, memories, and proclivities seem to speak the loudest to you. Write it all out, and then see if you can connect any dots to past lives.

And how can you spot an old soul? The older soul has experienced many a rattled cage, and has lived to tell the tale over and over again. They've gone through a good deal of hurt, challenge, and hardship, and have used it to grow and become wiser instead of letting it get them down and curse them to repeating the same patterns over and over. An old soul takes the world's challenges in stride and learns to work around or with them, while a young soul fights them.

Think about the challenges in your life. Yep, I mean that one ex who still gets under your skin, those extra ten pounds you can't seem to shake, or that one nagging coworker who just won't stop telling you in exhaustive detail about his weekend-warrior exploits that you couldn't care less about. How do you handle these things? Do you let them continue to get to you, or do you actively look for ways to move past them and onto things that are more worth your divine time? Think about especially stressful situations, people, and objects. Do you allow yourself to be overwhelmed by your fight-or-flight response instead of facing them? I don't want to sound like I'm being judgmental here, because believe me, I was, and sometimes still am, there. The key is to not judge yourself. Go easy on your soul, it's still learning! But don't let it get away with any BS, either. This is how our souls grow.

What about intuition? I think that intuition's more directly connected to your soul's past lives than instinct, even though instinct definitely plays a big role too. Intuition's about knowing what we have no way of knowing. Huh? Yeah, I get that that sentence is a bit of an oxymoron. Intuition is that unexplained sense of pure knowing that you feel when everything inside of you tells you not to trust someone, to take a different route to work, to go up and talk to someone you wouldn't normally talk to—it's a direct message from your soul's past lives. For example, say you get an overwhelming gut feeling about a connection between two friends of yours who don't know each other and even though these two friends seem to have nothing in common. You can't explain it, but you just know they're going to get along famously, so you introduce them. Then, years later, these two friends get married. You sensed their connection way back when, and you still can't explain it, but it was just *there*. Your soul has a language of its own, and it'll speak to you if you listen.

"Trust your intuition and let your instincts guide your path."
>Gabrielle Bernstein

So how do we tell the difference between instinct and intuition? If you find yourself in a situation of inner conflict, allow yourself to step out of your head and gain some perspective. Simply pause a moment to breathe in silence, and then ask yourself: What is my soul trying to tell me? Am I reacting bodily (instinct) or spiritually (intuition)? Why? Remember, neither one of these things is good or bad—they simply are. Both instinct and intuition are mouthpieces through which your soul speaks. Listen to your soul's truth. By allowing your soul to speak, you will find that you feel much more supported in those times of inner conflict, and it will help give you clarity in tapping into what your past lives are trying to communicate.

"The reason why the universe is eternal is that it does not live for itself; it gives life to others as it transforms."

>**Lao Tzu**

Ultimately, we write the story of our souls through our thoughts, actions, reactions, emotions, and adventures through this life and all lives before and after it.

The Akashic Records give us a chance to change our perception of our past, present, and future. No one can change the past, but we can learn from it, and this includes learning from our past lives. Understanding where our souls came from and what they've experienced and learned makes our current trials and tribulations seem easier to deal with.

When we change the way we look at our life, our life changes. Our lives are like seeds, and they will only grow if we nurture them. The more nutrients, love, and positive energy we take in, the more we grow. So I challenge you to listen to your intuition and your instincts, but don't let one or the other rule you completely. Take heed of those moments when you just know your soul's speaking to you from across the astral plane. Understand that all the answers you seek are there for the taking in your soul's history, if only you remain curious and never stop asking questions. Use all the clues available to you to become the person you were destined to be at this point on your journey. Don't wait till the end to live your purpose.

"Beliefs have the power to create and the power to destroy. Human beings have the awesome ability to take any experience of their lives and create a meaning that disempowers them or one that can literally save their lives."

>**Tony Robbins**

YOUR LIGHT COUNCIL AND SOUL MATES

've always found it funny that even the people out there who don't believe in an afterlife, subscribe to a particular religion, or even consider themselves spiritual still believe in the concept of soul mates. It's *that* ingrained in our collective consciousness! Language and imagery about soul mates is in songs, movies, TV shows, books, advertising, you name it, not to mention it's included in many people's personal philosophies. Some believe we are reincarnated and our soul mates are destined to connect with us in each of our lifetimes. Others simply believe that there is "the one," that twin soul that completes us that we'll run into eventually in this lifetime. I bet you even have that friend who falls in love on every first date and always exclaims, "He is *totally* my soul mate!"

Still others believe in the concept of many possible soul mates, that there isn't just one person destined for us, but rather many who could potentially fill those shoes. The romantic notion of love can ignite our souls with a curiosity that awakens even the most practical Soul Searchers. The idea of experiencing a connection in love that is serendipitous, meaningful, and above all, spiritually profound, points us back to the original starting point of this book: the pursuit of goodness in all things.

As a Soul Searcher, you have been CEO of your soul's business for a long time now—including your love life. Think about it: like a CEO, you appoint the best people to advise you, guide you, and execute the jobs you need done in your life. You allocate the best lover to the position of partner, the best advisor to the position of best friend, and so on. This panel of advisors, guides, teachers, lovers, friends, and supporters is what I like to call your light council—people you have chosen to support and inspire your life and soul's journey.

Have you ever met someone and felt an overwhelming connection to him or her, one of those *have we met before?* moments? No, not as a cheesy pick-up line, but because you generally felt like you knew them from somewhere? This could be because that person is, on some level and in some way, a soul mate of yours. I'm not saying you should go and have intimate, passionate affairs with all of these people—whoa, nelly! I mean, you certainly *could*, but that's not looking at what and who a soul mate really is. Soul mates can be lovers, but they can also be the friends and family of your soul—souls who somehow share connections and experiences with you that perhaps stretch over centuries or that might have a sympathetic resonance that make you kindred spirits. And it is these soul kindred, people you are drawn to, confide in, are attracted to, love, and yes, sadly, at times even hate: these are the people who make up your light council.

Often we are destined to repeat lessons still unlearned from previous lifetimes and, in some cases, with the same souls. Where does the Big L—the lens through which most of us view soul mates—come in to this cosmic equation? I have personally spent most of my adult dating life in the quest of finding "the One." Upon stumbling upon my spirituality and my quest as a Soul Searcher, I was delighted when I learned from other Soul Searchers that you can have more than one soul mate in your lifetime.

One night during my travels, a group of girls from all corners of the globe had gathered to share wine and talk about love, life, and everything in between. By the second sip, heartbreak was the topic of discussion, and one of the girls was practically sobbing about how she had lost the "love of her life." Now, this is where things got interesting—about one third of the girls didn't believe in soul mates, one third believed in soul mates, and one third believed in multiple soul mates. Back then I was more of a the-One-is-out-there kind of a girl, but now I'm more of the latter, not in the least because of that night. One of the girls, an old soul, had been divorced and had read every spiritual breakup-put-your-life-back-together book in her local library. She explained that a soul mate is a person we have agreed to connect with in this lifetime to learn something from—a soul meeting with purpose. We can learn from many souls like this, female and male, through relationships and friendships alike. She finished, "It is a twin flame we only get one of, and they are the ones who are hardest to find."

This was an incredibly freeing and relaxing bit of information. I quickly realized that this raised the odds of me finding my soul mate. Cha-ching! However, I later learned that yes, while this was true, the universe also has your destiny in order, so no matter how you organize your light council or how hard you search, soul mates will not be delivered to your doorstep until you are ready to learn, experience, and grow at a particular time and in a particular way. Consequently, when you have learned everything there is to know from that soul mate, the relationship will organically come to an end, allowing you to continue to grow and find your next soul mate.

Stories of soul mates date back thousands of years. For many of us, it is an unspoken, untaught, inherited wisdom of knowing that assures us that our other half, or halves, exist. As children, we develop the awareness of romantic love through a combination of intuition, instinct, and external influences, from Disney movies to seeing our parents kiss each other. Plato wrote in his *Symposium* that we have been searching for our soul mates since Zeus struck all humans—who, according to the story, were originally created with four legs, four arms, and a head with two faces—in half. People aspired to conquer the gods, and the gods retaliated by literally splitting human beings in two, dooming them to forever wander the world searching for their other half. Splitting people's bodies and souls meant that humans would be more focused on finding their matching souls rather than taking over the heavens.[1] Think about how much time you have spent looking for a partner or twin soul in life. Well played, Zeus, you big jerk.

Throughout our existence on this planet, romance has been intertwined with spirituality, and they both involve and can bring us wholeness, connection, and fulfillment. Many of us are torn between great love and heartbreak throughout our lives. The Buddhists believe that attachment is the root of our anguish—attachment to things, to outcomes, to people. In fact, many believe that sexual love is an obstacle on the path to enlightenment. But all religions highlight the power of love in some way—both the positive and the negative aspects of it. One thing is certain: we cannot live without love, romantic or otherwise. As Soul Searchers, our purpose is to search, find, and appreciate the highs, lows, and lessons of love as we walk our spiritual path.

> "Your task is not to seek for love, but merely to seek and find all the barriers within yourself that you have built against it."
>
> **>Rumi**

Ancient Egyptians believed that the spirit or soul was carried in the breath, and that a kiss united souls.[2] The story of Zeus and the splitting of the human soul implies that true oneness is now found through intercourse, a physical connection of two bodies. Saint Augustine believed he was in "love with love," and sought to help people by teaching the difference between love and lust, which he saw as a line between indulgence (lust) and a mutual return to care for and be cared for in return (love). He found love through his relationship with spirituality.

So what is your soul's personal journey with love? Have you learned from your lessons and relationships, or are you in a rut and repeat the same mistakes, attracting the same type of souls and relationships while never finding your soul mates? You will continue to experience the same thing in many different kinds of ways until you have mastered the lessons your spirit is destined to learn. For example, if you need to learn trust, your trust will keep being tried and tested during your relationships. The same goes for patience, faithfulness, selflessness, compassion—any attribute your soul feels it is lacking. So do yourself a huge favor and be open to learning from these experiences. This is the path that leads to opening up your heart and soul to your light council and soul mates.

"Being deeply loved by someone gives you strength, while loving someone deeply gives you courage."

>**Lao Tzu**

A Personal Lesson

In the spirit of opening up our hearts, I thought it important to share the "doomed" cycle of love I experienced before I got spat out the other side a wiser woman. Ever since I was quite young, I found myself around men who had been, well, sneaky, for lack of a better word. They lied, kept secrets, and were crafty masterminds at pushing my buttons, touching my weak points, and hurting me. If they weren't what we will classify as "bad boys" exactly, then they were too intense, too needy, or too attentive, which resulted in me completely losing interest altogether. In essence, there was no balance to my relationships.

I had convinced myself that the barriers I was facing in love and having a balanced relationship were all just part and parcel of relationships, and so I committed myself to relationship after relationship that lacked connection, depth, understanding, and most important of all, love. During one such partnership, the universe tried to help me realize that my relationship was no longer serving me by deliberately making the road rocky—we had constant arguments and challenges, and nothing seemed to be easy or natural or even fun. I was happy maybe 10 percent of the time. It took the possibility of marriage—and the subsequent "*nooooooooooooo!*" from my soul—for me to shake myself out of it, pull out of the engagement, and walk away from someone whom I did love in some ways, but who wasn't a soul mate.

There was a series of signs that helped guide me to leaving, some more obvious than others. The first was a reading from an astrologer who warned of my approaching Saturn Return. He mentioned that anything I had gut reservations about would come to a head, and that unless I faced it, I would be doomed to repeat it. When he said that to me, my soul screamed, "Emma, it's over!"

"What's over?" I asked myself, knowing in my heart what my soul was getting at but not yet ready to face it head-on. "Your relationship," said my soul, "but you already knew that, didn't you?" The second was an angel-card reading that I pulled the night before I finally left. The card was simple, loud, and clear. The card read: "Time to go." No room for misinterpretation there. The final sign was a song that came on the radio when I was driving away, leaving my partner. The lyrics "we are done" repeated over and over in a very happy, upbeat melody that made me feel like I was back on track to finding my twin soul, despite the pain I was in at that moment. It had taken some doing, but I'd broken the cycle.

These days, it can be pretty tough to find your soul mate. Sure, internet dating, Tinder, singles clubs, and the like can be helpful, but with all the noise and pressure and anxiety surrounding finding a mate, it can get exhausting! The trick, I think, is to focus less on things like the constraints of time and the expectations of society or your family, and more on seeking out souls that resonate with yours. Sign up for some classes, join a sports team or a book club, take a diving class, learn a language, go on a retreat or hike—put yourself in the path of like-minded souls and see what happens. One thing's for damn sure: if you never try, you'll never know.

In the spirit of sharing wisdom with my fellow Soul (mate) Searchers, I have shared my personal list of what I put in my diary below. I hope that these words might help inspire you in your quest to find what you are searching for in a partner. I wrote this list just four days before it manifested into a partner. When he entered my life, my jaw

EXPLORE THIS!

Write down a list of attributes you're looking for in a soul mate. Be specific and clear about what you do and don't want, will and won't put up with, and what are your must haves or deal breakers. Before you go out for drinks with friends or hit up your local Sunday-morning Frisbee golf practice, read over your list to keep it fresh in your mind. Spy somebody who's exuding some of those traits? Strike up a conversation and see where it leads. Remember: you only receive what you believe you deserve, so don't sell yourself short. Believe that you deserve someone amazing? You bet your ass you do! And the universe will listen and deliver if you don't compromise on putting what you know you deserve first.

hit the ground—not only because he was everything on my list, but also because I felt the universe had also supersized my order and added whipped cream, sprinkles, and a cherry on top as a reward for putting my priorities front and center. Get writing, friends, and once you write your list, be prepared for the universe to deliver.

My soul mate—or even better, twin flame—has these qualities, and I ask the universe to please connect me with him.

▷ RESPECTFUL
▷ LOVING
▷ TENDER
▷ LOYAL
▷ HONEST
▷ ADMIRING
▷ ROMANTIC
▷ THOUGHTFUL
▷ ACTIVE
▷ CULTURED
▷ WANTS KIDS
▷ SUPPORTIVE
▷ UNDERSTANDING
▷ MUTUAL LOVE FOR THE WATER
▷ MUTUAL LOVE FOR THE ENVIRONMENT AND ANIMALS
▷ FUNNY, HAS TO MAKE ME LAUGH
▷ SOUL MATE, HAVE A SPECIAL CONNECTION
▷ SUCCESSFUL, HAS TO LOVE WHAT THEY DO
▷ OPEN TO SPIRITUALITY
▷ A BIT OF A CAVEMAN, MASCULINE, AND A FIVE-O'CLOCK SHADOW OR BEARD IS PREFERABLE (MORE OF A WANT THAN A NEED THERE, BUT STILL!)

Let's not stop with list making, friends. We've got a long way to go yet. There are also a few things you can do to help keep your energy levels high, so you are attracting people on the same energy level. Here are a few tips to get you going and keep you going on your search.

Heart Mantra

WOO-WOO SCALE: ▲▲▲▲▲▲▲▲△△△
EXPLORE-IT SCALE: ▲▲▲▲▲▲▲△△△△

As we learned in Part I, affirmations and mantras are powerful! Think of them as magic spells—chants sent out to the universe that awaken, dust off, and kick-start your wish-making campaign. You can simply think it to yourself, speak it to yourself, or write it down and keep it by a mirror as a reminder sent to you at a certain time every day (preferably at 11:11, the wishing hour). Any way you do it, make sure you focus on opening, healing, and loving yourself first and foremost. It sounds a little hokey, sure, but loving yourself is truly the first step toward finding the love you seek elsewhere.

Some good examples for heart mantras are:

I open up my heart to receiving love.
I deserve love.
I create the love I wish to receive.
Love flows easily and naturally to and from me.
I am love.

Heart Opener/Wheel Pose

WOO-WOO SCALE: ▲▲△△△△△△△△△
EXPLORE-IT SCALE: ▲▲▲▲▲▲▲▲▲△

This is a goody if you are a doer rather than a thinker. You can jump-start your heart back into action. In yoga, the Heart Pose, also known as Wheel Pose, is when you lie on your back and bring your heels in close to your buttocks and the palms of your hands onto the floor under your shoulders and lift your body up off the floor, arching your body into the shape of a bridge. This position opens up the heart chakra and helps to stimulate blood flow, and relax and recharge the body's heart energy center.

Heartstrings

WOO-WOO SCALE: ▲▲▲▲▲△△△△△△
EXPLORE-IT SCALE: ▲▲▲▲▲▲▲▲▲△

What pulls at your heartstrings and makes them sing? Keep an ear out for music that has messages in it about what to do, not do, where to go, how to be, and how to see, because these musical messages are your guides giving you clues to help find your soul mate. Think of it like a musical treasure hunt. Many guides have a great sense of humor and will know what will resonate, or "sing," to you, so do yourself a favor and listen to music with your gut instead of your ears. One time, while readying myself to go out, I had superbad pre-date jitters and had gone through everything in my wardrobe in search of a "statement" first-date outfit, when a song came on with lyrics about an angel in blue jeans. I wore jeans. It was a great date, and I felt gorgeous.

Heart Feng Shui

WOO-WOO SCALE: ▲▲▲▲▲▲▲▲△△△
EXPLORE-IT SCALE: ▲▲▲▲▲▲▲▲△△△

Remember back in the chapter on Feng Shui, how what we put in the rear right corner of a room is what we attract into our relationships and love life? This has never been truer than in the context of the search for your soul mate.

EXPLORE THIS!

Stand facing in from your doorway and pay attention to what is in the far right corner of your room. Now think about what you want in a partnership. Love, passion, tenderness, support, adventure? You could put anything there from travel books if you want a partner who likes to explore, your surfboards or sports gear if you want an action-packed relationship, a book of famous love letters, your soul-mate wish list, and more. Personal tip: place a clear quartz crystal there to help clear out any negative energy from your past relationships and cleanse the path into your new one. That's the great thing about many of these spiritual practices we're exploring; you can mix and match all you want!

Love without Need for Return

WOO-WOO SCALE: ▲▲▲▲▲▲▲▲▲▲
EXPLORE-IT SCALE: ▲▲▲▲▲▲▲▲▲▲▲

We are lonely when we lack love, so naturally we search ways to get our needs met. We ache because we feel something is missing in our lives, and this causes us to fold inward on ourselves instead of reaching out. While this is a natural way to react, it's never gonna get us anywhere positive in the long run.

If you are lonely, longing, aching, heartbroken, or generally just in a crap place where love's concerned, I have one piece of advice for you: become a love slut. Um, excuse me? Okay, that came out a little wrong . . . but the sentiment stands. Offer your love, compliments, smile, and positivity to as many people as you can, as often as you can. You get back what you put out into the world, and eventually your positive energy will bring positive things back into your life like a cosmic boomerang. The key here is also to detach yourself from what you expect to receive in return as well. You know how you always find something you're looking for when you're not actively looking, or something drops into your lap that you've sorely needed for a long time when you're least expecting it? That's how this works too. Put your heart forward, and good things and people will gravitate toward and into your life.

So, feeling loved up? Aww, you big softy, you. The most important role of a Soul Searcher is to never stop seeking and to never stop believing, so if you have given up on finding your soul mate or twin flame, then boo hiss to that, my friend! Okay, I can't stay mad at you—but let's be honest. If I were in front of you right now, I would grab you by both of your shoulders and give you a shake—a friendly one; no teeth rattling to be had here. Why? To check if you're *awake*. Not just your-eyes-open awake, but really, truly awake—in your body, your mind, and your spirit. This is how we must be in order to welcome our soul mates into our lives. So keep your eyes, mind, and heart open; put it out there, think about it, wish it, will it, and make it so. One last confession of a fellow soul-mate searcher before we move on—remember how I told you that I made that list, and then I found my soul mate and twin flame? Well, guess where I found him? This stays between us . . . promise? Tinder. So go on, put yourself on the soul-mate market and turn on your heart's "room available" sign. And promise me one thing: that you'll never stop searching.

"One is loved because one is loved. No reason is needed for loving."
>Paulo Coelho

YOUR PROTECTION CEREMONIES

As a Soul Searcher, you will be operating at a higher vibration in your daily life than a lot of folks around you, and that's okay. Some will feel your higher vibration and be attracted to and curious about your vibes as you pull them into your bliss. Some, however, will not. Some will scoff at you, roll their eyes, and move along. Not everyone's destiny includes spiritual enlightenment through everyday practice like yours, and those are the people you have to let go on their way with no harm done to either party.

Sometimes, though, no matter how hard you try, that negative energy—whether from individuals, events, or sometimes even the world at large—can get you feeling down on yourself and distract you from your soul search. As with all things in life, everything must come in balance, so this chapter seeks to help you manage and protect yourself from any negative or dark energy that you may encounter in your day-to-day life.

"People take different roads seeking fulfillment and happiness. Just because they're not on your road doesn't mean they've gotten lost."
>His Holiness the Dalai Lama

One of the things I was confronted with when writing this book was the often-judgmental opinions of others—usually from people I least expected it from. The most accurate way I can think to describe the feeling it engendered in me is to draw an analogy to how it feels when you're a child and an adult looks at you like you've done something they don't approve of—not necessarily something bad, just something they don't feel is worth your time and energy. Sure, it might not hurt like a physical blow, but it can still be damaging to the soul. I could feel the hit, like a tsunami of negativity washing over me, drowning me.

Please know that while you explore and discover this new sense of spirituality and start to see the world in a lighter, brighter, broader way, that there are people—even spiritual people—who may feel threatened by your light and seek to challenge your views and practices. Let them. The key thing to remember—and I recommend making this your mantra for when you are confronted with this sort of negativity—is that, while we may walk some paths together, our spiritual journeys are our own. In fact, I would argue that someone who tells you that your approach to spirituality is wrong is not a spiritual person at all. People's opinions and views on you or your spirituality have nothing to do with you, so just let them be—as hard as that can be sometimes! As author Paulo Coelho said, "This is the reason that critics don't hurt me, because it is me. If it was not me, if I was pretending to be someone else, then this could unbalance my world, but I know who I am."[1]

One of the most groundbreaking things I was taught while exploring my spirituality was protection techniques. It blew my mind to learn that you could pretty much tap into a cosmic superpower that made you invisible, impenetrable, and invincible to all the naysayers, grumps, and negative-energy purveyors out there. My friends and I call it "white lighting." These techniques will transform your approach to energy vampires and, in my experience, have come in very handy for office-place harmony, family gatherings such as the holidays, and handling conflict or confrontation of any kind.

Angel Protection

WOO-WOO SCALE: ▲▲▲▲▲▲▲▲▲▲
EXPLORE-IT SCALE: ▲▲▲▲▲▲▲▲▲▲

This one is as simple as giving a shout-out to your guides to protect you. Archangel Michael is the man when it comes to protection, so if you are really feeling like you need backup, ask for him to stick with you. You can ask him to wrap his wings around you to help shield you from any attacks and negativity, or even to watch over you as you travel or simply move through your day. Another great way to seek out protection of this sort is to go back to your deck of angel cards. Use them to ground yourself into a stable place and reconnect with your angelic guides.

Light Protection

WOO-WOO SCALE: ▲▲▲▲▲▲▲▲▲▲
EXPLORE-IT SCALE: ▲▲▲▲▲▲▲▲▲▲

There are all different shades and colors of light protection, similar to the various colors of auras and chakras. Each color helps protect us in different ways. I like to sneak off to a quiet, private space and reach my hands up high above my head, palms touching, and visualize a beam of light shooting out of my fingertips to the heavens; then, when I can see the color I need in that particular moment, I slowly open my hands, creating a big, slow circle of light that encompasses me. Sometimes my fingertips even tingle as I do it!

Here are some colors to visualize, thus inviting in positive, protective energy:

White Light—The purist of the pure, white light is your go-to color for the ultimate protection, as nothing gets through white light. You can use it to surround yourself, your car, home, or other material possessions, and it will keep both you and them safe from harm and robbery.

Pink Light—Imagine yourself in a love bubble; pink light is the love protection shield so only love can touch you. Pink light is a great shield when we are surrounded by negative, passive-aggressive people, or even bullies.

Green Light—Green represents healing and is used as first aid for people who are ill, run down, or in need of some extra energy and support. Green is also the color of Archangel Raphael—an angel of healing—so when you see or think green, he usually makes an appearance too.

EXPLORE THIS!

If light protection resonates with you, I recommend reading more about the different colors, shields, balls, and pyramids you can use to help protect yourself. The examples here are three simple introductory color shields that everyone should know, but there are a variety of shields out there, so I highly recommend seeking out other methods and protection techniques that can help serve you in your day-to-day life, because the colors and techniques are practically endless.[2]

Crystal and Gemstone Protection

WOO-WOO SCALE: ▲▲▲▲▲▲▲▲▲▲▲
EXPLORE-IT SCALE: ▲▲▲▲▲▲▲▲▲▲▲

EXPLORE THIS!

Pick a crystal that speaks to you in a specific way (love, courage, peace— whatever your soul craves most at this moment), and then buy two. Give the other crystal to a friend, a lover, or a family member. Take the plunge and be honest about what this crystal means both to you and what it means to have an important person in your life owning the stone's twin. A friend of mine gave her mother a small rose quartz heart to carry around in her purse after her mother suffered (and thankfully made a full recovery from) a heart attack. My friend carries around an identical one in her purse, so their hearts are always connected!

Say it with me, guys: the more crystals, the better! Like light protection, the list of crystal and gemstone protection options is a long one, so I also recommend diving deeper into the world of crystal protection if it resonates with you. Crystal protection can be a really great protective practice to work into your daily routine because it is nearly effortless—you can keep a crystal in your pocket, handbag, by your bedside table, or even wear one on you to help shield you from any negativity or hurtful situations. Here are several examples to get you started. You can also hop back to chapter 2 on crystals and gemstones to get you on the right path.

Amber—Used by ancient Romans to bring about positive outcomes in battle, amber is a stone that attracts good luck and dissolves negative energy so is a great stone for daily protection.

Agate—As good for Feng Shui in the home or workspace as it is good for balancing energies and clearing perception while also clearing and protecting against negative energies. Agate is also an especially good stone for protection of children.

Tigereye—My personal favorite, tigereye is an energizing stone that radiates clearing, balancing, and protective energy in the form of a watchful eye so that you always feel grounded, secure, and stable, no matter what your day may bring.

Clear Quartz—If your bedroom does not have a clear quartz, I want you to put this book down and go buy one. Hang it in your window, so the sun can charge it daily, helping to clear your bedroom from any negative energy so that your room is always a clear, safe, harmonious sanctuary for you to rest in.

Rose Quartz—Carry rose quartz with you or place it under your pillow to welcome unconditional love in all aspects of your life. Rose quartz is tied to the heart chakra, and supports and enhances all kinds of love, from sexual and romantic to familial and community centered.

Cutting the Cord on Negativity

WOO–WOO SCALE: ▲▲▲▲▲▲▲▲▲△△
EXPLORE–IT SCALE: ▲▲▲▲▲▲▲▲▲▲

The need to protect ourselves is driven by our instinctual fight-or-flight response, when our minds, bodies, and souls tell us a person or situation is potentially harmful. Fear is a common energy drain for us all, and it is important we cut down on any associations we may have to fear in order to ensure we are not constantly being unnecessarily drained of energy.

An energetic cord is like an emotional umbilical cord that runs between you and the people in your life. These are natural, and can be very positive and nurturing; however, it is important to do some cord trimming every now and again to ensure people who are no longer serving us are no longer connected to us energetically. In order for us to cut an energetic cord, we must . . . simply let go! Release it, toss it, delete it, discard it. Turn it to dust: POOF! You can call upon your guides to help you make this change, or simply say a small prayer or mantra to yourself as you burn some cleansing sage, signifying the release of the negativity in your life that's been bringing you down. You must think of the person you no longer want to be connected to while enacting whatever ceremonial uncoupling you choose to do, and ask that the cord be cut, preferably aloud, so that your guides can hear you and lend a helping hand.

> "We must assume every event has significance and contains a message that pertains to our questions . . . this especially applies to what we used to call bad things . . . the challenge is to find the silver lining in every event, no matter how negative."
> **>James Redfield**

While negativity is obviously an icky business, we must remember that on our path toward spiritual goodness, there is always balance to be sought as well—happiness needs sadness, good energy needs bad energy, love even needs hate. As you take steps

EXPLORE THIS!

Saying that you're cutting a negative person out of your life is all well and good—and a very important step—but actually doing it? Honey, that's easier said than done. My advice is to be honest, even if it's hard and even if it hurts some feelings. Place the focus on you and your needs, not on the toxic person. For example, if you're cutting communication with an old friend who's turned into more of a frenemy, or a family member who's always caused you pain but whom you've never worked up the courage to tell off, try approaching it in these terms: "I have no wish to cause you pain or offend you, but what I need right now in my life is to separate myself from your energy in order to focus on my own growth and peace. Please be well, and know that I don't wish you any ill will."

to remove the negative influences in your life, you will be shocked by how different you feel in a very short amount of time. You will also be surprised by how obviously pervasive the negativity was, which is easier to see now that you've said good-bye to it and it's removed from your day-to-day existence. I encourage you to also challenge yourself to learn from these experiences so as not to repeat them later on down the road. Is there something you can learn from that guy at work you used to take your coffee breaks with who was always badmouthing your other coworkers? What about from your judgmental aunt who never had a nice thing to say about anyone who wasn't exactly like her? When you look at every situation, good or bad, as a lesson, they all become opportunities to learn rather than challenges to overcome.

You and I? We don't have time for anyone's bad vibes. Ours is the search for goodness, wholeness, and everyday spiritual bliss. Anyone who spends their energy challenging or attacking your love and light isn't deserving of it. Cutting yourself free from the tethers of negativity is a liberating and rewarding experience, as is the ability to be able to love, understand, and offer forgiveness to someone who is none the wiser. Your positive energy is your power. Use it wisely.

EXPLORE THIS!

Become a practitioner of everyday blessings. You don't have to be a priest or a healer to incorporate powerful blessings into your life. What are your most treasured possessions? Your surfboard? Offer up a little protective prayer to it before you head out into the waves. Your laptop? Who's to say it doesn't need a little positive energy directed its way? How about your great grandmother's collection of pressed flowers? Ask her to watch over and bless them with you, and thank her when she does. Your everyday blessings can incorporate aroma-therapy, your crystals and gemstones, you guides—whatever and whoever you feel will bring the most protective good to you and the things you care about. Experiment, have fun, and be blessed!

YOUR CELEBRATION

As we walk down the often-bumpy road of life, it's important to take time to celebrate, to let go, to combine the energies of your mind, body, and soul into one joyous whole. You have been grounding, meditating, and connecting with yourself to receive wisdom, guidance, and energy—now it's time to let some of that awesome energy out! Think of it as a two-way walkie-talkie: the message has been received; now you get to reply to the universe. *But how do I do it?* one might ask one's self. One of the best and, best of all, totally easy ways to do this is to just dive right in by immersing yourself with other people united in a common joy.

I totally get my joy sharing on by attending festivals, concerts, and other large events that bring together positive energy and people. For me, this is the easiest and most enjoyable way to incorporate celebration into my life. I also try to make room for small, everyday celebrations—something as tiny as

buying myself a beautiful new crystal or watching the clouds drift along in between my daily obligations is enough to remind me of my place in the universe, and how lucky I am to have it.

And, truly, there's nothing quite like feeling the collective pulse of so much positive energy in once place as you do when you're in the thick of a collective celebration. For me, it's been important to take a global perspective on this—there are amazing opportunities all over the globe to tap into this particular brand of collective celebration—and I encourage you to expand out of your locality and check it out . . . but don't kick yourself for not being able to travel to Brazil for Carnaval or hitchhike to Coachella. If there's a festival or show or gathering somewhere near you that's more practical for you to attend, focus on that. The energy will be just as good as if you traveled halfway around the world. Also, feel free to incorporate elements of global celebrations and traditions into your life. Draw on themes and ideologies from around the world to inspire and nurture your own daily celebrations.

Many people connect traveling with self-discovery and Soul Searching, so a trip or adventure might be something to think about as a component for your spiritual adventure. But, if a spiritual pilgrimage is not in the offing for you in the immediate future, there are still great lessons to be had without even having to get up off your seat right now. Just check out the list below, where you will find a variety of festivals, traditions, and celebrations from around the world for you to feast your spirit on.

Have a look; you never know what your next adventure might be! If something jumps out at you, think of it as a party invitation from your soul, worthy of an RSVP.

A Global Soul Celebration: Joy From Around the Globe

WOO-WOO SCALE: ▲▲▲▲▲▲▲▲▲▲▲
EXPLORE-IT SCALE: ▲▲▲▲▲▲▲▲▲▲▲

Unite your Body, Mind, and Spirit: The Wanderlust Festival (*USA, Canada, Australia, and New Zealand*)

The Wanderlust Festival brings together like-minded Soul Searchers through yoga, art, holistic healing, food, and wisdom with group meditation, various styles of yoga, international instructors, teachers, speakers, and bands to make for a menu that caters to every soul. The festival is all about discovery and stepping into the spiritual community, meeting like-minded souls, and trying new things. They call it "finding your true north" and, after experiencing this fest first hand on many occasions, it has my Soul Searcher seal of approval. While Wanderlust would blow your mind, if you cannot get to a festival, you can always join local yoga classes, meditation groups, or visit spiritual markets to connect with souls to learn, grow, and share your experiences and wisdom.

Offering Up Your Desires in a Shinto Temple (*Japan*)

In Japan, you can find Shinto temples that, for a small fee, allow people to draw and write out their desires on wooden plaques called *ema* and present them to the gods, called *kami*. Like any dream or goal, when we draw or write it down, it becomes more of a vision, something tangible, like we are physically turning it into our reality.

EXPLORE THIS!

Regardless of whether you make it to an actual temple in Japan or not, take a few minutes to write down your spiritual and personal goals on a piece of paper. Once you've compiled your list, go to a place that is sacred to you and have a conversation with your guides, offering up your desires to their influence.

Release Your Worries: Yi Peng (*Northern Thailand*)

The Yi Peng festival in Thailand celebrates the art of releasing your fears, doubts, and sorrows to the heavens by lighting a lantern and releasing it, letting it float away. Yi Peng refers to the full moon day in the second month according to the Lanna (northern Thai) lunar calendar—early November.

EXPLORE THIS!

Write your fears, worries, and baggage on a piece of paper. At nighttime, burn your piece of paper and watch the embers and ashes float toward the heavens, disappearing out of your life so you can focus on the continued soul search ahead of you. Be sure to do this on a wet night or during the fall or winter, so that nothing but your piece of paper catches fire!

Seek Forgiveness: Paryushan
(*held throughout India at Jain temples*)

Paryushan is an eight- to ten-day Jainist festival in India where people meditate and pray in a ceremony focusing on asking for and releasing forgiveness. During Paryushan, Janist monks often fast, meditate, and request forgiveness from each other for any offenses committed over the past year. It is believed to be the ultimate way to release hostility, anger, and to cleanse the soul of negativity.

EXPLORE THIS!

Write out all the crap you have buried inside of you, list out who you feel is responsible, and then write a forgiveness note to them. You don't have to do anything with the letter if you don't want to, but mentally forgive them all the same—this is the important part. You will feel a weight lift off your shoulders, and your energy will start to swing back toward the positive side of the cosmic pendulum right away.

Channel Your Inner Hippie: Coachella
(*Coachella Valley, California, USA*)

Music and art are two meditative and creative ways to express the soul. The Coachella festival encompasses everything free flowing and fun about modern-day life: communal music, community, art, dance, and all-around vibrant culture. If your soul craves liberation, freedom, and expression, Coachella is for you.

Allow Yourself Space to Grow:
Tu BiShvat Festival (*Israel*)

This Israeli festival begins early in the year and means "new year of the trees" in Hebrew. This holiday focuses on bringing the community together with the planting of trees to symbolize new beginnings and growth.

EXPLORE THIS!
<----«===--->

The act of planting a garden can be very therapeutic and is a great way to remind yourself that growth takes time. So get planting! Whether it's in your own backyard or in a community garden or urban tree initiative, as you grow into your spirituality, so too will the seeds, trees, and other green things you sow. Remind yourself that spirituality is an ever-evolving journey, a personal experience of growth that is unique to everyone.

Slow It Down: T'ai chi (*China*)

Think *meditation in motion* as you experience slow-moving, fluent stretches to help slow the mind and balance the body while awakening the soul. T'ai chi is an example of a tradition that helps to slow down the stress and pressure of everyday life and allow you the space to collect and recharge yourself.

EXPLORE THIS!
<----«===--->

Can't get to a class? Try YouTube-ing some starter moves and go from there. Once you're ready and if you have the opportunity, seek out a group class and get the added benefits of group energy and group meditation.

Be Grateful: Thanksgiving
(*USA, fourth Thursday in November*)

For folks in the United States, Thanksgiving represents a time to recognize family, friends, and other things one appreciates in one's life—and usually over an elaborate, shared meal. By taking a day to reflect on and appreciate the abundance and successes of their lives instead of focusing on things they lack, Americans recognize the importance of appreciating and actively celebrating what one has.

EXPLORE THIS!

When you focus on and cherish what you already have, you tend to get more of the good stuff—go figure. So stop wasting all that time and energy on desiring things, and take some time to take stock of what you already have and appreciate in your life.

Cleanse Yourself: Songkran Festival (*Thailand*)

Songkran—"astrological passage" in Sanskrit—is a fun, fresh way to kick off the New Year, which lands in April on the Thai calendar. The tradition includes the throwing of water—in cups, buckets, and even in water pistols!—to symbolize cleansing and a new start.

EXPLORE THIS!

Water is naturally cleansing—it can rebalance our chakras, relax, and calm us—so make some time to submerge yourself. Have a swim, a bath, or a shower and visualize your worries, stress, and fears literally washing off and away from you. Even better, grab some friends on a hot day, head to your local park, and have a water balloon fight!

Connect to Nature: Celebrate the Summer Solstice (*Ireland, Sweden, Finland, Norway, the United Kingdom*)

The Summer Solstice—also called Midsummer or St. John's Day—is a festival that marks the natural flow and transition of the seasons, specifically from spring to summer around the summer solstice. It is celebrated across the globe, and especially in many Northern European nations. For example, many people across Ireland throw midsummer carnivals, fairs, concerts, bonfires, and fireworks in the days leading up to or coinciding with Midsummer.

EXPLORE THIS!

On Midsummer's Eve—around June 20 or 21— organize a (legal!) bonfire with friends and celebrate.

Celebrate Life through Honoring Death: Día de los Muertos, aka Day of the Dead (*Mexico*)

The Mexican festival of *Día de los Muertos* celebrates the lives of loved ones who have passed on. The festival focuses on positivity, vibrancy, and joy instead of mourning. The event is an excellent reminder to all of us to live our life to the fullest and leave a legacy we would be proud of. What will your legacy be?

Expand Your Mind: Saraswati Day, aka Knowledge Day (*Bali*)

Observed in the fall, Balinese Hindus celebrate the goddess Saraswati by honoring her themes—knowledge, wisdom, and education—through offerings in schools, homes, and offices with flowers and incense. The celebration is a reminder that we can be as smart, wise, and spiritually curious as we choose to be and that our well of knowledge is bottomless. So go out, learn something new, and push yourself to keep growing and expanding your mind!

Spring-Clean Your Life: *Chun Jie* (Spring Festival, or Chinese New Year) (*China*)

Taking place from late January through early to mid-February, the Spring Festival in China is a time for renewal, change, transitions, and growth, and a time to allow for change and to make room for it. The festival is a time for people to cleanse, declutter, and rid their environment of anything unneeded or that no longer serves them.

Give and Expect Nothing in Return: Burning Man
(*Black Rock City, Nevada, USA*)

Burning Man's belief in radical self-expression, community, and selfless gifting is truly a thing to behold. Every year, the Nevada desert is transformed into an arts, cultural, and musical festival that welcomes all and hosts an ethos of generosity, creativity, and community—all elements vital to the development of a Soul Searcher. The festival welcomes radical creativity and will be sure to open your mind to new and exciting things that will help you express and develop yourself.

Visit Your Light Council:
The Third Day of Tet (*Vietnam*)

Teachers are honored in Vietnamese communities, and on the third day of the Vietnamese New Year, called Tet, they are visited and verbally thanked for the impact they have had on their life or the life of their children. Your light council of advisors, guides, and teachers can vary from angels to life coaches, and from mentors to spiritual friends, and you can choose to thank them verbally, write an email or text, or mentally send them thanks for the wisdom and love they have shared with you though your spiritual journey.

Fear Less: *N'gol* (land diving) (*Vanuatu*)

The N'gol ritual involves boys and men taking a "leap of faith" to face their fears as a right of passage and fertility ritual. Vines are strapped to the feet of the jumper who leaps off a man-made tower of sticks and branches before landing on the mud below, the vines helping to reduce impact.

EXPLORE THIS!

Now, please don't concoct your own bungee jumping platform—I can't see that ending well for anyone. Instead, think about something that stops you from fully living and make some choices to change that blockage in your life. Then take your leap of faith.

Face the Sun: Midsummer Festival (*Sweden*)

Vitamin D, anyone? In Sweden, the longest day of the year is celebrated with everyone simply enjoying the outdoors and taking time to be in nature and under the sun, if it's indeed shining that day. This is one of my favorite tools to re-center and ground myself, and it is so easy. Simply take your shoes off, go outside, stand on a patch of dirt or grass, and point your face at the sun. It actually feels like your batteries are charging!

Face Your Fears: La Mercè Festival (*Spain*)

Taking place in September, *La Mercè* is held in honor of Mare de Dèu de la Mercè, the patron saint of Barcelona. The festivities fill the streets of Barcelona with parades, folk dancing, and music. As the day darkens, so too do the celebrations, with hundreds of people dressed as devils walking the streets, setting off fireworks, waving pitchforks, and beating on drums, aiming to frighten the innocent. The festival is a great reminder for us to face our demons and confront our fears.

EXPLORE THIS!

Imagine your fears exploding like a firework and vanishing into vapor.

Give It Up: Ramadan (*Morocco*)

For Muslims in North Africa and around the world, Ramadan is a practice that reflects on the blessings in someone's life. For the holy month, from mid-June through mid-July, based on lunar cycles, the person must not eat or drink from dawn to dusk, fasting to show their thanks. Ramadan is similar to the Christian practice of Lent.

EXPLORE THIS!

Sometimes we need to give up something for us to truly understand what our life would be like without it, and to be grateful for our luck and sympathetic to others who maybe aren't so lucky. You could give up the internet, alcohol, or put a dollar a day away for a month to give to someone in need or to a worthy cause.

Live It Up: *Carnaval* (*Brazil*)

Yep, Brazilians sure know how to have a good time, and guess what? Spirituality is meant to be fun too! *Carnaval*, a festival held all over the world but most famously in Brazil, especially Rio, on the days leading up to Lent, is a euphoric celebration of diversity and self-expression, allowing everyone to love, enjoy, and celebrate themselves and each other through dance, music, community events, and parades. Make sure you follow the Brazilians' lead on this one. Wherever you are, whatever you're doing, make time to celebrate before things get serious!

Show Pride: Haka (*New Zealand*)

The Maori haka is a ceremonial dance used to intimidate, welcome, or congratulate people. Pretty versatile, huh? The haka, performed traditionally by men, unifies a team, group, or tribe of people through an ancient war song. Look up some haka videos on YouTube: it is definitely intimidating and also totally awesome!

EXPLORE THIS!

Think about your tribe—your family, a work unit, or a group of friends, and try to offer ways to uplift, unify, and motivate them through song. Take pride in spreading positivity and making others feel better after leaving your presence.

Make Time for Play: Holi (*India*)

Holi, taking place in March and also known as "the festival of colors," is a Hindu celebration in which colored powder is playfully thrown to color people's clothes, skin, and hair—it's even dusted on animal companions as well! Kicking off with a bonfire the night before *Holi* festivities begin, all ages take part in the festival, and festivities are a reflection of love, fun, and the vibrancy of life.

EXPLORE THIS!

When was the last time you had a worry-free, fun day that was all about being happy, positive, and playful? Introduce laughter back into your life if it's gone missing lately. Watch a funny movie, do something you loved doing when you were younger, dance and sing, or even get into a food fight!

Celebrating Soul Sisters and Brothers:
Ubuntu (*Southern Africa*)

The Nguni people of Southern Africa believe in the philosophy of *Ubuntu*—that we are only people through other people, and that our actions and behaviors in relation to others defines humanity. The presence of *Ubuntu* in day-to-day life ensures that generosity, selflessness, and moral responsibilities are always kept at the front of the mind.

EXPLORE THIS!

What do your actions say about you? Are you kind, compassionate, and giving? Try to offer your time, support, service, and love to others more freely—no strings attached.

Self-Love: Hygge (*Denmark*)

The Danes are always topping the charts on the happiness scale, so it is no surprise that they know how to indulge and nourish the soul. *Hygge* is about basic pleasures—lying in the sun, sitting by a fire, cuddling into a warm bed, or going off the grid for a few days to recharge and reconnect with nature. It's also about connecting with your fellow human beings in small but significant ways, and taking pleasure in and giving thanks for these connections.

EXPLORE THIS!

What recharges you and makes you feel like you have hit the reset button? A bath? A massage? A snuggle with your sweetie? Give yourself permission to self-love!

Ignite Your Light: Up Helly Aa (*Scotland*)

The Up Helly Aa festival is actually a variety of festivals that take place in winter across Scotland, especially in the Shetlands, which consist of parades through the streets with heritage costumes, flaming torches, and even burning Viking ships to remember and honor ancestry, history, and the life-giving nature of fire in the unforgiving winter months. It is a reminder to be proud of your roots and your life experiences, both good and bad.

EXPLORE THIS!

Take a day to reconnect with your ancestry. Ask family members if they have any special memories, objects, or wisdom they've gathered from your family's past.

Celebrate Stillness:
International Bali Meditators Festival (*Bali*)

Held once a year in Ubud, the festival brings yogis, meditators, healers, poets, musicians, and artists from across the globe where the barriers to different faiths, religions, practices, and lifestyles are brought down, so everyone can share wisdom, experiences, and practices with each other. It is the ultimate fusion of spirituality. Perfect for the Soul Searcher open to all beliefs and interested in learning kinetically about different styles of yoga, meditation, mantras, and prayer.

I'm sure that, by this time in our journey, the perks of being a Soul Searcher have made themselves abundantly clear. My hope is that you have had an awesome adventure as you discovered new things. Hopefully, all of your experimenting has lead you to a place where you feel informed and are able to see more deeply, love more deeply, and above all, know how to celebrate everything that life encompasses, welcoming exponential amounts of joy into your spirit as you go. On my soul search, I too experienced the benefits of actively seeking a path of discovery, regular wisdom injections from those I met along the way, and the glory of letting my hair down at many a celebration.

My parting challenge for this chapter is to do this: I ask you to mix in some festivities into your goals, your dreams, heck, even your holiday plans. Round up your light council and spiritual entourage if you need support, or fly solo. Once you open up your soul to merriment—in both the small, daily ways we all need more of and the big, bombastic, amphitheater excursions—you will organically meet people and find yourself surrounded by like-minded souls. Turn up the music, raise your hands in the air, and celebrate!

CONCLUSION: YOUR SOUL SEARCH

"The purpose of life, after all, is to love it, to taste experience to the utmost, to reach out eagerly and without fear for newer and richer experience."
>**Eleanor Roosevelt**

Look at you—all wised up and ready to venture out into the world with your arsenal of spiritual wisdom. You're graduating from spirit school! From here on out, you will continue to find a smorgasbord of spiritual enrichment everywhere you look because you now have the tools to spot and make use of life's buried spiritual treasure with your new bestie, your soul, as your guide.

I've got one more "Explore This!" for you. Ask yourself: What serves my personal spiritual journey right now?

It could be as simple as signing up for a few yoga classes; it could be a one-way ticket to the other side of the world. It may be an adventure like a surf camp or spiritual retreat, or it could even be as easy as tromping down to your local bookstore or library and picking out your next book. The trick is listening to your deeper self and actually hearing what your soul is trying to tell

you—and then doing it! Hopefully, you now have the tools to translate what it's been whispering or maybe even hollering at you all along.

Keeping up with the whole spiritual-growth/soul-searching stuff can be a little intimidating. You don't have to do it all at once. You can do it slowly, over time, and in little, bite-size pieces, or you can do it intermittently in giant-sized gulps, or a combo of the two. My point being that there is no destination, really; we can only truly say we've found the journey to . . . someplace that makes our souls feel right.

During my own journey, in order for me to really connect to my spirituality and myself as a spiritual being, I had to resign from my corporate job, bundle up my savings, sell everything I had to my name, and fly to the other side of the world, all on my own. I had to go via the freak-out route. It ended up being a good freak-out though, so I wouldn't change it for the world. What I do wish someone had told me back then is that the universe had my back all along, that I had guides by my side the whole time, and that I would eventually be rewarded for being brave enough to take that leap in the direction of my future, toward the unknown, into my new spiritual self. It would have also been nice to get a heads-up on the sweaty-yoga-butt thing.

"Wherever you go, go with all your heart."
>Confucius

Sweaty yoga butt or no, your soul search doesn't have to venture out of your living room if it doesn't want to. But please, promise your soul and yourself this—be honest, be brave, and be good to yourself!

Looking back, if I've learned a definitive thing, and end-all-be-all truism, it's that we are forever growing, learning, and expanding. Let the things you have learned here grow, give knowledge to, and expand your spiritual real estate, but don't make this book the final step in your spiritual expansion! Now that you've planted the seeds of spiritual awakening, you can continue to nourish your modern-day holistic lifestyle with new experiences and new wisdoms—and in doing so, your body will be healthier and more in balance, your thoughts will be more positive and centered, and your spirit will sing.

A final hope to share with you before we part. I hope, whatever your background, whatever your destiny, and whatever your religion or spiritual path, that you experience spirituality in every being you meet, that kindness is given and received throughout all parts of your life, and that respect and goodness abounds within you and around you. Let this last page be the first page of your new spiritually invigorated life. Good luck on your journey, my friend, and always but always, live well.

"This is my simple religion. There is no need for temples; no need for complicated philosophy. Our own brain, our own heart is our temple; the philosophy is kindness."
>His Holiness the Dalai Lama

ACKNOWLEDGMENTS

For privacy purposes, last names have been left out. You know who you are…

Anna, thank you for believing in me, and this book. Without you, this book would have never reached the hands of so many yearning Soul Searchers; thank you for changing their and my life. I could not have done this without you and the Beyond Words team. I'm eternally grateful. A special thank you also to the Editorial team including Sylvia, Lindsay, and Gretchen.

James, for his unwavering patience, support and allowing me the time and space to write this book, which essentially became the third person in our relationship.

Marg and Merv, for gifting me the freedom to explore my own spirituality and nurturing my weirdness while encouraging my quirkiness. I picked the best parents to raise me, thank you.

Tash, whom I have come to call the CEO of Emma Mildon dot com. Thank you for your frank, straight-shooting feedback on what is hip and what is whack.

Aunty Jane, for welcoming spiritual conversations into my life. You are like a mother to me, and for that I am grateful.

Nana Mildon, for all of the pearls of wisdom over the years, thank you.

Louise, Doreen, and Gabby, for sharing your words, wisdom, and inspiration with me, and the readers.

Celine, for allowing me to fashion her amazingly elegant designs. Sarah, for styling me and polishing up this old spiritual gangster into a goddess. Kenrick, for capturing me through his talented lens.

The O'Hara sisters, for your spiritual and business brainstorming sessions, support, and friendship. Babara, for sharing your wisdom with me, which gave me the courage to spark a new chapter in my life. Thank you for helping me "walk my talk."

Sharad, thank you for being such a humble and inspiring mentor. Tim, for teaching me the joys of SUP yoga, AcroYoga, and yoga friendships. Diane and Halo Smith, for your partnership, foresight and insight into spiritual entrepreneurship. Ish, for sharing his X factor and public speaking finesse to help transform the way I communicate with an audience, in person and on paper. Sacha, for giving me the low down on being my authentic self and helping to inspire the last line of the book. Live well . . .

Dione, for supporting my work and helping to connect me with wisdom and fellow Soul Searchers. Guy, Vanessa, Katherine, Leigh, and Lauren for putting up with my daily antics and curiosity. Ayla, for starting the movement. Thank you for being one of my first supporters and followers. Abbylee, thank you for being a shining light and like-minded spiritual hustler. Twyla, thank you for being a grounding, wise, and nurturing influence.

The team at Lululemon Ponsonby for their endless support, collective vision, and for welcoming me into their spiritual family. Special mention to Mo, Bex, Prism, Emily, and Poppy.

Tiffany, for teaching me that yoga really is medicine.

Jade and Charlotte, for giving me inspiration straight from my target audience.

Jacque and Jonnie, thank you for giving me my first opportunity to spread my public speaking wings at Wanderlust New Zealand. Wanderlust Festival, for your partnership and for allowing me to help Wanderlusters find their true north.

BookYogaRetreats, for your partnership and for sharing such a holistic view and attitude towards business.

Emm, for gifting connecting me to Wayne Dyer and helping me to make a shift! Rowan, for your patience and Personal Training. Imogen, for being a sister and family to me while I found refuge. Persephone, for showing me both courage and love.

Philip, for your Astrology reading that changed the course of my life and had a severe impact on this book. Narelle, for your support and most importantly for teaching me how to dance! Michelle, for your Numerology reading which sparked the start of my whole spiritual and writing career merging into this very book.

Richard, for showing me that spiritual world domination can happen from a small spark of curiosity in the smallest of countries like New Zealand. Jasmine, thank you for taking me under your wing as a life coach and spiritual teacher. Peter, for teaching me the 1, 2, 3s of numerology. I haven't been able to stop counting time, dates and letterboxes since.

Eli, for showing me another world and connecting me to my past life through regression.

Suzanne, for your straight shooting chats and giving me a strategy and a strong sense of direction. Kay, for helping me learn to be sensibly selfish and inviting me into the Mallorca spiritual community. Melissa, for connecting me with my spirit angels and guides. Barbara, for talking me through my tea leaves and past lives. Carmel, for healings, readings, angel aura sprays, and foot detoxes. Thank you for your energy.

Eoin, for imparting effortless wisdom that both grounded and transformed me. Cathy, for sharing your dream dictionary and spiritual insight. Karen, for sharing your spirit guide wisdom and being so welcoming with cross pollinating spiritual wisdom. Martin and Kaye, for teaching me Transcendental Meditation.

Marilyn, thank you for being a superb agent, the seed of my opportunities.

Reid and Cheryl, for helping to mold me into the mover and shaker I have become. Your workshop changed my life.

Last, but certainly not least, thank you to Gabrielle, Malcolm, and my angel and spirit guides who have channeled this book and experience through me. I feel like your names should be on the cover of this book. I am ever privileged to have you with me. It is an honor to be your messenger.

NOTES

Introduction

1. "Padmasambhava," Rigpa Wiki, last modified February 6, 2014, http://www.rigpawiki.org/index.php?title=Padma sambhava.
2. Karen Armstrong, *Buddha* (London: Orion Books, Ltd., 2000), 7–8.
3. Jalal al-Din Rumi, *The Essential Rumi: New Expanded Edition* (San Francisco: HarperOne, 2004), 196.

Part I

Chapter 1

1. Melissa Eisler, "The History of Meditation," The Chopra Center, accessed November 29, 2014, http://www.chopra.com/ccl/the-history-of-meditation.
2. Jeff Wilson, *Mindful America: The Mutual Transformation of Buddhist Meditation and American Culture* (Oxford: Oxford University Press, 2014), 35.
3. Gertrud Hirschi, *Mudras: Yoga in Your Hands* (Newburyport, MA: Red Wheel/Weiser, LLC, 2002), 14, 60–62, 64–65, 70–75, 82–85, 96–103, 108–109, 112–117, 120–122, 136–140. Reprinted by permission of the Publisher.
4. Kundalini Mudra. Used by permission from The Kundalini Research Institute. For further information, contact www.kriteachings.org.
5. Buddha Mudra. Used by permission from The Kundalini Research Institute. For further information, contact www.kriteachings.org.

6. Louise L. Hay, *You Can Heal Your Life* (Carlsbad, CA: Hay House, Inc., 1984), 122–141. Reprinted by permission of the Publisher.

Chapter 2

1. Richard Webster, *Color Magic for Beginners* (Woodbury, MN: Llewellyn Worldwide, Ltd., 2006), 59–62. Reprinted by permission of the Publisher.
2. Ibid.
3. Tasmania Hobart, "Divine Feminine—Kundalini, Transpersonal and the Inner Feminine," Transpersonal Lifestreams, last modified March 21, 2011, http://www.transpersonal.com.au/kundalini/divine-feminine.htm.
4. Ibid.
5. Webster, *Color of Magic for Beginners*, 59–62.

Chapter 3

1. Lise Manniche, *Sacred Luxuries: Fragrance, Aromatherapy, and Cosmetics in Ancient Egypt* (Trowbridge, UK: Opus Publishing, Ltd., 1999), 36.
2. Scott Cunningham, *The Complete Book of Incense, Oils, and Brews* (Woodbury, MN: Llewellyn Worldwide, Ltd., 2002), 27–44. Reprinted by permission of the Publisher.
3. Ibid.
4. Debbie Allen, "Biblical Scripture References for Use of Essential Oils," Young Living Essential Oils, accessed November 15, 2015, http://www.yleo-oils.com/bible.htm.
5. Scott Cunningham, *The Complete Book of Incense, Oils, and Brews* (Woodbury, MN: Llewellyn Worldwide, Ltd., 2002), 45, 58, 62, 65. Reprinted by permission of the Publisher.
6. Ibid.
7. Ibid.

Chapter 4

1. Richard Webster, *Living In Your Soul's Light: Understanding Your Eternal Self* (Woodbury, MN: Llewellyn Worldwide, Ltd., 2012), 47, 51, 52, 53, 54. Reprinted by permission of the Publisher.
2. Richard Webster, *Living In Your Soul's Light: Understanding Your Eternal Self* (Woodbury, MN: Llewellyn Worldwide, Ltd., 2012), 54–55. Reprinted by permission of the Publisher.
3. Ibid.
4. "What Is TRE®," Bercelli Foundation, accessed February 15, 2015, http://traumaprevention.com.
5. "Napping: Do's And Don'ts for Healthy Adults," Mayo Clinic, last modified November 21, 2012, http://www.mayoclinic.org/healthy-living/adult-health/in-depth/napping/art-20048319.
6. Jane Maati Smith, *Chakra Healing Solfeggio Frequencies: Sound Medicine For Chakra Balancing of the Body, Mind, and Soul*, ChakraHealingSounds.com, 2013, MP3.

7. Mark and Elizabeth Clare Prophet, "Aquarian Path: the Seven Chakras," http://www.aquarianpath
   .com/chakraschart.php, accessed May 17, 2015.

8. Richard Webster, *Aura Reading for Beginners: Develop Your Psychic Awareness for Health & Success* (Woodbury, MN: Llewellyn Worldwide, Ltd., 2002), 3. Reprinted by permission of the Publisher.

9. Richard Webster, *Living In Your Soul's Light: Understanding Your Eternal Self* (Woodbury, MN: Llewellyn
   Worldwide, Ltd., 2012), 69, 71, 72, 73, 74. Reprinted by permission of the Publisher.

10. "Clairvoyant Band Aid," *Almost Famous*, directed by Cameron Crowe, (2000; Universal City, CA:
    Dreamworks, 2000), DVD.

11. Richard Webster, *Aura Reading for Beginners: Develop Your Psychic Awareness for Health & Success* (Wood-
    bury, MN: Llewellyn Worldwide, Ltd., 2002), 83–94. Reprinted by permission of the Publisher.

Chapter 5

1. Richard Webster, *Feng Shui for Beginners: Successful Living by Design* (Woodbury, MN: Llewellyn
   Worldwide, Ltd., 2002), 1–3. Reprinted by permission of the Publisher.

2. Ibid.

3. Deepak Chopra, *The Book of Secrets: Unlock the Hidden Dimensions of Your Life* (New York: Harmony
   Books, 2005). Reprinted by permission of the Publisher.

4. Richard Webster, *Color Magic for Beginners* (Woodbury, MN: Llewellyn Worldwide, Ltd., 2006), 217–
   228. Reprinted by permission of the Publisher.

5. Webster, *Feng Shui for Beginners*, 132.

6. Ibid., 112.

Part II

1. Louie E. Ross, Ingrid J. Hall, Temeika L. Fairley, Yhenneko J. Taylor, and Daniel L. Howard, "Prayer
   and Self-Reported Health Among Cancer Survivors in the United States, National Health Inter-
   view Survey, 2002" *Journal of Alternative and Complementary Medicine*, last modified on May 16, 2015,
   http://www.ncbi.nlm.nih.gov/pmc/articles/PMC3152800/.

Chapter 6

1. John Lennon, "Imagine," on *Imagine*, Apple Records, 1971, MP3.

2. Ian Parker, "The Big Sleep," *The New Yorker*, December 9, 2013, http://www.newyorker.com
   /magazine/2013/12/09/the-big-sleep-2.

3. J.F. Pagel, MD, "Nightmares and Disorders of Dreaming," *American Family Physician* 61, April 1, 2000,
   http://www.aafp.org/afp/2000/0401/.

4. Paulo Coelho, *The Pilgrimage*, trans. Alan R. Clarke (Rio de Janeiro: Editora Rocco, Ltd., 2006),
   61–62.

5. Cathy Hunsberger, *Dreams: Unlocking the Mystery* (Bloomington, IN: Balboa Press, 2013), 163–178.
   Reprinted by permission of the Publisher.

6. Ibid.

7. Cathy Hunsberger, *Dreams: Unlocking the Mystery* (Bloomington, IN: Balboa Press, 2013), 163–178. Reprinted by permission of the Publisher.

8. Jane Maati Smith, *Chakra Healing Solfeggio Frequencies: Sound Medicine for Chakra Balancing of the Body, Mind, and Soul*, ChakraHealingSounds.com, 2013, MP3.

9. "Insufficient Sleep Is a Public Health Epidemic," Centers For Disease Control and Prevention, last modified January 13, 2014, http://www.cdc.gov/features/dssleep/.

10. Rudolf F. Graf, "Crystal oscillator," *Modern Dictionary of Electronics*, 7th Ed. (Boston: Newnes, 1999), 162, 163.

11. Rebecca Turner, "A History of Sleep," World of Lucid Dreaming, accessed December 11, 2014, http://www.world-of-lucid-dreaming.com/history-of-sleep.html.

Chapter 7

1. "Origin and Meaning of Emma," eBabyNames.com, accessed February 18, 2015, http://www.ebaby names.com/#!meaning-of-Emma.

2. "Chinese Vs. Western Numerology," Numerology.com, accessed February 14, 2015, http://www .numerology.com/numerology-news/chinese-vs-western-numerology.

3. Harish Johari, *Numerology with Tantra, Ayurveda, and Astrology* (Rochester, NY: Inner Traditions International, Ltd., 1990), 6–7.

4. Michelle Buchanan, *The Numerology Guidebook: Uncover Your Destiny and the Blueprint of Your Life* (Carlsbad, CA: Hay House, Inc., 2013), 3–16. Reprinted by permission of the Publisher.

5. Ibid.

6. Ibid.

7. Ibid.

8. Ibid.

Chapter 8

1. Ulla Koch-Westenholz, *Mesopotamian Astrology: An Introduction to Babylonian and Assyrian Celestial Divination* (Copenhagen: Museum Tusculanum Press, 1995), 11.

2. Nicholas Campion, *History of Western Astrology, Volume II: The Medieval and Modern Worlds* (London: Continuum International Publishing Group, 2009).

3. Robert Armour, *Gods and Myths of Ancient Egypt* (Cairo: American University in Cairo Press, 1986), 6–8.

4. Siegfried Morenz, *Egyptian Religion* (Ithaca, NY: Cornell University Press, 1973), 88–89.

5. April Holloway, "How Ancient People Marked the Equinox Around the World," Ancient Origins, March 20, 2014, http://www.ancient-origins.net/ancient-places/how-ancient-people-marked -equinox-around-world-001464.

6. Ibid.

7. Philip F. Young, *Astrology Unlocked* (Bloomington, IN: Balboa Press, 2013), 75–80. Reprinted by permission of the Publisher.

8. Carl Sagan, *Pale Blue Dot: A Vision of the Human Future in Space* (New York: Random House, 1994), 7.

9. Philip F. Young, *Astrology Unlocked* (Bloomington, IN: Balboa Press, 2013), 75–80. Reprinted by permission of the Publisher.

10. Ibid.

Chapter 9

1. G. E. M. Anscombe, "Modern Moral Philosophy," *Philosophy* vol. 33, no. 124 (1958): 12, www.jstor.org/stable/3749051.

2. Immanuel Kant, *The Metaphysical Elements of Ethics*, Trans. Thomas Kingsmill Abbott (Hazleton, PA: Pennsylvania State University, 2005), 5.

3. Mario Livio, *The Golden Ratio: The Story of PHI, the World's Most Astonishing Number* (New York: Broadway Books, 2002), 124–125.

4. Rhonda Byrne, *The Secret* (New York: Simon & Schuster, 2006).

5. Esther Hicks and Jerry Hicks, *The Law of Attraction: The Basics of the Teachings of Abraham* (Carlsbad, CA: Hay House, 2006).

Part III

Chapter 10

1. Associated Press, "Poll: Nearly 8 in 10 Americans Believe in Angels," CBS News, December 23, 2011, http://www.cbsnews.com/news/poll-nearly-8-in-10-americans-believe-in-angels/.

2. Max Martin, Savan Kotecha, and Shellback, "I Wanna Go," performed by Britney Spears, Jive Records, 1999, MP3.

3. Richard Webster, *Spirit Guides and Angel Guardians: Contact Your Invisible Helpers* (Woodbury, MN: Llewellyn Worldwide, Ltd., 2002), 18, 20–21. Reprinted by permission of the Publisher.

4. Brigit Goldworthy, *Totem Animal Messages: Channelled Messages from the Animal Kingdom* (Bloomington, IN: Balboa Press, 2013). Reprinted by permission of the Publisher.

5. Doreen Virtue, *Angel Numbers 101: An Introduction to Connecting, Working, and Healing with the Angels*, Hay House, Inc., Carlsbad, CA: Hay House, 2006), 9–37. Reprinted by permission of the Publisher.

6. James Redfield, *The Celestine Prophecy: A Pocket Guide to the Nine Insights* (New York: Grand Central Publishing, 1993), 112. Copyright © 1993 by James Redfield. Reprinted by permission of Grand Central Publishing. All rights reserved.

Chapter 11

1. "Akashic Records—The Book of Life," Edgar Cayce's Association for Research and Enlightenment, accessed on February 18, 2015, http://www.edgarcayce.org/are/spiritualGrowth.aspx?id=2078.

2. A. Pablo Iannone, *Dictionary of World Philosophy* (Abingdon, UK: Taylor and Francis, 2001), 30.

3. Katharina Brandt, "Rudolf Steiner and Theosophy," *Handbook of the Theosophical Current*, Olav Hammer and Mikael Rothstein, eds., (Boston: Brill, 2013), 122–3.

4. Richard Webster, *Practical Guide to Past-Life Memories: Twelve Proven Methods* (Woodbury, MN: Llewellyn Worldwide, Ltd., 2001), 13, 185. Reprinted by permission of the Publisher.

5. Richard Webster, *Living in Your Soul's Light: Understanding Your Eternal Self* (Woodbury, MN: Llewellyn Worldwide, Ltd., 2012), 14–16. Reprinted by permission of the Publisher.

6. Jennifer Longmore, "Akashic Records: A Sacred Tool to Facilitate the Deepest Level of Healing for Your Soul," Vital Spark: Canada's New Consciousness Network, accessed November 12, 2014, http://www.mcs.ca/vitalspark/2040_therapies/501akas.html.

7. Sylvia Browne, *Insight: Case Files from the Psychic World* (New York: Dutton, 2006).

Chapter 12

1. Richard Webster, *Living in Your Soul's Light: Understanding Your Eternal Self* (Woodbury, MN: Llewellyn Worldwide, Ltd., 2012), 178. Reprinted by permission of the Publisher.

2. Ibid.

Chapter 13

1. Elizabeth Day, "A Mystery Even to Himself," *The Telegraph*, June 13, 2005, http://www.telegraph.co.uk/culture/donotmigrate/3643720/A-mystery-even-to-himself.html.

2. Doreen Virtue, *Goddesses and Angels* (Carlsbad, CA: Hay House, 2005). Reprinted by permission of the Publisher.

SPIRITUAL TERMS GLOSSARY

A

Affirmation: A repeated mantra or statement to the universe that mentally reinforces positive feelings or goals, and triggers a request from the universe, helping you manifest the goal into reality. Affirmations can help heal; increase happiness, love, and success in your life; and focus the direction of your energy.

Afterlife: The experience of life after earthly death, tied to the belief that our souls live on after our corporeal existence ends.

Akashic Records: The Akashic Records, also known as the "book of life," are the collective memories and histories of every thought, physical and emotional vibration, sound, interaction, event, and journey of every soul throughout every lifetime.

Angels: Angels, or spirit guides, appear in many religions, in particular, Christianity. Angels are said to guide, protect, heal, and help us from the other side.

Anoint: To cleanse or heal, traditionally with an oil, often in the context of a religious or spiritual ceremony.

Archangels: The second choir of high-ranking angels in many branches of Christianity and Judaism, including Archangels Michael, Gabriel, and Raphael.

Aries: The first astrological star sign of the zodiac, often represented by the ram.

Aquarius: The eleventh astrological star sign of the zodiac, often represented by two waves stacked on top of each other.

Aromatherapy: Commonly associated with complementary and alternative medicine (CAM), aromatherapy is the use of liquid plant materials, known as essential oils (EOs), and other scented compounds from plants for the purpose of affecting a person's mood or health.

Astrology: Astrology is the science of charting the cycles of the earth, planets, and universe to connect with our soul's journey. The zodiac is used in astrology and consists of twelve star signs, each with its own ruling planet and a specific segment of the calendar. Each star has its own traits and pros and cons that connect to personality, challenges, and purpose.

Aum: The most sacred syllable in Hinduism, regarded as the seed of all mantras, and commonly spoken as *om*.

Aura: The aura contains all the colors of the spectrum, and represents our state of body and mind with a specific color, helping to represent our current status of well-being, our energy levels, and our moods. When someone speaks about another person's "vibes" or "energy," they are often actually referring to that person's aura.

Ayurveda/Ayurvedic Principles: The ancient Hindu science of health and medicine. In Ayurvedic medicine, keeping one's constitution in balance is considered important in maintaining good health and prolonging life. Ayurvedic principles are founded chiefly on naturopathy and homeopathy.

B

Birth Sign: Your birth sign is also known as your star sign in astrology. This is the astrological sign that represents where the sun and moon were at the exact time of your birth.

Buddha: Gautama Buddha (*Buddha* means "awakened one" or "enlightened one"), also known as Siddhartha Gautama, was a sage who lived between the sixth and fourth centuries BCE. Buddhism was founded in accordance with his teachings.

Buddhism: Buddhism is a dharmic, nontheistic religion, and a philosophy. Buddhism is also known as *Buddha Dharma* or *Dhamma*, which means the "teachings of the Awakened One" in Sanskrit and Pali, languages of ancient Buddhist texts.

C

Capricorn: The tenth astrological star sign of the zodiac, often represented by the goat.

Cancer: The fourth astrological star sign of the zodiac, often represented by the crab.

Chakras: The word *chakra* is Sanskrit for "vortex" or "wheel." The chakras are energy centers within our physical bodies. There are seven major chakras between the crown of the head and the base of the spine. There are another forty-two or so minor chakras, and more in our auras.

Channel/Channeling: A channel or channeler, also known as a *medium*, is someone who is able to communicate with spirit or the other side. This process is known as channeling.

Chant/Chanting: Repetitive, short, simple words; an affirmation; or other sounds produced to help the chanter attain a deeper spiritual or meditative state.

Chi: Chi is the energy that flows through the body's vital organs and circulates through the entire body. Chi is positive energy, and is also used in ancient methods of Feng Shui.

Crystals: Crystals and other natural gems are formed in the earth over countless millennia. The energy they have absorbed during their formation is ancient, rich, and potent, and many use them for a variety of purposes, including healing and overall spiritual wellness.

D

Dharma: The word *dharma* originated in the ancient Sanskrit language, and its basic meaning is "duty" or "a universal order/law."

Dogma: A teaching that is at the core of a tradition or religion.

Dreams: The ability to experience and, at times, transcend daydreaming or dreaming in sleep to connect to messages from loved ones who have crossed over or messages from your spirit guides and angels.

E

Enlightenment: In a religious context, enlightenment is most closely associated with South and East Asian religious experiences of reaching a state of complete knowing, freedom, and awakening.

F

Feng Shui: Feng Shui is the ancient Chinese system for creating harmony in the environment by unblocking and ushering out negative energies. It is the practice of balancing energies in any physical space one inhabits.

G

Gemini: The third astrological star sign of the zodiac, often represented by a set of twins.

God: The word *God*, when capitalized, usually refers to the deity held by monotheists to be the supreme reality. God is generally regarded as the sole creator of the universe. Theologians have ascribed certain attributes to God, including omniscience, omnipotence, omnipresence, perfect goodness, divine simplicity, and eternal and necessary existence. When used with a lowercase g, the word can refer to any number of mono- or polytheistic deities across cultures and religious traditions.

Goddess: A goddess is a female deity. Similar to *god*, it can refer to any number of mono- or polytheistic deities across cultures and religious traditions.

Guardian Angels/Spirit: The guardian angel/spirit guide's job is to urge, encourage, nudge, support, advise, protect, and guide us on our life's path.

Guided Meditation: Guided meditation involves verbal guidance, either recorded or live, into and then back out of a state of meditative consciousness.

Guru: *Guru* is Sanskrit for "teacher" or "master," and is recognized in Hinduism, Buddhism, and Sikhism, as well as in many new religious movements. Based on a long, traditional line of philosophical understanding as to the importance of knowledge, the guru is seen in these religions as a sacred conduit to self-realization.

H

Hatha Yoga: Hatha is a system of yoga that is widely used today. It is said that Shiva himself invented Hatha Yoga, but its earliest known appearance is in the *Hatha Yoga Pradipika*, a compilation of earlier sources by Yogi Swatmarama, a fifteenth-century Indian sage. In this treatise, Swatmarama introduces Hatha Yoga as "a stairway to the heights of Raja Yoga," hence a preparatory stage of physical purification that renders the body fit for the practice of higher meditation. Hatha Yoga is what most people in the West associate with the word *yoga*.

Heaven: Heaven is a plane of existence in many religions and spiritual philosophies, typically described as the holiest possible place accessible according to various standards of divinity (goodness, piety, etc.). Christians generally hold that it is the afterlife destination of those who have accepted Jesus Christ as their savior.

Hell: Hell, according to many religious beliefs, is an afterlife of suffering where the wicked or unrighteous dead are punished. Hells are almost always depicted as underground. Christianity and Islam traditionally depict hell as fiery; hells from other traditions, however, are sometimes cold and gloomy. Alternatively, hell is sometimes not a place or locality but rather a state of being, where one is separated from God and thought to be held back by unrepented sin and corruption of spirit.

Healer: A healer is a person who is able to channel healing energies and direct them to someone in need of healing—physically, mentally, or spiritually.

Hinduism: Hinduism is a religion that originated on the Indian subcontinent. It has no known founder, being itself a conglomerate of diverse beliefs and traditions, and contains a vast body of scriptures. Developed over millennia, these scriptures expound on a broad of range of theology, philosophy, and mythology, providing spiritual insights and guidance on the practice of dharma (religious living). Among such texts, Hindus consider the Vedas and the Upanishads as being among the foremost in authority, importance, and antiquity.

Holism (Holistic): Holism is the idea that all the properties of a given system cannot be determined or explained by the sum of its component parts alone. Instead, the system as a whole determines in an important way how the parts behave. For example, *holistic health/healing* means paying comprehensive attention to the health of the body, mind, and spirit, as well as the influences of environment and society on a person's health.

Horoscope: The studying of the horoscope is an ancient art charting the cycles of the universe and the positions of the planets at the time of birth to forecast, predict, and draw a distinct impression of one's personality and life path. The horoscope (also called the astrology chart or zodiac chart) is made up of twelve sun or natal signs, each with its own ruling planet and a specific segment of the calendar, called *houses*.

I

Incarnation: Incarnation, which literally means "embodiment" refers to the conception and live birth of a sentient creature (generally a human being) who is the material manifestation of an entity or force whose original nature is immaterial.

Intuition: Your intuition is your own personal early warning system. It alerts you to dangers, changing energies, knowledge, and relevant information. Our job is to listen to what it is telling us and take heed of the messages.

Invocation: A formal greeting or prayer to call upon the presence of spirits.

K

Karma: The concept of "action" or "deed" in dharmic religions understood as denoting the entire cycle of cause and effect described in Hindu, Jain, Sikh, and Buddhist philosophies. Karma is believed to be a sum of all that an individual has done, is currently doing, and will do. The effects of all deeds actively create past, present, and future experiences, thus making one responsible for one's own life and the pain and joy it brings to others.

Kundalini: Kundalini, according to various teachings, is believed to be a type of "corporeal energy." It is envisioned as a serpent coiled at the base of the spine. According to Hindu tradition, through specific meditative exercises, Kundalini rises from the root chakra up through the spinal channel, called *sushumna*, and it is believed to activate each chakra it goes through.

Kundalini Yoga: Kundalini Yoga is a system of meditative techniques and movements within the yogic tradition that focuses on psycho-spiritual growth and the body's potential for maturation.

L

Law of Attraction: The law of attraction is commonly associated with New Age and New Thought theories. It states people experience the corresponding manifestations of their predominant thoughts, feelings, words, and actions, and that people therefore have direct control over reality and their lives through thought alone.

Leo: The fifth astrological star sign of the zodiac, often represented by the lion.

Libra: The seventh astrological star sign of the zodiac, often represented by the scales.

Life Force: The energy within us and the entirety of creation that makes us alive.

M

Magic: Magic and sorcery are the influencing of events, objects, people, and physical phenomena by mystical, paranormal, or supernatural means. The terms can also refer to the practices employed by a person to wield this influence, and to beliefs that explain various events and phenomena in such terms.

Mandala: Mandala is of Hindu origin, but is also used in other dharmic religions, such as Buddhism. In practice, *mandala* has become a generic term for any plan, chart, or geometric pattern that represents the cosmos metaphysically or symbolically, a microcosm of the universe from the human perspective. A mandala, especially its center, can be used during meditation as an object for focusing attention.

Manifesting: Manifesting is a term often used in New Thought and New Age circles to refer to the belief that one can, by force of will, desire, and focused energy, make something come true on the physical level. It is often tied to the law of attraction.

Mantra: Religious or mystical syllable or poem, typically from the Sanskrit language. They are primarily used as spiritual conduits, words, or vibrations that instill one-pointed concentration in the devotee. For example, *aum* is a common mantra.

Meditation: A state in which the body is consciously relaxed and the mind is able to become calm, focused, and free from distraction.

Metaphysics: Metaphysics is the branch of philosophy concerned with explaining the ultimate nature of reality, being, and the world. More recently, the term *metaphysics* has also been used more loosely to refer to subjects that are beyond the physical world.

Miracles: Sensibly perceptible interruptions of the laws of nature, such that can only be explained by divine intervention, and are sometimes associated with a miracle worker.

Mudra: Meaning "mark," "seal," or "gesture" in Sanskrit, mudras are symbolic hand symbols and gestures said to activate different body parts and thus promote healing and well-being.

Myth/Mythology: Mythology consists of a collection of stories or legends used by cultures to explain the unknown and the unexplainable. Broadly, the word *myth* can refer to any traditional story.

N

Numerology: Numerology is "the science of numbers," or the study of numbers and their effect on our lives. Practiced across cultures and throughout recorded history, numerology tells of our potential destiny and natural talents, and helps us gain a better understanding of ourselves and others.

New Age: *New Age* is the term commonly used to designate the broad movement of late twentieth century and contemporary Western culture, characterized by an eclectic and individual approach to spiritual exploration.

Nirvana: Sanskrit word that means "extinguishing of the passions." It is a mode of being that is free from mind contaminants such as lust, anger, and craving; a state of pure consciousness and bliss unobstructed by all passions and emotions, free from human suffering. In the *Dhammapada*, the Buddha says of nirvana that it is "the highest happiness." This is not the sense-based happiness of everyday life but rather an enduring, transcendental happiness integral to the calmness attained through enlightenment.

O

Other Side, The: The other side is thought by some to be where our spirits come from when we enter the womb. It is also where our spirits go when our physical bodies die. It is the realm of spirit.

Out-of-Body Experience: An out-of-body experience is when a person's consciousness is able to see the world from a perspective that transcends the physical body and bypasses the physical senses.

P

Paganism: *Paganism* is a term that, from a mostly Western perspective, has come to connote a broad set of spiritual or cultic practices or beliefs of any folk religion, and of historical and contemporary polytheism religions in particular.

Past-Life Regression (Therapy): Past-life regression is a technique used by some hypnotherapists to attempt to get clients to remember their past lives. Implicit in this procedure is the spiritual belief that souls exist and come back many times, living in different times and places, experiencing different genders, races, social classes, and so forth in an attempt to learn from these past experiences.

Phenomenon: Dictionary.reference.com defines the word *phenomenon* as: "an observable event, particularly one that is remarkable or in some way extraordinary." This term can mean a variety of things in a spiritual context and is often tied to the concepts of miracles and mystical/magical events and happenings.

Pisces: The twelfth astrological star sign of the zodiac, often represented by the fish.

Power Animal: A power animal (or totem or spirit animal) is the animal spirit or energy with particular characteristics and attributes that represent traits or qualities you resonate with.

Prana: *Prana* is a Sanskrit word meaning "breath" and refers to a vital, life-sustaining force of living beings and vital energy in natural processes of the universe.

Prayer: An active effort to communicate with a deity or spirit either to offer praise, make a request, seek guidance, confess sins, or simply to express one's thoughts and emotions.

Predestination: A religious concept that involves the relationship between the beginning of a thing and its destiny. Predestination concerns God's decision to determine ahead of time what the destiny of groups or individuals will be and also includes all of creation.

Prophecy/Prophetic: Knowledge or information that comes in the form of a vision or dream before it happens.

Prophetic Dreams: Prophetic dreams are dreams in which a future event or events are detailed. People of all creeds and cultures throughout the ages have accepted that dreams can foretell the future or reveal long-forgotten images of the past.

Psychic: A person who possess extrasensory abilities, including clairvoyance, psychometry, and precognition, and who can sometimes communicate with spirits, ghosts, or other spiritual entities.

Psychoanalysis: Psychoanalysis is a methodical approach used to examine the unconscious mind as a form of mental and emotional healing.

R

Reflexology: Reflexology is a method of hands-on healing using massage to activate points on the feet and hands that directly relate to organs of the physical body through channels of energy. Healers use these energy channels or points to heal physically, emotionally, and mentally. Reflexology is often used in conjunction with Reiki, aromatherapy, massage, and other alternative therapies.

Reiki: Mikao Usui developed Reiki in early-twentieth-century Japan, where he said he received the ability of "healing without energy depletion" after three weeks of fasting and meditating on Mount Kurama. Practitioners use a technique similar to the laying on of hands as well as gestures in the air and the use of crystals, gems, and stones, with which they assert channels' healing energies (*chi*).

Reincarnation: The belief that the human spirit survives the death of the physical body and returns to recurring lifetimes in a variety of chosen circumstances and bodies for the purpose of the soul's growth and learning in an effort to finally ascend to heaven.

Religion: A set of beliefs and practices generally held by a community, involving adherence to codified beliefs and rituals, and the study of ancestral or cultural traditions, writings, history, and mythology, as well as personal faith and mystic experience.

Ritual: A practice incorporated into a ceremony in which a set of actions are performed mainly for their symbolic value, which is prescribed by a religion or by the traditions of a community.

S

Sacred (Holiness): Holiness, or sanctity, is the state of being holy or sacred, that is, set apart for the worship or service of God or gods. It is most usually ascribed to people but can be and often is ascribed to objects, times, or places. The word *holy* is related to the word *whole*.

Sagittarius: The ninth astrological star sign of the zodiac, often represented by the archer.

Sanskrit: Sanskrit is a historical Indo-Aryan language, one of the liturgical languages of Hinduism and Buddhism, and one of the twenty-two official languages of India.

Scorpio: The eighth astrological star sign of the zodiac, often represented by the scorpion.

Self: The self is a complex and core subject in many forms of spirituality. Two types of self are commonly considered—the self that is the ego, also called the learned, superficial self of mind and body, an egocentric creation; and the self which is sometimes called the "True Self," the "I" (or "I AM"), the "Atman," the "Observing Self," or the "Witness."

Soul: The soul, according to many religious and philosophical traditions, is the self-aware essence unique to a particular living being. In these traditions, the soul is thought to incorporate the inner essence of each living being, and to be the true basis for consciousness.

Spirit: The true essence of who we are; the real and eternal part of ourselves that, according to some beliefs, lives on after corporeal death.

Spirit Guides: A term used by mediums and spirituals to describe an entity that remains a disincarnate spirit in order to act as a spiritual counselor or protector to a living incarnated human being.

Spirituality: Spirituality, in a narrow sense, concerns itself with matters of the spirit. The spiritual, involving perceived eternal truths regarding humankind's ultimate nature, often contrasts with the realities, or perceived realities, of material existence. Spirituality in the context of the New Age movement often focuses on personal experience. Many spiritual traditions share a common spiritual theme: the "path," "work," practice, or tradition of perceiving, internalizing, and becoming closer aligned with one's true nature and relationship to the rest of existence (God, creation, the universe, and life).

Supernatural: A term that refers to forces and phenomena that are not observed in nature and are, therefore, beyond verifiable measurement.

T

T'ai Chi: T'ai chi is an internal Chinese martial art often practiced with the aim of promoting health and longevity. T'ai chi is considered a soft-style martial art—an art applied with internal power—to distinguish its theory and application from that of the hard martial art styles.

Tao Te Ching: The *Tao Te Ching*, roughly translated as "The Book of the Way and Its Virtue," is a Chinese classic text. According to tradition, it was written around 600 BCE by the Taoist sage Laozi (or Lao Tzu, "Old Master"), a record keeper at the Zhou dynasty court.

Taoism: Taoism (Daoism) is the English name referring to a variety of related Chinese philosophical and religious traditions and concepts. These traditions influenced East Asia for over two thousand years and some have spread internationally. Taoist propriety and ethics emphasize the Three Jewels of the Tao: love, moderation, and humility. Taoist thought focuses on *wu wei* (nonaction), spontaneity, humanism, and emptiness. The *Tao Te Ching* is widely considered to be the most influential Taoist text.

Tarot: One etymological theory for the origin of the word *Tarot* is that it was devised from two Egyptian words: *tar* meaning road and *to* meaning royal. Thus, we have the "royal road" to wisdom. Over the centuries, Tarot decks have been used both as simple playing cards and as a form of spiritual guidance. Today, Tarot is often used as a tool for self-development, especially when used with meditation for clarity, insight, and for the highest good. Tarot cards reflect life's journey from birth to death, mirroring the path from naïvety to experience and self-knowledge. Most aspects of human experience are found in Tarot.

Taurus: The second astrological star sign of the zodiac, often represented by the bull.

Tibetan Book of the Dead (*Bardo Thodol*): The *Bardo Thodol* is a funerary text that describes the experiences of the consciousness after death during the interval known as *bardo* between death and rebirth. The *Bardo Thodol* is recited by lamas over a dying or recently deceased person, or sometimes over an effigy of the deceased.

V

Vedas: The Vedas are a large corpus of texts originating in Ancient India. They are the oldest scriptural texts of Hinduism.

Virgo: The sixth astrological star sign of the zodiac, often represented by the virgin maiden.

Y

Yin and Yang: The dual concepts of yin and yang originated in ancient Chinese philosophy and metaphysics, which describe two primal, opposing but complementary principles or cosmic forces said to be found in all non-static objects and processes in the universe. The concept is the cornerstone for Taoism and traditional Chinese medicine.

Yoga: Yoga is a family of ancient spiritual practices originating in India. Hindu texts discussing different aspects of yoga include the Upanishads, the Bhagavad Gita, the *Yoga Sutras of Patanjali*, the *Hatha Yoga Pradipika*, and many others. Major branches of yoga include: Hatha Yoga, Karma Yoga, Jñāna Yoga, Bhakti Yoga, and Raja Yoga.

Yogi: A yogi or yogin is a term for one who practices yoga. These designations are mostly reserved for advanced practitioners. The word *yogi* has also evolved into a general term for a spiritually knowledgeable or enlightened person.

Z

Zen: Zen is a school of Mahayana Buddhism notable for its emphasis on practice and experiential wisdom, particularly as realized in the form of meditation known as zazen, in the attainment of awakening. As such, it de-emphasizes both theoretical knowledge and the study of religious texts in favor of direct individual experience of one's own true nature. The word *Zen* is also used today to connote a desirable general state of peace, clarity, and spiritual health.

SOUL SEARCHING EXTRAS

Your online spiritual library awaits you. You can find all of the spiritual extras sitting in this one, easy-to-navigate, interactive, online spiritual hub. Just visit WWW.EMMAMILDON.COM and explore the *Spirituality, Explore it!* section. There you will discover spiritual-inspired resources including recommended books, videos, and even products you can purchase to keep "soul searching" and apply your newfound knowledge from this book!

Channels to further your soul searching journey include:

Aromatherapy ⟶ For the ones who follow their nose.

Astrology ⟶ For the seekers who wish to be guided by the stars.

Body ⟶ For those keen to get active with Yoga or Detox.

Chakras ⟶ For those of you wanting to learn more about good vibes.

Crystals ⟶ For those of you curious about all things shiny.

Dreams ⟶ For the ones who are guided on clouds and pillows.

Feng Shui ⟶ For those who need a sanctuary.

Guides ⟶ For those who seek to connect to their guiding source.

Numerology ⟶ For the finger counters out there!

Past Life ⟶ For the seekers looking to connect to their previous self.

Protection ⟶ For those looking to use energy work to protect themselves on their journey.

Soul ⟶ For those of you whose souls crave more!

Soul Mate ⟶ For those who seek their twin flame.

Universal ⟶ For the ones ready for an adventure.

Need a Soul Search Mentor?

Visit the guides channel on emmamildon.com under the *Spirituality, Explore it!* section and watch online tutorials from yoga teachers, life coaches, and motivational speakers. Connect with other Soul Searchers via Emma Mildon's social media channels including Facebook, Twitter, Instagram, and Pinterest. Meet other Soul Searchers and get guidance on more recommended reading, recommended life coaches, mentors, or events in your area. Remember, the best guide is the wise guide inside, so listen to your inner guide. Read the books it draws you to and connect with the people they put on your path.

Need a Soul Search Adventure?

Visit the universal channel under the *Spirituality, Explore it!* section of the website and visit travel sites, spiritual festivals, expos, and retreats. They key is to follow what resonates with you and have the courage to follow your intuition!

1/13/2016

BookYogaRetreats.com

This is a one-stop-onl̶ taways. With thousands of retreats across the g̶ ̶ ̶ ̶ ̶ ̶ ̶ ̶ ̶ ̶ ̶ ̶ ̶ ̶ ̶ ̶ ̶ ̶ .

Visit the meditation s̶ ̶ ̶ ̶ ̶ ̶ ̶ ̶ ̶ ̶ ̶ ̶ ̶ ̶ ̶ ̶ ̶ ̶ drop down. Get a free guided meditation (tr̶ ̶ ̶ ̶ ̶ ̶ ̶ ̶ ̶ ̶ ̶ ̶ ̶ ̶ ̶ ̶ plus a meditation recommended books list̶ ̶ ̶ ̶ ̶ ̶ ̶ ̶ ̶ ̶ ̶ ̶ ̶ to help you meditate and help guide you t̶ ̶ ̶ ̶ ̶ ̶ ̶ ̶ ̶ ̶ ̶ ̶ .

Download the free a̶ ̶ ̶ ̶ ̶ ̶ ̶ ̶ ̶ ̶ ̶ ̶ ̶ ̶ ̶ ̶ reminders about full moons, new moons, a̶ ̶ ̶ ̶ ̶ ̶ ̶ ̶ ̶ ̶ ̶ ̶ ̶ cted for future books and offers.

Visit the *Books and Be̶ ̶ ̶ ̶ ̶ ̶ ̶ ̶ ̶ ̶ ̶ ̶ ̶ avorite soul searching music. You can even w̶ ̶ ̶ ̶ ̶ ̶ ̶ ̶ ̶ ̶ ̶ ̶ ̶ books to add to your bookshelf.